The Evolution of a UCC Style

the Evolution of a UCC Style

History, Ecclesiology, and Culture of the United Church of Christ

Randi Jones Walker

Cleveland

dedication

To the members of my UCC History classes, 1992–2003, especially, Jeanette Zaragoza, Bea Morris, Evelyn Vigil, Roger Barkley, Christopher Hayward, Johari Jabir, Brenda Brown, Andrea Hartman, and Diana Coberly who asked genuinely new questions.

United Church Press, 700 Prospect Avenue, Cleveland, Ohio 44115
unitedchurchpress.com

Printed in the United States of America on acid-free paper

10 09 08 07 06 05 5 4 3 2 1

Library of Congress Cataloging-in-Publication Data

Walker, Randi Jones.
The evolution of a UCC style : history, ecclesiology, and culture of the United Church of Christ / by Randi Jones Walker.
p. cm.
<Includes bibliographical references and index.
ISBN 0-8298-1493-0 (pbk. : alk. paper)
1. United Church of Christ. I. Title.

BX9885.W35 2005
285.8'34—dc22

2005044019

CONTENTS

ACKNOWLEDGMENTS

This book has steeped a long time in my head. It is more than anything else, the product of conversations with people within and outside of the United Church of Christ who really wanted to understand what kind of Christian community we are. These conversations number literally thousands and I would be a fool to try to record them all here, but the ones that stay in my mind most, I do want to acknowledge with public gratitude. This does not mean that I value the others less, but that I have a finite, all too human memory. I also want to be clear that I have in this work proposed some ideas that I believe emerge out of these conversations, but I could be quite mistaken in what I think I have heard. In the next few years, I really look forward to reading and hearing what others, perhaps more deeply rooted in this United Church of Christ, have to say about the nature and purpose of our life together. Whatever in this work does not ring true should not be laid at the feet of any whose wisdom I sought.

The conversations began when I was a student at two different United Methodist seminaries, in the mid 1970s, as word began to filter out about such things as the ordination of Bill Johnson. Mitzi Eilts, Ann Appley, Les Strathern and the Arcadia Congregational UCC, Roger and Pat Robbenault, Fred Register, Michio Oyakawa, Dan Romero, Carol Keim, Bob Arnott, and many others shaped my decision to join the United Church of Christ and began to spark my ecclesiological questions.

During my decade in pastoral ministry, compelling questions from ecumenical dialogue partners continued to drive me to try to understand this church I had been allowed to represent. My particular memories include the day Canon Harold Hultgren, the Ecumenical Officer for the Episcopal Diocese of Los Angeles, asked me where we located our episcopé in the UCC. He also kept pressing me to explain to him how we could describe ourselves as a church at all given our (what he regarded as) indefinite creedal commitments and amorphous authority structures.

As I began to teach the UCC History and Theology course at Pacific School of Religion, an entirely different set of conversations began to stir the eddies in my mind and force me to think more clearly about ecclesiology in the UCC. The students in my class, particularly the ones I mentioned in the dedication, the UCC History and Polity Teachers Group, the many members of various Ministry Issues Consultations, all pressed upon me the real lack of definition of our selves as Church. Continuing ecumenical conversations only made the question more urgent, as the UCC began to enter serious ecumenical partnerships, particularly with the Disciples of Christ, the Lutheran and Reformed churches, the Churches Uniting in Christ, and the UEK (Die Union Evangelischer Kirchen) formerly the EKU.

I value particularly conversations with Lydia Veliko, John Thomas, Fred Plumer, Barbara Brown Zikmund, Beth Nordbeck, Jack Jackson, Kekapa Lee, Hector López, Wayne Wilson, Toni Dunbar, Harland Hogue, John von Rohr, Doug Adams, Clyde Steckle, Don Freeman, Henrietta Andrews, David Finster, Harold Rucker, Bill Hulteen, Loren Cope, Lowell Zuck, Thomas Dipko, and friends outside the UCC, Lewis Mudge, Lynn Rhodes, Archie Smith Jr, Joe Driskill, and many from the Disciples of Christ.

No one does any research on a book without the assistance of librarians and the hospitality of many people. I want particularly to thank Kris Veldheer at the GTU Library, helpful correspondence with the librarians at Elon College and Lancaster Seminary, Lowell Zuck at the Eden Seminary archives, George Hing Ng, Bridgette Kelly, and Edward Cade of the UCC Archives, Harold Worthley of the Congregational Archives, the hospitality of Beth Nordbeck, Lowell Zuck, and Loren Cope, and a timely financial grant from the Graduate Theological Union Dean, Margaret Miles, and Pacific School of Religion's provision of travel funds for faculty which enabled me to make two long research trips. Thanks, also, to Audrey Englert and Renee Williams for helping with the index.

The encouragement of the History and Polity Teachers group and the enthusiasm of Timothy Staveteig, the Pilgrim Press publisher, for this project have sustained me. The most helpful comments of the three readers of the manuscript shaped the text in ways they will recognize. And the never-failing love of my spouse Jerry Walker, an Episcopalian, makes my life as I know it possible.

Thank you to all.

One

A Critique of the Four-Tradition Origin Myth of the United Church of Christ

It seemed so easy, or at least logical at the time. The ecumenical momentum of the early twentieth century propelled four denominations together within two and a half short decades. The Congregational and Christian denominations seemed scarcely to have any differences, the Reformed Church in the United States and the Evangelical Synod of North America shared a German ecumenical heritage, and courageously united before sorting out their common beliefs and the organizational form under which they would live together. Almost immediately, encouraged by their success, the two new churches began to talk to one another. Though the road to their union would prove unexpectedly rough, it did not take them long in the great sweep of Christian history, to form the United Church of Christ. Dedicated to making visible the unity Christ prayed for among his disciples as depicted in the Gospel of John, "That they all may be one . . ." (John 17:11). Represented among these four traditions are almost all the diverse streams of the Reformation. Could this new American denomination be the one to heal these old, old breaches of Christian communion? It seemed that perhaps it might.

And perhaps it could have done this if these theological and organizational differences were all that needed healing in the post–World War II world. Already in the conversations about union, the four denominations encountered divisions of class and culture.[1] Soon after the new denomination settled the matter of a constitution and a statement of faith, the question of race surfaced. Could a church talk credibly about unity, human or ecclesiastical, if it remained divided by race? The UCC had been, it turned out, a union forged largely by white folks. It did not occur to most of the white majority to ask about the question of race in this great project of Christian unity.[2] There were exceptions. In a few places, notably in the Southern Conference where racial tensions could run high, the African American Convention of the South made its own decision to join the UCC.[3]

Scarcely was the ink dry on the Statement of Faith, when another question arose in the context of a larger cultural debate about language and social gender roles. Did this Statement of Faith, or indeed any Christian statement include women? Two women, Mary Ely Lyman and Bernice Buehler, had a hand in writing the Statement of Faith but no one thought to represent women specifically in its language. As the white race included or represented the others, so men represented women and no one was aware of an alternative.[4] Thus class, race, and gender divisions in American culture and in all of humanity claimed consideration by those who prayed with Christ, "that all may be one." Other divisions appeared, divisions of sexual orientation, biblical interpretation, language, generation, region, and politics. If the United Church of Christ claimed as its vocation the unity of the Church, it did so just in time to face the late twentieth century onslaught of plurality and divisions of humanity.

While these issues faced every institution in the United States at this time, the United Church of Christ felt them keenly because the emerging view of society as divided along many lines countered so clearly the ideal of oneness in Christ. Where did this unity lie? Was it in the church as an organization with a common purpose? Was it in the basic Christian beliefs shared by the people? Was it in the network of covenants that held the congregations and all the disparate parts of the whole together? The church preached acceptance of diverse practices and views, just as it included diverse races, genders, generations and cultures, but such acceptance was hard to practice. The ideal that seemed so easy at first, challenged the denomination to its core. Could the simple four stream history of the United Church of Christ carry the freight of healing a far wider range of division?

One might of course simply dismiss the United Church of Christ as a failure for not finding a theological and practical way to carry out its idealized vocation. But the divisions of humanity were not created by the founders of the UCC. They existed before, and perhaps it was the church's willingness to articulate the ideal of unity, and go beyond current divisions to try to realize unity in practice that brought those same divisions so starkly to light. In the first chapter I want to outline what has come to be the Four Stream Origin Myth of the United Church of Christ along with the unfinished ecclesiological business left by our founding mothers and fathers. I want to point out the continued rhetorical value of the Myth as well as understand its limitations.

The first histories of the United Church of Christ, written in the period from 1962 to 1990, appeared at a time when the UCC was reeling from the impact of events that challenged its original core identity. Some of these events were internal developments, questions affecting the United Church of Christ community alone, and others were national and world-wide events and trends. These first historical works strove to reestablish denominational identity in an effort to guide the changes taking place within the church during this time. It is as if the United Church of Christ, in its formation, attempted the culmination of several movements in the late nineteenth century and early twentieth century, blending together the ecumenical optimism, the evangelical enthusiasm for the growth of Christianity, the liberal theological project of making Christian thought accessible to the modern mind, and the social gospel's concern for human justice only to find that this culmination happened just as three of these movements collapsed as driving forces in American and perhaps also world Christianity.

The historical treatments of the life of the United Church of Christ written in the 1970s and 1980s[5] reflected these concerns. Among these are Louis Gunnemann's, *The Shaping of the United Church of Christ* and *United and Uniting: The Meaning of an Ecclesial Journey*, and Dorothy Bass and Kenneth Smith's, *United Church of Christ: Studies in Identity and Polity*. Gunnemann's two books focused their attention on the ecumenical vocation of the new denomination and the developments of a national structure in the church. They also gave attention to the new cultural and political developments, but saw these mostly as concerns which deflected attention away from this foundational ecumenical vocation and fragmented the church's community life. Dorothy Bass and Kenneth Smith edited a collection of essays by Chicago Theological Seminary faculty. Collectively they were a study of UCC identity, and focused on theological and sociological reflections on the contemporary situation of the church, but one essay by Dorothy Bass presented the Reformation roots of the denomination with more depth than ever before, or since. Two further essays in the book share with Gunnemann interest in the ecumenical ideals and the dimensions of national institutional history as important for understanding the United Church of Christ. Perhaps the most widely used history of the UCC is the short summary written by Margaret Rowland Post for the pamphlet, "History and Program of the United Church of Christ" (1986). Post's is a statement of the classic four-tradition origin story of the denomination beginning in Jerusalem with the Judaism of Jesus and the first disciples, briefly tracing the fragmentation of Christendom in the Reformation, and the development of each of the four traditions as Protestantism developed in North America. She echoed Gunnemann in highlighting the ecumenical vocation of the denominations that formed the UCC, and though she listed the cultural issues pressing on the church in the 1980s, she returned to the ecumenical ideal at the end.

> The United Church of Christ continues, a united and uniting church. God alone is its author, Christ alone its head. A biblical church, it continues to witness by the power of the Holy Spirit, remembering that 'truths hitherto guarded in separateness become imperiled by their separateness, because they are in essence 'catholic' truths, not 'sectarian."[6]

Barbara Brown Zikmund's two volume collection of essays, *Hidden Histories in the United Church of Christ* (1984 and 1987), complicated the traditional four-stream history by introducing numerous smaller groups within and uniting with the main churches over the course of two hundred years. While Zikmund's books make clear the limited focus of the other works, mainly on institutional developments, male characters, and European origins, the publication of *Hidden Histories* illustrated the fragmented and patchy nature of our understanding of United Church of Christ history.

In 1990, there was a flurry of activity in publishing or reprinting historical works on the United Church of Christ and its forebears. Williston Walker's *Creeds and Platforms of Congregationalism,* originally compiled in 1893 and reprinted in 1990, presented a documentary history of the Congregational Churches. Two years later John von

Rohr's *The Shaping of American Congregationalism* (1992) appeared. He concentrated on the period before the Congregational union with the General Christian Convention. David Dunn and several others edited *A History of the Evangelical and Reformed Church* (first published in 1961 and also reprinted in 1990). This was a more balanced presentation of narrative essays in the histories of both the Reformed Church in the United States and the Evangelical Synod.[7] Johnson and Hambrick-Stowe's *Theology and Identity,* appearing at the end of the troubled decade of the 1980s, began with the traditional recital of short histories of each of the four main traditions. The theological essays that follow turn again and again to the founding ecumenical vision even as they point out the difficult points of diversity within the church.

The union-of-four-traditions approach to the history of the United Church of Christ served the denomination well when most people in it came from one of the four traditions and could remember their lives as separate churches. It acknowledged the gifts each tradition brought into the formation of an entirely new kind of church, and it fostered the use of these traditions in developing the new institutional forms and rituals of common life that hold a Christian communion together. The United Church of Christ histories written in this period also emphasized the ecumenical enterprise that lay behind the church's formation. Rightly they pointed out the roots of the union effort in that generation's lifelong work for Protestant church unity in the service of a coherent Christian message for the difficult times of the early twentieth century. Unfortunately, the post–World War II era opened up challenges that were not easily answered by ecumenical enthusiasm or by reciting the gifts brought forward by the Reformed, the Congregationalists, the Christians and the Evangelical people who now together had to face the redefinition of Christianity itself from the outside world no longer much interested in its institutional life.

At this point it will be helpful to look at the United Church of Christ in the context of world Christianity. Looking for underlying patterns of ecclesiology, spoken or unspoken, I wish to open up some questions about the development of United Church of Christ self-identity in the last half of the twentieth century and to take our understanding more deeply into the American and world cultural issues of the twentieth century than has been attempted yet. Louis Gunnemann hinted that this would be necessary at several points in his classic history, *The Shaping of the United Church of Christ*.[8]

Louis Gunnemann wrote the first historical treatment of the United Church of Christ. Douglas Horton's earlier work, *The United Church of Christ*,[9] essentially a commentary on the UCC Constitution, contains a summary history of the formation of the church, but at that point the United Church was only five years old. Gunnemann traced the history of the denominations that formed the United Church of Christ and examined some of the context in which the union proceeded. Gunnemann's focus in this book and its sequel *United and Uniting*[10] was on the ecumenical aspects of the union, its ties to the larger ecumenical movements of the day and the necessity of attending to that ecumenical heritage as the church evolves in new times. Both histories focus on the national setting of the church, the actions of the General Synods and the activities of the national boards. Both also focus on the American mainline Protestant context of the story. However, the issues that were just emerging to trouble Gunnemann in the 1970s and 1980s, racial justice issues, feminism, and the question of sexual orientation as a criteria for ministry, originated in the local settings of the church. The increasingly complex dilemmas of economics and world peace spilled in from beyond the borders of the United States and mainline Protestantism, and were not particularly well addressed by an emphasis on ecumenical developments. These issues presented themselves urgently, one right after another, and called for practical response rather than simply theological discourse. So urgent were they that the theological discourse, needed though it was, was postponed.

In contrast to perceptions of the state of the church in the 1980s as distracted, obsessed with lack of identity, and focused on what feels good rather than careful thinking,[11] I see a church, rooted in the activism born of a pietist culture, exhausted not so much from lack of identity as lack of clear connection of that identity with the world concerns. In addition, the initial structure of the United Church of Christ isolated the national church from the local congregations causing their senses of identity to drift apart.[12] The problem was not so much that the church lacked a sense of identity as that it lacked a common one. In the chapters that follow, I would like to point to an emerging sense of common style based in both the Reformation traditions undergirding the church as well as the shared recent history of disharmony. This requires a look at the place of the UCC in the context of world Christianity as well as a consideration of factors outside Christianity, regional differences, increasing cultural diversity in American society, and changes in culture that have shaped all American religions, indeed most world religions. In addition, it will be necessary to view the history of the United Church of Christ from the local and regional point of view. Many issues arose locally to trouble the national church. In the remainder of this first chapter, I would like to discuss several aspects of this background of the United Church of Christ story that are rooted in culture and yet have called forth theological responses or should do so because they have ecclesiological implications.

UCC in the Context of World Christianity

The United Church of Christ is only a small branch of global Christianity. At just over one million members, it is overshadowed by the Roman Catholic Church with some sixty million members just in the United States, or by other Protestant churches, the various Baptist, Methodist, and Pentecostal churches in particular. In 2000, the United Church of Christ represented only 1.2 percent of those in the United States who claim to be adherents of organized religious bodies.[13] Its history lies in the sixteenth-century Reformation traditions of Western Christianity, most particularly among the Reformed tradition. Ulrich Zwingli and later John Calvin are important early figures in these traditions, but their thought is rooted even further back in ecclesiological concerns and ecumenical ideas of early Christianity, especially the theological tradition extending from the apostle Paul to the fourth-century theologian Augustine of Hippo. Though the UCC is situated historically in this Reformed confessional family (those churches sharing the Heidelberg Catechism and the Westminster Confession among their theological tradition's resources) it incorporates Lutheran, Anabaptist, and Wesleyan resources as well. The UCC is a member of the World Alliance of Reformed Churches because it was formed out of church bodies that were predominantly Reformed in their heritage and it carries on their previous memberships in that Alliance. However, the UCC does not fit neatly into that body.

Though it claims particular historical confessions of faith as its own, the United Church of Christ fits into that category of churches defined by loyalty to Jesus Christ but adverse to using dogmatic formulations as tests of faith, even if there may be general agreement among the churches about some matters of theology.[14] In this sense, the United Church of Christ is not purely a Reformed church though it stands in that tradition. The principle is stated in the Evangelical Synod's "Bekenntnisparagraph" (Confessional Statement).

> We recognize the Evangelical Church as that communion which acknowledged the Holy Scriptures of the Old and New Testament as the Word of God and as the sole and infallible rule of faith and life, and accepts the interpretation of the Holy Scriptures as given in the symbolic books of the Lutheran and Reformed Church, the most important being: The Augsburg Confession, Luther's and the Heidelberg Catechisms, in so far as they agree; but where they disagree, we adhere strictly to the passages of Holy Scripture bearing on the subject, and avail ourselves of the liberty of conscience prevailing in the Evangelical Church.[15]

The United Church of Christ is one of a handful of united and uniting churches in the world, churches united across confessional lines; among them are the Church of South India, the Evangelical Church of the Union in Germany, the United Church of Canada, and the United Church of Christ in the Philippines as well as movements such as the Churches Uniting in Christ in the United States. These churches share a number of distinct characteristics which in turn make it difficult to form internal clarity about theological and cultural matters. These characteristics were identified by three theologians participating in the Sixth International Consultation of United and Uniting Churches in Ocho Rios, Jamaica in 1995, Reinhard Groscurth of the Evangelische Kirche der Union, Roderick Hewitt from the United Church in Jamaica and the Cayman Islands, and Rena Karefa-Smart of the Episcopal Church, one of the members of the Churches Uniting in Christ (formerly the Consultation on Church Union).[16] Among these characteristics are a consciousness of unity as a demand of the gospel, a sense that every one of the denomination's partners in union has had to die to achieve a fuller life (Groscurth called it a morphological life),[17] understanding identity as an ongoing process shaped by the work of the Holy Spirit and expressed in mission, and not as a confessional stance that clarifies essential beliefs of the faith. All of these things mark the church as a uniting church, and all of them create difficulties. United churches do not find an easy road, and have trouble with issues of identity. They are open and accessible, but also vulnerable in order to heal the wounds of the world.[18] However, Groscurth affirms that "difficult as it is, the life of a united church keeps the question of church unity alive."

The essential ecclesiological questions facing United and Uniting Churches center on the question, for what purpose are we united? Hewitt suggests that the purpose is two fold, to share the Gospel with the world, and to be a blessing to the nations.[19] The united church is focused on the way of life required by the Gospel, the mission of the church, rather than in legalities of what the church "should" or "ought" or "must" do.[20] However, Hewitt laments that too often united churches become preoccupied with intraecclesial concerns instead of mission. Their organizational life is complex and these churches use precious energy trying to preserve and put together the various forms of church life represented in the union rather than concentrating on becoming in all things new for the sake of the mission of the gospel. In addition, all of the united and uniting churches tend to perpetuate Eurocentric ways of thinking and devalue indigenous roots and new patterns of theology and church life coming especially from communities outside the European traditions. This is especially troubling when the indigenous and emerging patterns are more responsive to current social concerns.[21]

There is a certain logic to the development in the United Church of Christ, a united church, of a multiracial, multicultural ethos. While I do not want to suggest that we fully know how to do this, it fits into two current day intellectual patterns. These patterns echo long-standing historical concerns within the traditions of the UCC as well. One is that sense of radical openness in the earliest churches. In these early ecclesia, the beloved community, beloved by Christ, beloved by each other, across lines of gender, class, and culture, came into being. The Gospel theme of eating together seems to have preceded mission. The biblical scholar Burton Mack put it this way.

> . . . To have been invited to a *koinonia* that cut across conventional barriers would in itself have been a slightly enticing experience. To find oneself in mixed company, having a good

> time talking about mixed company, might have been all the challenge one could stand. For the business of this association was just about itself as a new social configuration. It took its place on the borders of traditions breaking down, and filled in the spaces left vacant by the institutional fragmentation that was becoming obvious at the end of the Hellenistic era. People who felt lost or displaced may have found the association in the name of Christ appealing. . . .[22]

The self or community that serves its neighbors is formed for that service at the table where grace is extended to everyone who will accept it. The biblical record breathes an openness to the displaced, the marginal. Jesus seems to have chosen the margins of society rather than the center as the place from which to invite us to join the meal. This is a disconcerting reflection for a denomination that until recently was among the churches that shaped American culture. We have grown used to a place in the center.

In addition, as I write this book, we hear everywhere of a post-modern and even post-Christian culture. While modern and Christian do not belong together in any essential sense, the United Church of Christ is among those American Protestant denominations who fully embraced the modern as the best way to proclaim the gospel in the twentieth century. I would argue that while our historians still view the UCC as an appropriately modern church, able to carry on conversations with science and technology, able to translate the faith into frames of reference derived from political democracy, evolution, modern business, and capitalist economics, that lately we have entered into serious criticism of modernity, not as our Fundamentalist Christian sisters and brothers do, but in our own way. Our critique of modernity stems from our interest in the theological possibilities of the margins even if we are not able to stand there fully. As a united church and as a multiracial, multicultural church we begin to renew the early Christian dismissal of social barriers. Even more so, in the growing embrace of a radically open and affirming stance toward those displaced from the center of society due to gender or sexual orientation identities, or handicaps which require significant and visible accommodation by the majority, the UCC is willing to entertain a world view at odds with modernity. On behalf of those who suffer from the ill effects of modernity, environmental deterioration, the vast destructive possibilities of modern weapons, and the oppression of technology, the UCC is among those who raise a voice for justice and compassion.

The contemporary political philosopher Ernesto Laclau describes the basis of a democracy that gives difference an equal opportunity to shape society as "the attempt to preserve the conflictive character of all personal/social processes so as to stave off a total(itarian) social formation whilst at the same time aiming for a polity of "equality and equivalence."[23] The UCC has been moving in this direction, recognizing the tyranny of the majority of modernist democracy and aiming for a Christian culture in which each voice is valuable, regardless of the continual necessity of working through conflicting points of view. In this kind of polity, as Groscurth points out, a definite settled identity is not possible, only a constant process of pressing onward toward the beloved community sitting down together with a Christ who embraces the whole world. The United Church of Christ is not simply interested in the institutional union of churches, but in the unity of humanity.

The United Church of Christ is the product of a particular kind of ecumenical concern sharing this larger interest in human society outside of the church institutions. Louis Gunnemann points out in *The Shaping of the United Church of Christ* that the founders of the church came from the Life and Work Movement of the twentieth-century ecumenical project. This was the movement focused on the unitive possibilities in shared life and service. The Life and Work people tended to downplay questions of confessional unity and institutional form.[24] Instead they saw the path to Christian unity lying in the struggle for a just society. At the first World Conference on Christian Life and Work meeting in Stockholm 1925, the delegates issued "A Message to All Christians."[25]

> The struggles, losses, and anxieties of the Christian church during and after the war [the First World War] have led to the humiliating acknowledgment that the world is stronger than a divided Christendom. Before God and the world, we confess the sins and neglect of duty of which the church has become guilty through lack of love and sympathetic understanding. The call of this hour to the church must, therefore, be a call to repentance, and at the same time also a call for a cheerful new

> beginning through the inexhaustible source of power, Jesus Christ. . . . We have also considered these moral and social problems: the lack of proper dwellings, unemployment, immorality, intemperance and crime. We have been led to realize that these different problems can not be really solved through the strength of any individual but that the community must assume the responsibility for them and exercise social control over the acts of the individual insofar as it may be necessary in certain cases for the common good. We have also occupied ourselves with questions which arise from the higher valuation of woman, childhood, and labor in the field of education, the family and the every-day task. The church must not interfere in the rights of the individual but must represent the rights of the moral personality as well as anything else which enriches humanity through the complete enfolding of every individual soul.[26]

I believe Louis Gunnemann is right, that the founding of the UCC was fundamentally an ecumenical project and that ecumenical ideals, particularly those derived from the Life and Work Movement in the world ecumenical developments of the twentieth century, provided the energy and theological underpinnings of our beginnings. While I think many of the issues that face our denomination today may be framed in ecumenical terms, I do not think they all can be. An ecclesiology that functioned well to hold our disparate traditions based in creed and polity together ecumenically, is not always supple enough to help us with concerns of wider, more secular, plural divisions of class, race, culture, gender and sexual orientation. At the end of this first chapter, I would like to delineate the concerns that need attention if we are to understand fully the history of the UCC in the last forty years, and to begin to deepen our thinking about the nature of the Church and its ministry. These issues include regional differences, cultural diversity, race, gender, class, and political differences, the effects of the world wars, the Great Depression, and technology on everyday life, rising environmental concerns, and the disintegration of old empires and the rise of new ones. Not all of these issues will be treated with equal attention in these chapters, but all have importance for discerning the new roles the Church is called to play in and for society.

Let us turn first to locating the United Church of Christ within the larger picture of world Christianity, and then look at its situation within American religion.

It is an open question whether or not the United States might still be named among the Christian nations though Christianity is by far its largest religious tradition. By the end of the twentieth century, Christianity had spread to most of the world, though in most places it was also a minority religious tradition. Though Christianity is the largest religious tradition in Europe and North America, it lost its sense of being the majority as secularization grew. Christians, even in the most churched areas of the United States, cannot necessarily count on economic or cultural support for the expression of their religious faith. For instance, stores are open on Sunday, meaning some Christians work that day. On the other hand, Christianity is most prevalent in Latin America and is growing fastest in Africa. Europe and North America are no longer the center of the Christian universe if they ever were. The typical Christian today is a young Latin American, Roman Catholic, woman, poor or working class. The typical United Church of Christ member is North American, woman, over forty, middle class, with a greater than high-school education. The North American UCC woman may possibly believe her faith includes the Latin American Roman Catholic woman as a sister. The Latina Christian, however, most likely does not sense the hospitality or sisterhood.

Once recently, I overheard someone at a UCC meeting comment that there were more Muslims in the United States than members of the UCC. Indeed there are. In 2004, the UCC has a little over 1.3 million members. Estimates of the number of Muslims in the United States are hard to come by and vary widely. One source, the *World Christian Encyclopedia*, Second Edition, where the source of the numbers appears to be United Nations demographic databases, gives a 1995 total of 3.8 million expected to expand to 4.3 million by 2005.[27] Another source, *Religious Congregations and Membership in the United States 2000* using data based on organizational self-reporting of 416 of 1,209 mosques and surveys, puts the number of Muslims in the United States at 1.55 million.[28] This illustrates how different the twenty-first century context of the UCC is in relationship to its roots in earlier centuries. It is hard particularly for those UCC people from the Congregational tradition who for so long held cultural hegemony in this country, to find they are no longer at the centre of religious life in the United States. While the Congregational and Reformed traditions in America Protestantism could once claim cultural hegemony they are no longer at the center of the American Protestant universe. The people of the United Church of Christ have moved within one century from the center to the periphery of American religious culture, and that shifting social location has shaped us in profound ways.

Regional differences pervade the life of the United Church of Christ. A geographical review of the denomination reveals that while the Congregational and Reformed churches were among the big church families of the Colonial Era, by the time of the creation of the United Church of Christ both had been eclipsed by the Roman Catholics, Baptists, and Methodists, and the growing number of those disinterested in organized religion. In the 1950s, Congregationalists remained concentrated in New England, were smoothly spread in the upper Midwest and existed in small concentrations on the West Coast and in the South. The Reformed Church in the United States in the 1930s was most numerous in Pennsylvania and the Ohio Valley, scattered in the upper Midwest, and also existed in pockets in the South and the West Coast. The Christian Churches that found their affinity with the United Church of Christ concentrated in North Carolina, Virginia, New York, Ohio, and Indiana, with some concentrations in New England, and a few in the upper Midwest, Alabama, and Georgia. The Evangelical Synod churches clustered in the Mississippi, Missouri, and Ohio valleys, around the shores of the Great Lakes, and a few found their way to Texas or California. The United Church of Christ remains essentially a northern church which may explain why it has suffered less division on the social issues facing society. It is also located mostly in areas where church membership across all groups is falling.[29]

The origin of the United Church of Christ in the Midwest may be significant. It was not the cosmopolitan cities of Boston and New York, nor the sparsely populated synods and conferences of the West that produced the impetus for union, but rather the Midwest. Samuel Press and Truman Douglass from St. Louis, and Douglas Horton from Chicago were major figures in the initial conversations. While not from the centers of establishment in the cities of the East Coast, nor from the weaker communities of the West Coast, these Midwesterners had perhaps the best foundation from which to think about church unity, a stable social situation, and the lack of a tradition to protect. The uniting Synod was held in Cleveland and it is in this geographical region that all four of the uniting traditions had representation.

Geographical differences in the United Church of Christ continue to be apparent. The northern Midwestern conferences continue to be among the strongest. New England, Pennsylvania, and Missouri are still the heartlands of the Congregational, Reformed and Evangelical traditions respectively. In New England, the Associations are strong, because they were the initial organization congregations formed in their efforts to express a larger sense of the Church. Generally, in the West, synods or conferences are stronger. Either the Home Missionary Society's influence in Congregationalism kept the conference organization strong, or the Evangelical and Reformed synods served as the basic organization. In both cases, Associations and Coetus groups were usually formed as secondary bodies in the West, whereas they arose originally as the primary bodies in the East.

Besides geographical diversity in denominational culture, layers of immigration have created increasing cultural diversity that has shaped all American religions. The initial cultural diversities in the United Church of Christ were rooted in the predominantly Anglo, or British heritage of the colonial Congregationalists, and the older German American culture of the Reformed Church (among the many German groups William Penn invited to settle in Pennsylvania) and to some degree also the Christians. Additional cultural diversity appeared with the nineteenth century German heritage of the Evangelical Synod, the African American congregations within the Christian and Congregational churches and the mission churches in the Native communities of North America and Hawaii, the Hispanic communities of the Southwest and Puerto Rico, among the immigrants from China, Japan, and the Pacific Islands, and a handful of European immigrant Congregationalists from Germany, Finland, or other places. In the beginning of the twentieth century, The Hungarian Reformed Churches became associated with the German Reformed Church, by then the Reformed Church in the United States. The majority Anglo or American churches in any of these traditions assumed that eventually the others would worship in English and participate in the larger American culture, while retaining and celebrating aspects of their original language and culture. That this was not always necessarily the plan of the churches representing a cultural minority, did not often surface for conversation. The United Church of Christ came into being despite what some saw as an impossible barrier between German and English cultural and church traditions. These would not prove to be the most difficult cultural differences facing the new church.[30]

In other kinds of cultural terms—class cultures, urban/rural cultures, the question of what it means to be Christian in America has shifted in a secularized society. The move from center, carrier and former of culture to outsider directly challenges the mainstream ethos of the United Church of Christ. The historian R. Laurence Moore, holds that outsiderhood is a mark of American identity, and that religious institutions serve to help communities preserve their individual identities by perpetuating that sense of outsiderhood.[31] Our Reformed and Puritan ancestors carried this sense with them when they arrived on the continent as exiles. Outsiderhood may prove more fruitful to our faith in the long run, provided we can avoid the Reformed/Puritan habit of seeking dominance and longing to create theocracy. The better part of the half century since the UCC was formed has been spent negotiating the cultural transition from mainstream to marginal religious identity. That transition has been rocky and appears differently from various settings within the Church. In addition, this transition has strongly affected the ways in which UCC people have perceived and struggled with the issues of the late twentieth century: race, war, poverty, gender, and sexual orientation issues, women's roles, technology, the environment, and the decline in institutional life in America.

From the local point of view, the issues facing twentieth-century American Christians in the Congregational Christian churches and the Evangelical and Reformed Church were not the ecumenical ones that galvanized the leadership of the union effort. This is not to say that local church people did not participate in the ecumenical enthusiasm of the time, they did. But other concerns were foremost in their minds. The world was changing rapidly and their economic and community lives were touched, raising concerns unanticipated by earlier generations. The two World Wars and the Great Depression had changed the relationship of national government to local life, they had changed people's understanding of themselves as workers as well as affected their sense of security. The relationship of America's different racial communities was brought to the consciousness of the nation as more than a north/south, black/white question, but rather a constellation of issues of race, class, and culture that affected everyone. Women's role in society was transformed and neither they nor their families could go back to the mythical times of the Victorian separate spheres. Vast migrations of people from one part of the world to another brought the world in some personal way to nearly every local community, and the automobile and airplane made shorter, more personal migrations easy and comfortable. Technology, especially television, opened a window onto the world in every house that had one, especially the world of violence, power, money, and sex. While much of this violence and power seemed far away and contained, the vast new threat of nuclear destruction and the more subtle but discernable decline in the natural environment disturbed their sleep and shook their faith in science and industry. In this cultural context, people who had been used to assuming that their Christian beliefs were congruent with their culture, found suddenly, within a generation or two, that their culture no longer held their Christian beliefs and values in high regard, and in fact had become indifferent to and ignorant of them. In addition, in the churches forming the United Church of Christ, the people had been used to being part of the influential group of churches in this country, and found by the end of the century that they were in the minority and on the margins of American Christian culture.

To give this change some form, we can look at the progress of these concerns within the United Church of Christ from the early fifties through the end of the 1980s and view the evolution of a UCC style of church life and thinking. The foundation of UCC church life in the 1950s was late nineteenth-century evangelical Protestantism overlaid by liberal theology and ecumenical enthusiasm of the early twentieth century. The Congregational Christian Churches and the Evangelical and Reformed Church embraced modernity. Leonard Sweet, an American religious historian, has characterized the modernist Protestants of this era, including the UCC as wholeheartedly adopting the modernist values of efficiency, exhibited in good business management and therefore bureaucracy and advocacy of ecumenism because it would eliminate duplication of services; activism which valued accomplishment over the repetitive non-productive forms of religious life such as worship and prayer; and pluralism both in terms of theology and demographics, opening boundaries but consequently in danger of losing identity.[32]

Though even in the thinking of the theologians who formed the earliest United Church ideas, the word liberal was somewhat suspect. It was nonetheless the foundation of the ecumenical ideal and social concerns that emerged with the new denomination. The nineteenth-century liberal and evangelical Protestant had been an optimistic soul, viewing Christianity as the most advanced religion, dispensing benefits unselfishly to the whole world, everything from vital, saving religion to better agriculture and political systems. This Protestant was concerned above all with the cultivation of Christian character and virtue and the cultivation of a good society.[33] And society reflected back an affirmation of these values and projects. However, our nineteenth-century Protestants, evangelical about both their religion and culture, and liberal and generous in their theology regarding social issues, were nevertheless imbued with the racism of the day, and neglected to take account of their privileged position in their own society. They genuinely believed they had earned a privilege, and that tended to make them paternalistic to those toward whom they directed their missions, and made them equally reluctant to admit those they 'helped' into full participation in the life of their churches. In short, they were middle-class Christians, open minded, but prone to thinking of their ways as best for everyone.

By the end of the 1950s, the Protestant churches sharing this legacy seemed to have proved their superiority. They were building congregations and churches at unprecedented rates, their numbers were soaring, and they seemed to be in rapport with their culture, fitting in, feeling comfortable. Mainline Protestant ministers were respected members of their communities, and with the prosperity of their congregations came a warm-hearted ecumenical spirit. These were people who, in Amanda Porterfield's words, "took the rightness of their world for granted."[34] Some decades have passed since then, and historians such as Leonard Sweet now point out that there were cracks in this comfortable facade.[35]

> Behind the picture window, it was a different scene—the furniture of faith formless and in confusion, the table of devotional observance on its last legs. Menacing yellow and black "civil defense" triangles on church walls across America showed just how carefree this happy decade really was. Behind

> closed doors it was "the haunted fifties," as I. F. Stone put it. Religious and biblical literacy had seldom been lower. Denominational identities were eroded by the forces of public religion, bureaucratization, and modernism's devaluation of tradition. Allegiances were becoming less to denominations than to movements and causes within denominations. The fifties were the triumphant decade for the definition of church membership as going to church rather than being the church, with the individualistic notion of the church as one's private chapel so rampant that gambits had to be devised to thaw the cold wars going on inside the sanctuaries themselves—guest registration pads passed down the pews, "rituals of friendship," during worship, and their more stylish updating in the 1960s as "the kiss of peace."[36]

The United Church of Christ was born in this paradoxical era. That same year, 1957, riding a wave of enthusiasm for evangelical religion, the Billy Graham crusade in New York netted over two million dollars and almost sixty thousand decisions for Christ. At the same time, the court-ordered integration of Central Union High School in Little Rock, Arkansas stirred civil rights concerns. The two events illustrate contrasting aspects of the times.[37]

The facade of religious prosperity seemed sound to the founding generations of the United Church of Christ. It was not until the decade from 1965–1975 that its weaknesses appeared and not until the end of the century that the full situation became apparent. The year 1973 serves as a particularly dense example of the kinds of assaults the facade of the fifties received. Those who were alive then will remember that many things happened that year. It was a General Synod year in the United Church of Christ, but it was also the year of the Roe vs. Wade decision, the AIM occupation of Wounded Knee, the Arab/Israeli war and the oil embargo, the United States's withdrawal from Vietnam, and Watergate. Just the previous year the Golden Gate Association ordained William Johnson and the Executive Council received the concerns of women in the church about the exclusively masculine language of the Statement of Faith and the words of the newly published *Hymnal of the United Church of Christ.* As this flood of urgent issues swept over the UCC, what became of its initial sense of its life as an ecumenical witness?

General Synod IX meeting in 1973 was, according to Gunnemann, a turning point in the church's recovery of its ecumenical vocation. That Synod issued a statement entitled "The Ecumenical Stance of the United Church of Christ," created the Council for Ecumenism, and discontinued the Theology Commission, moving its work to the Office of Church Life and Leadership.[38]

Important as these moves were to the ecumenical life of a church dedicated to Christian unity, the larger issues of society weighed on a local church membership ill equipped through the neglect of biblical and theological study to formulate a coherent mainline Protestant response to these events. All the historians of this period note the growing distance between the clergy and professional leadership in the Protestant churches and the people in the pews.[39] Over the course of the twentieth century, the professionalization of the clergy encouraged them to develop business models for organizing church work and to use the methods of psychology in their pastoral care, creating a distance between traditional theological understandings of church life and leadership and the actual practice of ministry. The laity became more and more isolated from the clergy, making appointments to see the pastor rather than receiving pastoral visits. The business style reassured the laity from the business world that the structure of the church was sound, but little by little the role of the pastor as spiritual leader and advisor was lost. A mystic in the United Church of Christ had virtually nowhere to go for spiritual counsel or understanding of intense religious experiences.

In addition, the gulf between the academic study of theology and the practice of theological thinking in the churches was growing. The gap between the concerns of the laity and the professed public agenda of the national church, the seminaries, and the clergy threatened to unravel the ecumenical ideals and vocation of the denomination. While these trends were only becoming apparent in Gunnemann's work, they now need more sustained attention from historians in order for the United Church of Christ to have a deeper understanding of its past and its future calling. While the tale of four denominations coming together serves to introduce this new church, its history has by no means simply followed that initial agenda. In the following chapters we will take a closer look at several of these issues in an effort to come to understand how the United Church of Christ understands its ecclesiology, and how these issues in society have influenced its development.

Out of the United Church of Christ engagement with the social and ecumenical issues of the late-twentieth century world, an ecclesiology has emerged that is characterized by three emphases, covenant, community, and mission. However, there has as yet been no complete articulation of the ecclesiological thinking of the UCC, nor has a consensus developed. Thus, the picture I present here is an ecclesiology in progress. It will serve to help us understand the ways the UCC has been shaped in its almost fifty years, and I hope also will encourage further refinement in our theological thinking about the nature and purpose of the Church.

The United Church of Christ locates itself within the broad Trinitarian family of Christian confessions, though it does not insist on a particular theological understanding. It also takes Scripture as its inspiration and guide, though not for a century and a half has any of its traditions taken the words of Scripture in a literal or magical way. While it does not fully share the Catholic understanding of the Scripture as a product of the church and thus the most important, but not the only source of Christian faith and practice, it does not follow the strict doctrine of the words of Scripture alone being sufficient. Following Calvin and supported in the newer historical critical study of the Scriptures, we understand the necessity of discernment of the context in which the parts of what became the Scriptures were written, what purpose they served, and how to translate them into the language of a culture almost unimaginably different from those in Late Antiquity.[40] Any ecclesiology in the UCC has to be faithful to the Biblical record, and recognizable within the traditions that make up the denomination. The Biblical record also leaves many questions open, and thus leave us continually free to rethink the meaning of the texts for our new contexts. The tension between a recognizable faithfulness to the Biblical tradition and the discernment of new insight for contemporary questions is characteristic of our denominational life. The ecclesiological ideas I have developed here in order to help me discern what is going on in the history of the United Church of Christ are by no means to be taken as settled doctrine among us, but rather as some possibly useful ways of understanding ourselves that both keep us within the broad traditions of Christianity we claim to stand within, and also as a source of fresh ways of understanding the meaning of the "ecclesial journey" in our own time.[41]

In addition, the development of any ecclesiology for the United Church of Christ inevitably entails attention to the growing ecumenical conversation about the nature and purpose of the church growing out of both the Faith and Order projects within the World Council of Churches, and the increasing need for the churches to give an account of themselves to a secular society. In both conversations, Louis Gunnemann noted more than a decade ago a developing ecclesiological deficit in the UCC, that is we failed to develop an understanding of the nature of the church.

While I have heard it argued that ecclesiology means simply polity, the UCC has come to no consensus about the theology of the nature of the church which underlies our polity. In UCC conversations about ecclesiology three terms surface again and again. One is Beloved Community, whose origins are obscure to me, but the outline of the ecclesiology people seem to mean when using this term has been laid out beautifully by the Presbyterian ecumenical theologian Lewis Mudge, in his book, *Rethinking the Beloved Community: Ecclesiology, Hermeneutics, Social Theory.* "[T]he reality of *ekklesia* is *given* through God's calling, through Jesus Christ and in the power of the Spirit, of the human race into 'beloved community.'"[42] A second common term arising in conversations about ecclesiology in the UCC is covenant, stated in the UCC Statement of Faith this way, "God bestows upon us the Holy Spirit, creating and renewing the church of Jesus Christ, binding in covenant faithful people of all ages, tongues, and races." Missio Dei, stated in unaccustomed Latin by Norman Jackson, the idea of the mission of God as the fundamental principle defining the church and its ministry is the third common ecclesiology put forward in recent UCC discussions. This definition is rooted in our long history within the social gospel and the Life and Work branch of world ecumenism.[43] The UCC Statement of Faith puts it this way, "God calls us into the church to accept the cost and joy of discipleship, to be servants in the service of the whole human family, to proclaim the gospel to all the world and resist the powers of evil, to share in Christ's baptism and eat at his table, to join him in his passion and victory."

The ecclesiology I find myself facing in the UCC is rooted in a paradox evident in the Gospels. First the radical openness of the UCC understanding of the Church is an outgrowth of Jesus' continual violation of the boundaries that excluded people from society—illness, gender, occupation. In his great sermon he says not to judge, not to worry, that all who mourn, all who are meek, all who hunger and thirst for righteousness, all who are merciful, all who are pure in heart, all who are peacemakers, all those who are persecuted for righteousness' sake will be blessed. Or as Luke has it, those who are poor and who are mourning will be rich and happy. It is clear that this openness will bring conflict. On the other hand, it is equally clear in the gospels that not all who are invited to this company respond positively to the invitation. Not even all who are healed choose to join the company. Generally in the Gospels it seems to me that for Jesus there are no boundaries to the table, or the community, but it is equally clear that people put up such boundaries all the time, and many refuse the invitation because of their discomfort with the unbounded table.

The same paradox seems also to exist in Paul. For instance in the letter to the Romans, Paul wrote, "God shows no partiality." On the other hand, while there will be honor and peace for those who do good, there will be anguish for those who do evil. Paul, and after him the Gospel writers are not completely clear about the nature and purpose of the Church. At times it is simply a community of people gathered to remember Jesus Christ. At other times, it is clear that the central nature of the church is a community dedicated to proclamation of the resurrection and that this proclamation leads to a life of love. But over and over in Paul's letters we find the notion of invitation or election. God invites an unlikely group to the table—Jesus invited an unlikely group to the table. It is the startling invitation of God that crosses the social barriers recognized by human beings that characterizes the Church and its paradoxical radical inclusiveness and apparently stringent requirements for membership.

The paradox continues throughout the history of Christianity, and the community called by God that is the church has moments when it forgets the balance. Sometimes, the boundary is obscure, and while the table is fully welcoming, love does not reign because people come to the feast only to feast. Sometimes the church has forgotten that the church is not simply an invitation to party, but a costly invitation to discipleship. In other times the church has forgotten that the invitation has no bounds because God's love has no bounds, and has tried to restrict the love of God to only certain people, who behave in well-controlled ways, mistaking custom for morality. We live still in this paradox within the UCC. We tend (thankfully, I think) to err on the side of an unbounded feast, but the beloved community is called into being, and lives in covenant in order to give witness to the resurrection, to the living reality of God's love for the world. That witness involves both the safer proclamations of sacrament and study and the familiar fellowship of our congregations and the more dangerous public witness in the face of personal and systemic evil and indifference. The covenant keeps us from mistaking our own desires for the mission of God, the beloved community sustains our hope and love even as our work for the mission of God can go for so many years unrewarded. The covenant is formed by love, for those who love us and are beloved by us are sustained by God's unending love. That love cannot rest contented within a sanctuary but must go forth in mission to embrace the world.

In the following chapters, I wish to put this emerging ecclesiological thinking into dialogue with the social and internal political issues the United Church of Christ has considered of greatest importance in its corporate life. In the next chapter, I ask how we came to identify ourselves as a multiracial, multicultural church, how this is a requirement for the beloved community, what it requires in terms of our covenantal life, and to what work it calls us in proclaiming the Gospel and bearing witness in our deeds as a church. In the third chapter I search out the theological foundations of our ecclesiological ideas in the Reformation, the Pietist movements and the Enlightenment. In the fourth chapter I turn to the development of a liberal style in the theological thinking in the traditions of the UCC and how this development shaped our thinking about the nature and purpose of the church. The fifth chapter focuses on the nature of covenant in relation to community, and some particular legacies from our Congregational forbears. And the conclusion will be a reprise of the United Church of Christ as an ecumenical project.

Two

Becoming a Multiracial, Multicultural Church[1]

History is often marked in the United Church of Christ by General Synod Resolutions, the product of a collective thinking process, answering some pressing need to speak to or about the times. These resolutions rarely represent complete consensus. They may represent only the thoughts of the majority of the people assembled in that General Synod, but they all are rooted in concerns that arise somewhere else in the church. When in 1993 the Nineteenth General Synod in St. Louis passed the resolution "Calling the United Church of Christ to be a Multiracial, Multicultural Church,"[2] it was not pulling an issue out of thin air, but putting forward a widespread dream of a church rich in cultural traditions in which the one body of Christ was undivided by society's distinctions of race or language. Though this dream was stated over and over again in the United Church of Christ, clearly it has been hard to achieve. In this chapter I have no intention of trying to say how we might actually become a multiracial, multicultural church, open and affirming, and accessible to all—as our phrase runs. This is a communal enterprise, and certainly one white woman has no business suggesting the process. United Church people have always been engaged in this project in some way, sometimes more successfully than other times. As a historian, I believe I can offer some ruminations on how racial and cultural difference has been identified and valued in our past traditions and what wisdom can be derived from such an exploration.[3]

> They, therefore, brought me to the church, to the place where the word of God would confront and transcend the hostile forces of hate, violence, prejudice, and even the law of the land. They believed that the gospel had the power to bring together, in one transformed community, people of all ages, races, and tongues. They believed that membership in the household of Jesus Christ transformed persons to become the new creation. It was their belief and hope that the church would become that new creation and that it would use its moral and spiritual force to eliminate racism and to create a wholistic and inclusive society. . . . The division of the human family because of race challenges the Church of Jesus Christ to renew its foundational commitment to the faith. God's promise to us is that we are one people because we are reconciled to God in one body through the cross. Therefore, we cannot support any pattern of subordination or domination that separates and divides.[4]

With these words, theologian and activist Rev. Yvonne Delk, made clear the nature of the church as a community in which transformation, resurrection, liberation are possible, indeed to be expected. This concern for the broken nature of the Christian community along the lines of race had very early superceded the traditional ecumenical concerns of faith and order in the United Church of Christ. The ecclesiological issues Delk raised so clearly in her 1989 article "The Unfinished Agenda," are that racism is a profound violation of the beloved community, a breach of the covenant with each other and with God (and therefore is sin) and a failure to undertake the reconciling mission of God.

The main development leading us to the 1993 resolution has a simple plot line, with complex subtexts. The traditions of the United Church of Christ, for the most part European in origin, thought of their cultures as the best, most advanced in the world, largely, they believed, as a result of the application of Christianity to the structures of society. Their approach as Christians to other cultures was that of enthusiastic efforts to convert them to both their Christian religion and their European American culture. As they developed long-term relationships with people of other cultures, both at home and away from home, some of them came to appreciate the ways of others and to have a critical perspective on their own culture's habits and structures. In addition, many converts to the traditions represented in the United Church of Christ chose the religion, but did not take on its cultural forms. Nevertheless, predominantly, converts to the traditions of the United Church of Christ adopted European cultural forms as well as Christian religious content. While there have always been some who could navigate cross-cultural waters with grace, most of us have been uncomfortable outside of our own people's ways and have chosen to remain in separate enclaves within the larger denomination.

By the end of the twentieth century, the major divisions within the United Church of Christ traditions were no longer theological (though those differences exist as well) as much as cultural. The denomination's initial efforts at creating a multicultural, multiracial church have resulted in some success, but primarily it has been on the surface. The irony of this superficial success lies in the church's request that those people, whose culture the European ancestors of the UCC worked hard to eliminate, now revive their culture to share with everyone. We enjoy this multicultural festival as long as it does not fundamentally change the way we do things. In the coming decades, the United Church of Christ must undertake the harder work of understanding and welcoming a wide range of ways of organizing, thinking and carrying on mission. It will take everyone together to do it. Enormous variety will be possible. I look for the day when gifts from all of us are valued by all of us. But it is not easy and so in this chapter I return to history for some perspective.

Church and Culture

The concept of culture needs some definition these days. A recent summary[5] by Fernando Segovia of the issues as they pertain to our topic of multiracial, multicultural forms of church life suggests that the particular definition of culture we use will inevitably have political overtones and, to be honest, they should be acknowledged. Is culture the art, literature, philosophy and science produced by a people with the leisure and means to "cultivate" these things? Is culture the way of life of a people organized into a national group living in a particular natural environment? Is culture shaped by economics? And are individuals independent from their culture, or in important ways determined by it? There are no simple answers to these questions because the idea of "culture" has at various points been identified in all these ways. In this chapter, when I use the word "culture" I mean primarily the habits and customary ways of thinking and living that groups of people develop over time in their lives together. These ways may include art and literature as well as political and economic structures. They are habits and become deeply ingrained, shaping people's sense of identity and their very personalities. However, culture is also cultivated and changeable. People do adopt new cultural forms, either because their environment changes, or they move to a new environment, or they simply are attracted to a new way of doing things.

In this chapter, I understand culture always to be a communal process, it is never simply a matter of individual choice and shaping, but rather the work of the individuals' webs of relationships, whether they act consciously in concert or not. Culture is also not explicitly associated with race. Particularly in the United States, because of the mixing of people, most cultures are shared by more than one race and people of any particular race practice more than one culture. Where more than one culture exist side by side, political relationships among them shape these cultures depending on their relative prosperity and power. Thus emerge terms such as mainstream or dominant culture and minority culture or subaltern culture. The United Church of Christ for the most part derives from "mainstream" American culture, a culture shaped over almost four hundred years from a British colonial base and English language literature with additional contributions from generations of European immigrants to the cities of the East Coast and Midwest. It includes the complex legacy of African slavery in its economic, political, and social structures. However, increasingly it contains minority cultures besides the African American ones that have also been viewed and valued as inferior to the mainstream culture, but are now declared in our 1993 resolution to be equally valuable. How will the United Church of Christ then create an inclusive denominational culture? And more importantly, as Christians in America, how will the UCC negotiate the difference between its denominational culture and the national culture(s) in which it lives?

The question of the relationships of Christianity and its institutional form, the church, with the culture in which it lives have been alive from the beginning of tradition. Paul in his letter to the church of Rome, a church he did not start and whose agreement he did not count on, deals primarily with cultural difference between Jew and Gentile and the unity of the church. As the church developed, it was not only the question of Jews and Gentiles, but Greek, Latin, Persian, Celtic, Arabic, Egyptian, Indian and Chinese cultural forms of Christianity. Where doctrinal discussions were often overshadowed with political concerns, and evangelism efforts followed trade routes and imperial expansion, various cultures shaped Christianity in many ways that had nothing to do with the Gospel. However, the basic stance of Christianity allowed it to take a variety of cultural forms without endangering its unity of belief. Pope Gregory's advice to the missionary Augustine in the sixth century is one illustration. Augustine wrote to Gregory in the year 598, "Whereas the faith is one and the same, are there different customs in different Churches? And is one custom of masses observed in the Holy Roman Church, and another in that of the Gauls?"[6] Gregory replied

> You know, my brother, the custom of the Roman Church, in which you remember you were brought up. But my advice is that you should make a careful selection of anything that you have found either in the Roman [Church] or [that] of the Gauls, or any other Church, which may be more acceptable to Almighty God, and diligently teach the Church of the English, which as yet is new in the faith, whatsoever you can gather from the several Churches. For things are not to be loved for the sake of places, but places for the sake of good things. Choose, therefore, from each Church those things that are pious, religious, and seemly, and when you have, as it were, incorporated them, let the minds of the English be accustomed thereto.[7]

In the Middle Ages, the main cultural question for European Christianity became the relationship of the religion to government. Christianity replaced the ancient household deities and imperial religion of Rome as the state religion by the end of the fourth century. Western Christianity thus became wedded to the Roman Empire first and afterward to the collection of small feudal nations that replaced it. The struggle of Popes and emperors and kings for ultimate authority in society defined a large portion of Church history in those centuries. In addition European Christianity in the Middle Ages developed from the monotheistic faith of the Jews, already rich in its cultural diversity, and incorporating elements from the older polytheistic traditions of the European peoples, molded yet another form of Christian religion equally rich in saints and angels as well as biblical apostles and prophets.

The traditions from which the United Church of Christ was formed were forged in the great sixteenth-century reform movements within this European Christianity and it's Church. Because the people of that time assumed the equation of religion and secular society, reform of the church inevitably required reform of social structure as well. The sixteenth century was not a tolerant age. The reformers focused single-mindedly on purifying the church and society from all that was not congruent with the New Testament.[8] The Reformers were persecuted where they were in the minority and where they had the upper hand became in turn persecutors. Multicultural expressions of Christian faith could not exist in such an environment. The equation of religion and culture was so completely assumed that few Protestants or Catholics could have entertained the idea.

The Reformed tradition, from which most of the UCC traces its roots, originated in the Swiss cities, the most important being Zurich and Geneva, and went further in theory than the German Lutheran tradition in changing church structures. Where Luther kept the episcopal polity in which the church had always been formed in Germany, including the role of the prince in the governance of the Church, Zwingli and Calvin looked to the New Testament for alternative models that would free the Church from secular authority. The Swiss reformers were not able to put this theory completely into effect and the city council, notably in Geneva, retained the ability to influence church affairs. In addition, Zwingli and Calvin derived the conciliar view of ecclesiastical governance from the New Testament tradition, that the Church was best governed by a council of its elders rather than a single person be it pastor or bishop. In doing this they followed contemporary calls within the late Medieval Church for a council to reform the papacy and the Church bureaucracy. Both Zurich and Geneva adopted a form of church government that became known as presbyterian, placing the governance of the church in the hands of lay and ordained elders (the presbyters), a church council. Where Luther kept the roles of bishop and prince in the governance of his culture,

Zwingli and Calvin also kept the model of secular government by city council, and they provided a role for the city council in church government. In both cases the city council authorized the reforms in the first place. However, Calvin insisted that the city council, made of up of lay people, was under the authority of the Church rather than the other way around. This conciliar form lies in the immediate background of the development of Congregational ecclesiology in the English Reformation as well as the presbyterial organization of the German Reformed Church.[9]

Though the conciliar polity increases the number of voices in deciding Church policy, it is not necessarily a guarantee of greater tolerance. While the Reformed tradition developed a form of Church governance that could increase diversity, it did not always function in that way. Both the German Reformed Church and the Congregational Churches in the British American colonies tended toward intolerance. Their project was not to forge a new and open society, but to forge a more tightly defined society in the interests of salvation of souls. Church and culture remained wedded in their minds.

The Traditions' Encounters with American Religious and Cultural Plurality

Colonial America, especially in the areas controlled by Great Britain, was not monolithic in culture. In the first place, England had a way of opening its colonies to its dissenters instead of trying to suppress them at home. Among those dissenters, the Congregationalist Puritans found a refuge in New England and there tried to mark out a geography ruled according to their understanding of God's plan. Others, Quakers, Baptists, Catholics, and even the Anglicans entered neighboring areas and forced the Puritans to come to terms with them. The Dutch, a Reformed people, were near by in New York. William Penn solicited colonists from the Palatinate in Germany, both Reformed and Lutheran people, to come to Pennsylvania. The Scottish Presbyterians came as well. All these Reformed groups settled close to New England, but being Presbyterian rather than Congregational, their agreement with the Congregationalists was limited to theological principles.

For both groups, their first significant encounter with another culture was their meeting with the Native American peoples in the area. The result of their wedding of Christianity and culture defined their approach to the other. Their approach assumed incorporation of the other into their religious culture. Some even characterized it as a commandment, *Cuius regio, eius religio,* the principle by which the religion of the ruler determined the religion of the people still pertained, though already Pennsylvania's religious diversity allowed no single group to dominate. Uniformly they assumed the right to incorporate the Native Americans into their own culture.

The Puritan Congregationalists started missionary work in the first generation of their migration, notably the missions of John Eliot and later David Brainerd. In this mission they undertook to convert the Algonquin, the Narraganset, the Massachusets and other Native Americans both to Christianity and to English colonial culture, though both the colonists and the Native Americans would have been hard pressed to separate the two. In 1671 Eliot composed a series of Dialogues designed to aid native missionaries in converting their neighbors. The dialogues serve to illustrate the way in which Eliot's culture was embedded in his idea of Christianity. Eliot painted the Massachuset culture as shameful and sinful. He envisioned their eventual incorporation into his own society and therefore wrote in English, even though he knew their language.

> KINSMAN. Well met, and welcome beloved cousin. I am glad you are still alive. Can you make shift to live in that new way of living that you have taken up at Natick? [One of the villages of Christian Indians founded by Eliot]
>
> PIUMBUKHOU. I am very glad that God hath guided my way so well, as that I should meet you, whom I have longed to see. . . . I am like a friend that has found honey, and plenty of food, and I come to call my friends to partake with me. But what noise is this that I hear?
>
> KINSMAN. I perceive you have quite left off those delights and fashions that your countrymen use, and which in your young time were accustomed to, because you have forgot the meaning of such noises. There is a great dancing, and sacrifice, and play, and that is the noise you hear.
>
> PIUMBUKHOU. You say right. We have indeed quite left off and cast away those works of darkness. For we have great light

> shining among us which discovers the filth and folly of those things. . . . We plainly see the sinfulness of our own former, and of your still continued ways, and I desire that God will help me to open among you some of the divine light which god hath showed us, that it may shame you from such filthy practices and shine them away forever, as the rising sun doth dissipate and drive away all the darkness of the night and maketh wolves, bears, and all other wild beasts hide themselves in thickets, and not dare to be seen in the day light.[10]

Living in an English-style house, keeping the Sabbath, and becoming educated in the faith as well as in "the ordinances of God; whereby we walk with God in ways of civil government, and good order,"[11] defined Christian life. The dialogue implies that the "praying Indians" were prosperous and healthy because they followed the true religion, while warning that praying for such things only showed a person to be interested in earthly matters.

Eliot portrays the cultural exchange as the absorption of the Massachuset into the English culture, as a one-way movement. He forgot that the cultural exchange was at first two-way. The Plymouth colonists had established their village on the site of a Native town which had been abandoned. Level places for buildings and some building materials were at hand. They used seed corn they took without asking from Indian stores (some from graves), and later learned from the Indians to use fish as fertilizer. The Pilgrims were marginal and outnumbered. Their anxiety was evident at that Thanksgiving day feast October 3, 1621 when the surviving Pilgrims (some fifty in number) invited the Indians, only to be overwhelmed by ninety-two visitors. The Indians brought with them five deer for the feast. After dinner the Pilgrim men discharged their firearms in a show of force.[12]

While for the most part the Puritans' only relationship to the Native Americans was that of enemy, the few missionaries who tried to establish a relationship expected conversion to include the adoption of their culture as well as Christianity. This pattern repeated itself over three hundred years whenever the Puritan Congregationalist met another culture. They incorporated the other into a general English sameness. This culture, Yankee Christianity one might call it, was Reformed Protestant in its theology, evangelical in its style (engaged in mission with the view of converting others), English in its language and literature, and fully supportive of and supported by American representative democracy and growing industrial economy. A. Knighton Stanley identified several characteristics of this style, particularly noticeable in Congregationalism. In a spirit Congregationalism consisted of a continuing desire to reform the church and transform society. This resulted in a tradition with a theocratic ideal (society should be guided by the church), and a covenant form of organization based on shared ideals of behavior rather than confession of certain beliefs. The heritage of Congregational hegemony in New England easily became cultural imperialism, and it also easily developed a weak sense of denominational identity because it had a propensity to equate itself with American culture.[13] A vision of this Yankee Christianity spread across the United States with the foundation of the American Home Missionary Society and the American Missionary Association. These mission societies undertook to win the whole society to this way of being religious in America. One hearty proponent of this Yankee Christianity as it moved West across the continent was Horace Bushnell who frankly celebrated the Saxon race. "Out of all the inhabitants of the world, a select stock, the Saxon, and out of this the British family, . . was chosen to people our country."[14]

Among the New England Yankee Congregationalists, anxiety about Roman Catholics was particularly high. The October 3 date for the first Thanksgiving Day was the anniversary of the Dutch overthrow of Spanish rule, and the consequent defeat of Catholicism. Early in the nineteenth century, Boston became a majority Catholic city, fueling this anxiety. After the Mexican War in 1848, the enormous territories annexed by the United States represented another Catholic threat inspiring missionary efforts by Congregationalists, Presbyterians, Christians, and Methodists to convert the Hispanic population to Protestantism in order to save the Protestant character of the Republic. The Congregationalists converted very few of the former Mexican citizens. They as well as the Christians were more successful in Puerto Rico and later with Puerto Rican immigrants to Florida and New York. In both the Mexican Southwest and the Caribbean, the Hispanic Congregationalists have always had to negotiate an ambiguous space between the Catholicism of their culture and the Protestantism they adopted.[15] In addition, the American Missionary Association work with the southern newly freed slaves was motivated in part by anxiety about the burgeoning Roman Catholic missions in the same area.[16]

The home mission efforts of the Congregationalists, the German Reformed, Christians and Evangelicals concentrated first on providing churches in the places to which their people migrated, but also offering to others not originally of their group an evangelical, educated, democratic form of church life they believed to be most consistent with the Gospel. While the Congregationalists engaged most of the major racial and ethnic groups in the United States at one time or another, both immigrants and those native to the territories annexed to the United States in the course of the nineteenth century, the German Reformed and Evangelicals worked most closely with other Reformed Christian people coming from Europe. The Christian Connection developed home mission work, focused largely on serving those Christians migrating west, but also engaging immigrants, Native Americans, and through their foreign missions, Japan, India, and Latin America. Of the four groups, the Congregationalists remained most inclined to equate their religion, particularly their church organization with their culture.

> As Congregationalists, while we hold ourselves in an honest and generous attitude towards all other bodies, it becomes us to set its full value upon our system and polity, as that which is most scriptural, and because most scriptural, best fitted to secure the highest state of vigor and prosperity to the church, not in New England alone, but at the West, and everywhere, where the divine laws prevail. What is so good a thing intrinsically, is good enough to be maintained and propagated by all lawful and honorable means.[17]

While the Christians held Christian unity to be their principle mission, they were also concerned with the growth of their tradition, whether for practical or theological reasons. Josiah Bishop outlined the theology underlying the Christian missionary work in *The Christians and the Great Commission.*

> The missionary idea grows out of the nature of things; it is the idea of propagation. . . The Church must propagate or it will become extinct. Here is a natural basis of missions. . . . But the

> enterprise of Christian missions does not rest on mere inferences that may be drawn from natural bases. *Christian missions is a divine institution, authorized and ordered by God Himself in His sacred Word. This is a pivotal point. . . .* From Genesis to Revelation the Bible is pregnant with the missionary idea.[18]

According to this thinking, the destiny of humanity lies in Christianity and the supreme business of the Church, its mission from God, is for it to expand until everyone in the world has heard the Word of God.

In the Evangelical Synod, concern grew about the increasing secularization of German and American society. One advocate for missionary activity in the church picked up the same idea that Josiah Bishop of the Christian Church put forward, that the Evangelical Synod would turn inward and die unless it undertook missionary activity. The immediate problem was the difficulty of the Christian India mission in the 1930s, a difficult financial time for all American churches. Some in the Synod wanted to curtail what they perceived to be an expensive program. Two advocates, Paul A. Menzel a pastor and Secretary of the Board of Foreign Missions and his son E. W. Menzel, a missionary in India, argued instead that such missionary activity was vital to the life of the church, growing out of an ecclesiology based in the mission of God.

> The cost of the missionary program has been emphasized out of all proportion to the other side of the ledger, namely, the benefits which have accrued to the Synod through its missionary program. It will take a lengthier chapter than the present one to trace out the full import of the influence on the Synod of the contacts with larger Christian fellowships which participation in mission work make inevitable, and the educational value of "giving" which no other branch of our work has been able to teach our constituency of German immigrants (who came from a country where the State supports the Church thus relieving the individual of obligations) quite as effectively as the appeal in foreign missions.[19]

The same concern is echoed in the Reformed tradition, when one writer expressed concern that almost as many people drop out of churches in three years as are added in two. Charles Schaefer, General

Secretary of the Board of Home Missions of the Reformed Church in the United States until the Board merged with that of the Evangelical Synod in 1934, wrote that the mission the churches were called to most strongly was the Christianization of their own country. Borrowing rhetoric from the Congregationalist Leonard Woods, he wrote an essay in 1914 pointing out that America so far had set a poor example, sending missionaries to foreign lands when the American churches could not manage to make their own society Christian. The mission of the church was to Christianize all of society. Growing cultural diversity worried him most.

> Great forces are marshaling themselves in this country. Two great civilizations are meeting on the Pacific Coast, which is destined to be the Mediterranean of the World—one is the civilization of the West, the other of the east. Occident and Orient meet each other in deadly combat. Which shall prevail? The issue depends upon the answer which the Christian forces of America give.[20]

The assumption of cultural superiority, more precisely Anglo or German-American (both Saxon) cultures, colored the encounter of all four churches with those outside European-America. Efforts to convert the Other grew out of their fears that other cultural expressions would somehow erode American social and political institutions in addition to their convictions that Christians should convert and transform the world for spiritual ends. Even the Social Gospel with its concerns for worker and city dweller was steeped in a sense of cultural superiority. Josiah Strong, one of the key Congregational figures in the early Social Gospel movement was clearly ambivalent about the diversity of cultures flowing into the United States at the turn of the nineteenth century.

> Long before the thousand millions are here, the mighty *centrifugal* tendency, inherent in the [Anglo-Saxon] stock and strengthened in the United States will assert itself. Then this race of unequaled energy, with all the majesty of numbers and the might of wealth behind it—the representative, let us hope, of the largest liberty, the purest Christianity, the highest civilization—having developed peculiarly aggressive traits calcu-

> lated to impress its institutions upon mankind, will spread itself over the earth. . . . And can any one doubt that the result of this competition of races will be the "survival of the fittest"?[21]

I suspect that much of the anxiety displayed among United Church of Christ people today regarding the decrease in our numbers is centered not so much in worry about our faithfulness to the Gospel as simply about whether we are among the "fittest" in the secular sense.

Throughout the nineteenth century, the multicultural question within the traditions of the United Church of Christ turned on the question of what it means to be American because the Congregational Churches, the Christians, and even the German Evangelical Synod and the Reformed Church in the United States assumed that to be American was to be Protestant Christian. As time passed, the German traditions and the other smaller European ethnic traditions that became part the United Church of Christ felt the pressure to assimilate into the widespread Anglo-Saxon ethos, adopting the English language, democratic structures, and modern optimism about economic and religious progress. If their only difference from the Anglo-Saxon American was language, the assimilation was much easier, if other factors were in play, such as race, it became more difficult.

In the late nineteenth century the New England home missionaries and the Social Gospel preachers worked to shape a particular kind of American culture. However, as A. Knighton Stanley pointed out, the original genius of the movement was lost in the project of creating a duplication of New England culture among especially the southern Blacks, instead of bringing the genius of New England tradition to bear in a new place as in a crucible where a new tradition could be born. But the same process is recognizable with other cultural groups as well. Stanley applauds the American Missionary Association, a largely Congregationalist society, for seeing that the freed Black's problem lay in acquired attitudes and life styles imposed by dehumanizing conditions rather than on a genetic deficiency. The problem, the American Missionary Association recognized, was history rather than biology—however their view of history was limited. They failed to note the way in which Congregationalism had collaborated in a culturally conditioned social and historical perspectives in its effort to preach the Gospel in the southern Black community. "White Americans particularly, and Europeans generally, have been reluctant to admit that cultural supremacy is the underside of white supremacy. This has been especially true when cultural supremacy could be obscured in some ideological framework which gave it sanction that made this framework appear to be absolute and divine."[22]

In the twentieth century, the question shifted, particularly after the Second World War. American culture and the role of religious traditions in shaping it changed as society became more culturally complex. The question of what it means to be Christian in America now requires a new look at what it means to be the Church. Until this point, the ecclesiology underlying the missionary movement envisioned a church constituted by willing converts bound together in covenant by a common set of broadly Reformed Protestant practices and doctrines. They advocated an Anglo-American culture they believed to be derived from this religious culture featuring nuclear families, industrious workers, democracy, education, and a high degree of personal freedom. They remained unaware of the source of many of their values in the expanding industrial business culture of the corporation. The highest mission of this church was to convert the whole world to its religious beliefs and way of life.

United Church of Christ Thinking about a Multiracial, Multicultural Ecclesiology

Several factors lay behind the rethinking of ecclesiology in the twentieth century in order to take account of cultural diversity. The first was the sustained experience of the missionaries worldwide. The encounter of the myriad forms of European and North American Christianity in other parts of the world showed an embarrassing lack of Christian unity. Much of that disunity was based in theological difference, but more was based in differences of language, national origin, and culture. In addition, Christianity was adopted by people of Asian, Pacific Island, Native American and African nations and given forms comfortable to them but foreign to those who came as missionaries. The problem of how to recognize Christianity in varieties of cultural dress became central to the growing ecumenical movements. The second factor was the deep questioning of Christian alliances with national policies. This was occasioned by industrialization, economic depression, world wars, racial strife, and discovery of the limits of Christian optimism in human progress. The third factor was the immigrants of many hitherto unfamiliar forms of Christianity along with other world religions coming to the United States after the Second World War. The Christian claim of superior culture in relation to their assumption of the basic weakness, ignorance and corruption of other religious cultures broke down with actual contact. New respect for other religions opened dialogue on the nature of Christianity and the purpose of mission.

The traditions of the United Church of Christ shared a principle of "liberal pluralism" in their approach to the cultural diversity increasing around them. This principle is still dominant in the denomination. Fernando Segovia characterizes the logic of the principle in this way.

> At the core . . . lies a project of assimilation undergirded by the following principles: the abstraction of ethnic cultural practices from the material conditions of their existence; the appropriation of these practices at the level of aesthetic culture, removed from any sort of political or economic considerations and thus confined to the realm of recreation; and the ongoing exercise of homogenization and rationalization in the political and economic spheres.[23]

In essence, the newcomers gradually enter the mainstream culture, learn its language and take on its social and economic forms, but contribute new varieties of food, holidays, literature and religious ritual which others feel free to appropriate. The "Others" melt into a larger "Same." The traditions of the United Church of Christ, though liberal in their tolerance for diverse cultural practices and advocating and celebrating pluralism, hoped for these diverse cultures to assimilate into mainstream American culture, while borrowing their songs, prayers, dances, and music for worship and decoration, but resisting any change in the way power and money were handled in the church. Our denominational policies mirror Segovia's definition of liberal pluralism. The 1993 resolution seeks to move beyond it to a change in ecclesiology that would undergird substantial change in the alignment of power in the church. The United Church of Christ, born in that immediate post-war period, had available to it the makings of an inclusive ecclesiology, but has only now begun to learn to live it out.

The elements of that inclusive ecclesiology are lodged in many of the early foundational documents of the churches. The Congregationalists' idea of the freedom and responsibility of the local church to be the church in its location, based in the covenant of believers, places no cultural barriers before the community. One of the earliest Puritan theologians, Robert Browne, wrote, "Wherefore are we called the people of God and Christians? Because that by a willing covenant made with our God, we are under the government of God and Christ, and thereby do lead a godly and Christian life."[24] Reaffirming the principle that "the Catholic Church is the whole company of those that are elected, redeemed, and in time effectually called from the state of sin and death unto a state of Grace and Salvation in Jesus Christ, . . . invisible in respect of their relation wherein they stand to Christ, . . . visible in respect of the profession of their faith, in their persons, and in particular churches,"[25] the Cambridge Platform of 1648 offered a mature Congregational definition of the Church. In particular the Platform sought to avoid connecting church structure with national political forms, although the Congregationalists did not always succeed in doing that.

> The state of the members of the Militant visible church walking in order, was either before the law, Oeconomical, that is in families; or under the law, National: or, since the coming of Christ, only congregational: (The term Independent, we approve not: Therefore neither national, provincial, nor classical.[26]

Based not in Paul's letters, but in the Gospels, the Platform states that "there were no ordinary officers appointed by Christ for any other than *Congregational* churches" and that there was the possibility of diversity among them, the church in each locality having its own character. This covenant ecclesiology left room for diversity of theological and cultural expression within a mutually supportive fellowship of churches and a basically Augustinian or Calvinist theological consensus.

The Heidelberg Catechism, a foundational document of the German Reformed Church, based in Reformed Protestant theology but recognized ecumenically by Lutherans as well, takes a more theological approach to the definition of the Church.

> Question 54: What do you believe concerning "the Holy Catholic Church"? I believe that, from the beginning to the end of the world, and from among the whole human race, the Son of God, by his Spirit and his Word, gathers, protects, and

> preserves for himself, in the unity of the true faith, a congregation chosen for eternal life. Moreover, I believe that I am and forever will remain a living member of it.[27]

Gathered from the whole human race, the next question affirms that believers "shall share in one fellowship." While concerns about translating the catechism into English marked cultural concerns among the Reformed from Germany, the catechism itself does not limit the Church to a single culture. Likewise, the Evangelical Catechism makes no mention of cultural differences among Christians as a significant problem. "What is meant by "Church" in the Apostles' Creed? By the one holy universal Christian Church we mean the entire body of true Christians."[28] The Church is called "universal" because "God meant it for all . . . and because everyone finds in it what he [or she] needs."[29]

The Christians were reluctant to develop an ecclesiology beyond reference to the New Testament. James O'Kelly's "Author's Apology" was written in 1798 to explain why his group, then known as the Republican Methodists, and later simply as Christians, left the Methodist Episcopal Church. Here O'Kelly put into words for the first time the Christian understanding of the Church. "We learn from the Book of God, that the church in general, includes all the real Christians in the world. Eph. 5:25. 1 Cor. 12:13,14. Any number of christians [his spelling] united in love, having Christ for their head, and center of union, constitutes a church."[30] While it may not be entirely clear why the verse from the passage on the Christian household as a metaphor for the church in Ephesians led him to this conclusion, the verses in Corinthians exhibit the characteristic ecumenical spirit of the Christian movement. "For in the one Spirit we were all baptized into one body—Jews or Greeks, slaves or free— and we were all made to drink of one Spirit. Indeed, the body does not consist of one member but of many." (NRSV) Rice Haggard, writing in 1804, clarified O'Kelly's initial thinking.

> Hence it follows that all Christians ought to be members of one church. Because we find but one foundation of a church, and that is Christ; "and other foundation can no man lay." All therefore that is built upon that foundation, is one superstructure, or one body in Christ. This is his mystical body, and no other. And the name of this body originates from its head, which makes it the christian [his spelling] church or church of Christ.[31]

Haggard derived his idea of the church directly from the New Testament, particularly from the metaphor of Christ the Vine and we the branches. In both the case of Haggard and O'Kelly, the church is not constituted at all by a body of shared belief, but rather by an organic experience of community. Having little spelled out, the Christian ecclesiology allowed for a variety of cultural expressions.

The theological heritage of the United Church of Christ suggests an open, culturally inclusive ecclesiology, but in practice it has not proved to be so open. Rosemary McCombs Maxey, a Native American (Muscogee) UCC theologian asks the Church, "Who can sit at the Lord's table?"[32] The answer, despite the many statements of better intentions, has been that those like us in manner and belief are welcome at the table in our churches. That has meant in mostly white congregations, mostly white people, mostly middle-class people, mostly well-educated people, mostly English-speaking people come to the table even when the invitation seems open. A rich cultural diversity exists among UCC congregations but not within them, and not always within the denomination's centers of power. What is missing? Why is the development of a multiracial, multicultural church so hard? Maxey's analysis of our history with Native American people serves as an example of a more generally applicable principle of missionary activity. The main missionary project was, as we saw above, and often still is in our efforts at church growth, assimilation of the other into white or European culture.[33] In the process of three and a half centuries of this project, the missionaries viewed the other cultures as something to overcome and change. By this missionary activity, people lost their languages and culture as the price for becoming Christian. Maxey speaks to a church that does not yet recognize the irony of its desire to celebrate cultural diversity after earlier generations of our missionaries tried to change or destroy the very cultures we now want to include in our ceremonial life.

When people gather for a banquet, in our case the foretaste of the heavenly banquet, they engage in conversation, not in one direction with only one listener, but in many directions with multiple speakers and listeners. The problem is that in the UCC the speaking mostly goes only one way. One thing missing at our tables is listening on the part of those used to doing the speaking.

> If this church can relinquish its defensive power posture and assume a listening posture, then we can sit at the Lord's Table

> as I believe God intends us to do. Let the United Church of Christ forthrightly say, We don't see one strand of commonality on which to base our unity, but let's be our unique selves at the Lord's Table. At the Lord's Table there is room to be, to be included, to be fed, to be forgiven, to be acknowledged, and to be at home in God's world. At the Lord's Table, there is a theology of listening toward mutual hearing.[34]

In summarizing Maxey's contribution, the Native American theologian, James Treat writes, "Her emphasis on relationships rather than doctrines or institutions suggests a distinctively native Christian understanding of "church" and of the connection between theory and practice."[35] Maxey calls us to move from an understanding of the church as proclaimer of the Gospel to the church as beloved community, listening to each other's witness. We share the Gospel rather than proclaim it.

An extension of the metaphor of the Table is that of family. In writing about theology among the Asian Americans of the United Church of Christ, David Hirano focused on the importance of family in Asian cultures. "The family is more important to Asian American and Pacific Island cultures than the individual. Families supersede the person, and individual identity is not as important as the family."[36] In a world filled with people who, in the eyes of the world are poor, unworthy, guilty, unlovable, shameful, or oppressed, the Church is called to offer family. "The church needs to become the extended family in which the losers as well as the winners are welcomed, where the sinner knows that God loves everyone. . . .The community of believers also becomes the locus in which displaced persons can find identity."[37]

The UCC ethicist Ismael García, in discussing the Hispanic/Latino Protestant understandings of *comunidad* defines the church in this way:

> The true church is constituted by all people of goodwill, no matter what the basis of their belief system. What matters is that they reveal a commitment to protecting the vulnerable from the power of death. This ecumenism is political not in the sense of seeking political power, but in the more fundamental sense of making power accessible to the powerless and keeping our power accountable to the weakest members of society. This church understands that God is not absent from

> any place and that we are all God's people. As a church, thus, we have as much to learn from the world as we have to teach to the world.[38]

He raises a danger when the *comunidad* becomes too focused on itself. "The danger is that we stop extending hospitality, recognition, and respect to strangers and to the future generations that our youth are forging."[39] His concern is echoed by Roger Shinn.

Responding to a lecture by Douglas Horton at Lancaster Theological Seminary in 1965, Shinn also entered a note of caution about this idea of family and its gifts and difficulties as a metaphor for the Church. Commenting on the 1963 General Synod debate[40] over a declaration of a policy to contribute funds only to institutions and churches that are open to all without respect to race, national background, or ethnic origin, he noted the following.

> One group, who opposed the resolution, frequently described the church as a family. This is a helpful description, harking back to the New Testament theme of the "household of God." This group pointed out that within a family nobody has to earn acceptance by his good behavior. . . . If my antennae reported correctly, this judgement came primarily from some churchmen of the Evangelical and Reformed tradition and its biblical force was mingled with notes of *Gemütlichkeit* [kindliness or cosiness]. The argument has unquestionable force. Its danger is that it makes the church a cozy fellowship instead of a fellowship of commitment.[41]

Another group opposed the resolution on the grounds of Christian freedom. Shinn identified this as a concern coming from some Congregationalists and pointed out its danger as well. "The danger is that it confuses biblical freedom with arbitrary assertion of will—that it remembers Paul when he says, "You were called to freedom" . . . and does not finish the sentence: "only do not use your freedom as an opportunity for the flesh, but through love be servants of one another" (Gal. 5:13)."[42] Shinn viewed the ultimate decision to pass this resolution as a defining point in the ecclesiology of the United Church of Christ. "Granted that the church is always subject to sin and error, the segregation of God's people by boundaries of race is so plainly a defiance of the very meaning of the church as to call for a decision."[43] He ended by warning however, that the danger in this decision is that we adopt the Donatist position of some in the fourth century African churches who defined the church in terms of moral purity forgetting "the sinful church always lives by the grace of God." The beloved community and the covenant of committed faithful people balance one another. Neither alone can adequately define our ecclesiology.

The image of a community gathered for a meal—at the Lord's Table—whether in the anxiety of the Upper Room or the festival of the Heavenly Banquet—runs through theological reflection on the nature of the Church among the minority traditions of the United Church of Christ.[44] The work of the Church lies with the people gathered at the table going out into the world to work for justice. The metaphor never leaves the people comfortably at the table among friends, but constantly sends them out to extend the community and to bring God's love to bear in human affairs. The movement from the table to the world is the subject of Norman Jackson's work on the *Missio Dei*.[45] In a country where Christian practice has come to mean "going to church," Jackson recovers an understanding of the activity of God in setting a people apart, and then sending them out to transform both the Church and the larger society, exemplifying justice and healing a broken world.[46] Despite the activist tradition claimed by the United Church of Christ, Jackson warns that we, along with the North American mainline Protestant traditions in general, tend to succumb to the cultural understanding of Christianity, to be content to sit in the pews, to meet around the Table even, but without comprehending the call of the restless Spirit of God for us to engage in the mission of God. Our understanding of ecclesiology is not complete unless we continually renew our activist style and that the activity "takes its character from the nature of God."[47]

In the African-American theologies in the United Church of Christ, a central conception of the work of God in the world is liberation. Some might say it is the central concept. In assessing the contribution of the Black churches to the United Church of Christ, Samuel Slie puts it this way, "Perhaps initially this could be said to have been passive, more a matter of presence in the midst of early American society, much of which claimed to be Christian, and, if Christian, thus concerned about the conversion of nonbelievers and setting captives free" but in the end, coming to see liberation as the essence of the Gospel. "God is not fully known by the parameters of our thoughts, but is alive, at work, and preeminently revealed in struggles for human liberation where people can come to know God as God has been made known in the existence of Jesus Christ."[48] Slie closes by quoting Benjamin Chavis, Jr.'s "Psalm 141."

> The church
> the faithful community
> of believers in Jesus Christ
> who come together to worship God
> to confess sin
> to share in everything
> who come together
> to take a stand for justice
> peace and liberation
> the faithful community
> the church of Christ
> continues
> to the remnant
> existing and struggling
> to reconcile the world
> to God.[49]

It is not only the world that needs reconciliation, but the Church as well. Bound together as "faithful people from all ages, tongues and races," we also bring with us our limitations and inability "to resist the powers of evil."[50] United Church of Christ theologian and historian, Lawrence Jones writes:

> Nevertheless, reconciliation within the body of Christ is a critical precondition for creditable pursuit of a reconciled society. It follows then that black theology issues a call to the United Church of Christ to embody the unity and oneness to which it summons its members in its formal statements. Unity and oneness are not synonymous with integration. In the search for unity and oneness one does not ask the other to "come and join us on the conditions we have established." On the contrary, one seeks that shared commitment to the purposes of

> God which is the primary challenge to every Christian as well as to the whole church.[51]

The United Church of Christ has paid attention to this challenge. In 1991, the national officers, Council of Instrumentality Executives, and the Council of Conference Ministers of the United Church of Christ issued their "Pastoral Letter on Contemporary Racism and the Role of the Church."[52] The letter signaled a recognition in the Church that despite considerable progress, racism seemed to be as entrenched as ever in society and in the churches. They reaffirmed the public witness of the United Church of Christ against racism and outlined again the things the churches needed to do, but offered little new advice on just how to do these things. Five years later, Bennie Whiten, Jr. offered this assessment and question.

> As I look back over the years, I think the United Church of Christ has made great strides forward in including persons of color. I can see the difference in General Synod delegations and attendance. The picture at General Synod 20 in Oakland in 1995 was much different than that of my first General Synod in 1963. A visitor would say that we are a multiracial and multicultural church—and in that setting we are. But what are the realities "back home?"[53]

Whiten asked further if a few conferences and congregations were asked to carry the burden of providing diversity so the rest of the church could feel they had achieved it. He had particular questions about the new structure that was developing for the national setting of the church.

> The new structure of the national setting of the church could reduce the participation and visibility of people of color even further. . . . For many persons of color, this was their introduction to the wider church, and that door is being closed. Perhaps others will open, but I am not particularly sanguine about that prospect. . . .[54]

In the same year as Whiten offered his reflections, a group of African-American and European-American United Church of Christ people presented a dialogue in *New Conversations*, entitled "Don't Ask the Question. . .if you don't want to hear the answer." The title of the issue came from a quote by Bernice Powell Jackson of what her mother used to say. And, suggested Jackson, "we don't want to hear the answer." Instead there is silence in our society about racism. "The first step, that very first baby step we must take to . . . finding common ground, is to talk."[55] An enormous educational task lies before the church. Jackson singles out education of all the races about themselves and each other as the basic first step in finding the common ground. In another essay, Jean Alexander, a white woman, plumbed the depths of the silence, but especially white silence.

> Writing about racism and the state of black/white relationships as a white person seems about as foolish as trying to run barefoot across a minefield. There is no doubt that no matter how carefully I say what I say I'm probably going to step on something and get blasted to kingdom come. . . . As a white person, I have to take more risks to be honest with those who I cannot assume will take what I say as spoken in love.[56]

Alexander also reminded her readers that the task is worth undertaking, and depends upon understanding this as a mandate of the Gospel, and, because racism is sin, depends also upon the conversation being grounded in the worship of God. Plumbing the issue of white silence about racism even further, Eleanor Scott Myers, a Disciples of Christ scholar, the author of another of the essays, confronted the "racialness of whiteness" and the inability of white people to talk about their experience of race and racism.[57] Myers went on to discuss the important aspect of power in relationships between the races.

> Maybe this unity we seek with persons of other colors is a continuing form of power-evasion; maybe as we seek to name it and define how to get there we are fighting to maintain our white power and control. After all it is what we know, perhaps all we know. And we feel comfortable being in charge.[58]

In the final essay of the collection, Hollis Wilson developed the idea of an ethos of diversity, suggesting the deliberate development of an alternative culture for the national setting of the United Church of Christ. It included the clear development of demographic diversity, but also a different way of working together. He applauded the consolidation of the national offices in Cleveland because it would foster contact, trust, and long-lasting relationships among those who serve in the national setting. Wilson suggested that the ethos of diversity is possible. "The diverse composition of the staff has reached a "critical mass." This fact requires the organization to find an alternate lifestyle which devalues conformity and values the critical nature of diversity."[59] He added one final point, *"Never underestimate the power of grace."*[60]

Geoffrey Black, writing in 1999 in *Prism*, followed Wilson's Ethos of Diversity line of thought and suggested that the church needs to move beyond the sociopolitical approach to inclusivity if it was to be able to talk about racism in a way that would lead to constructive change. "It also has to do with becoming a transformed people."[61] Thinking about Meyer's words about power, we can see that Black offers a way to equalize the power around the table. He suggested that one necessary change was in the way decisions are made. The process begins where Bernice Powell Jackson suggested it should, with shedding preconceived ideas and listening. In the United Church of Christ, partaking of two centuries or more of democratic political life, we have come to view the rule of the majority with a view to the rights of the minority as the proper and wise way to conduct business. It is effective and efficient without being autocratic. It gives us the sense that everyone has a voice and a vote and therefore a stake in the decision. However, we do not take account of the way in which the majority can become a tyranny. Black suggested a process of discernment that takes seriously everyone's point of view, and that a decision is not authentic until it answers everyone's concerns rather than only the concerns of the majority. In other words, no one is left behind. All remain around the table.

> In seeking to become a multiracial, multicultural church, we are challenged to become more relational in our approach to being church. In doing so, we must work at being in relationship with one another and in relationship with God in all ways, including the way we respond to the issues we encounter as the people of God. Perhaps when our decisions give way to our discernment, our corporate utterances and decisions will be received with the very highest regard by people of the church wherever they are shared.[62]

As I have read over the writings of United Church of Christ people from many cultures, I am struck by the way in which we are able to diagnose the problem of racism with clarity, denounce it with energy, but seem to get bogged down when trying to eliminate it. Certainly our theologians put forward suggestions, we develop affirmative action plans, we pay attention to public vocabulary and images, we may try listening and dialogue, and newer methods such as the discernment process outlined by Geoffrey Black. But the disconcerting thing is that none of these work without the transforming work of God among us. Jones calls the Church back to its origin in the Gospel asking the United Church of Christ to meditate and act again on the question "what do atonement, redemption, new birth, and reconciliation have to do with the *circumstances* of the "least" of these in the world?"[63] The word is that God is afoot among us, working for the "least" and molding a transformed world, a world of healing compassion and justice. This gospel is perennial. That word is either hopeful or disturbing depending on how much we have suffered from or benefited by the way things were and still are. Those of us who are disturbed need to meditate carefully on Jones' question. Living toward a multiracial, multicultural church requires bringing our polity into line with our theology of the welcome table.

Nothing in our historical theological consensus documents precludes the adoption of an Ethos of Diversity as our denominational style. Our ecclesiology supports a table open to all tongues and races. What gets in our way is simply human sin and therein lies the problem. Time and again, the thinkers of the United Church of Christ remind us that the way toward this vision is God's way and requires that we visit again the sources of our faith relying on the Holy Spirit rather than upon our human designs. The degree to which this Ethos of Diversity transcends the old liberal pluralism as the prevailing United Church of Christ style depends on the ability of those with power in the denomination to open their hands and let it go. I would like to close with these words from Cornel West. Where he speaks of the nation, we can apply the idea to the United Church of Christ.

> In these downbeat times, we need as much hope and courage as we do vision and analysis; . . . We are at a crucial crossroad in the history of this nation—and we either hang together by combating these forces that divide and degrade us or we hang

> separately. Do we have the intelligence, humor, imagination, courage, tolerance, love, respect, and will to meet the challenge? Time will tell. None of us alone can save the nation or the world. But each of us can make a positive difference if we commit ourselves to do so.[64]

I would add that Christ has already gone on before us to make a way.

✦

We gather around the table as the beloved community where we meet each other and the Risen Christ face to face. But Christ's love requires that we leave our comfortable community to undertake the mission to which God calls us, to work for liberation, the resurrection of all people, so that there are not barriers to the giving and receiving of love. We talk easily about justice in the UCC, but it often strikes me that we are a church afraid of the resurrection, the very idea of it and its power to transform community. This fear causes us to pull back from full participation in the beloved community. I think this fear is rooted in our intellectual tradition inherited from the Reformation and the Enlightenment and Pietist movements that followed it. The reconciliation of the churches to each other is not enough. If the church's nature is that of the beloved community called together by God's love, in love for each other, for the purpose of reconciliation, that reconciliation must go further than just churches in their relationship to each other, though that is critical to their ability to witness to the one body of Christ. The purpose of this unity of Christians with one another is for furthering the reconciliation of the whole world, all of humanity, all of creation, to God. In the next chapter I want to explore more deeply the ecclesiological heritage we have received and put it in dialogue with the multiplicity of denominational and theological traditions in the contemporary United Church of Christ. This emerging ecclesiology appears there as well as the ongoing, but evolving liberal cultural style of Christian life and thought of our traditions.

Three

Roots of Theological Diversity in the UCC

Reformation, Enlightenment, and Pietism

The Question of Theological Diversity in the United Church of Christ

Unquestionably the United Church of Christ is characterized by theological diversity. The volume of essays by Daniel Johnson and Charles Hambrick-Stowe, *Theology and Identity: Traditions Movements, and Polity in the United Church of Christ* suggests several kinds of diversity in the theological views of our denomination. First there are the theological traditions that were mainstream in each of the predecessor bodies, Congregational, Reformed, Christian, and Evangelical. Next are essays on several more kinds of theological traditions both intellectual or philosophical traditions as well as cultural traditions, process theology, feminist theology, liberation theology, biblical witness theology, and ecumenical theology. There are also issues presented that though not theologies themselves, raise questions for all the above mentioned kinds of theology, issues of sexual orientation and gender identity, mission, racial and cultural diversity, and the corporate structure of the church. The question for understanding the ecclesiology of the United Church of Christ is whether the inclusion of plural and diverse theological points of view and traditions is infinitely possible within our tradition, or does the UCC draw a boundary to this diversity? To what degree is the idea of the Church characterized by shared thinking about theology?

The United Church of Christ does profess certain shared ideas, but does not require strict conformity to them. As we noted in the first chapter, the tension between ecumenical and ethical inclusiveness and the desire for identity remains. Thus the question of the limits of diversity is always before us. In this chapter, I want to explore certain theological traditions in our historical roots that can lead to diversity in theological approach. In the end, the question will be whether the legacy of theological diversity can be supported when all of the traditions are gathered into one Church. The question of whether the UCC understands theological traditions of Christianity as given at a particular moment to be preserved, or whether they are the result of on-going processes of human interaction with the divine and thus expected to change with each new generation, is one that continues to surface in the UCC in various forms.

In the last chapter we considered that multicultural and multiracial issues represent a non-theological kind of diversity. We turn our attention now to theological issues that represent another kind of diversity. They are of course connected. Our understanding of the church is shaped theologically to take account of human experience. In the United Church of Christ, theological diversity is one of the main concerns throughout its history. The assumption of Christian unity as comprising among other things, some kind of theological unity, some agreement about the Gospel we share, the apostolic witness we pass on, lies in the background of our past and current theological thinking. This assumption is held by the majority in Christianity, not just in our church, and not just in our time. Christian unity as unity in belief underlies most of the theological developments of what the churches come to recognize as common doctrine—the teaching of the church. In the United Church of Christ the traditional formulations of doctrinal agreement from the history of Christianity, especially from the sixteenth-century Reformation, play a particular role. They do not, as in many other communions, define the boundaries of the church,[1] though we have congregations and Associations with confessional requirements for membership and ordination. The classical teachings of Christian doctrine are not simply put aside as irrelevant to the life of the church, though unquestionably we have members and congregations who do so.

The United Church of Christ is Christian in its affirmations, but even the Statement of Faith—coming as close as anything can to having universal acceptance in the UCC—exists in three forms and does not bind the conscience of any member to state the faith in precisely those ways.

In contrast to the United Church of Christ stand enormous numbers of Christians who define the Christian faith through particular creedal statements giving witness to a common confession of the truth about the Gospel. For many of them, the sacraments themselves are signs of agreement with the common confession and not open to those who think otherwise. The common plot line of the history of Christianity tells how the church after many struggles with error settled on the true statement of the faith in the course of the ecumenical councils of the first six centuries and after that engaged in constant defense of the faith against all manner of new errors. The story falters somewhat after the Enlightenment of the eighteenth century but overall, the mainstream of Christianity defended and still maintains the truth of the creeds, and in the twentieth century they became a focus in the growing ecumenical conversations.

Anyone who reads Eusebius, the fourth-century commentator and witness to the Council of Nicaea, cannot escape the knowledge of how political the ostensibly theological decisions of the Church were, and still are. By the time of the Reformation, the Christian humanists, both Catholic and Protestant, in their enthusiasm for a return to the sources, the earliest manuscripts they could find, discovered errors not only in Church documents but in the Biblical text itself. The transmission of authoritative texts had been subject to the same political influences as the creeds. Such findings did not immediately disturb the ongoing, particularly Protestant, proclamation of Scripture as the sufficient and even infallible rule of faith, but by the eighteenth century, additional scientific findings encouraged an alternative confidence in the power and authority of human reason. As the traditions of the United Church of Christ came into being in America, claims of biblical authority and the binding nature of the creeds as unquestionable representations of Christian truth faced increasing challenge. All of the UCC traditions held the Bible and some also the creeds to be authoritative, but all of them at the same time respected a critical approach to their interpretation based in a high regard for human reason. Thus all of the traditions had within them numerous schools of thought about the degrees and kinds of authority possessed by the Bible and the creeds. Among other theological questions, significant variation existed among the traditions on the matter of the Trinity, with some confessing the ancient creeds and others at the other end of the spectrum rejecting them altogether.

The United Church of Christ still situates itself among the Trinitarian Christian churches. However, I identify diversities among us that challenge an easy identification of the theology of the United Church of Christ with its Statement of Faith. First of all, a deep seated suspicion of the nature of creeds lies behind most of the traditions in the UCC. The Protestants still affirmed the traditional creeds of Christendom, but, in their defense of particular interpretations of Christian doctrine, they were willing to commit appalling crimes against those who disagreed with them, just as their rivals whether the Catholics, or other Protestants, were willing to do. In addition, the radical branch of the Reformation influenced part of the Puritan tradition, following the humanist interest in the origins and sources came to understand the creeds as merely human devices rather than divinely given. Particularly the Socinian or Unitarian branch of the Radical Reformation returned to an earlier view of the nature of Christ. Based on ambiguities in the Bible, they proclaimed a strictly monotheistic idea of God and clearly subordinated the person of Christ. They rejected the philosophical terminology of the creeds, and maintained that the concept of the Trinity as found in them was not biblical. The religious violence of the sixteenth and seventeenth centuries caused thinking Christians to reconsider the meaning of confessional definitions of the Church.

Both the Enlightenment and the Pietist movements shared a similar ambivalence about neat creedal statements delineating the basic required beliefs of Christians. Instead they favored a test of the fruits of one's life against one's claim to be a Christian. Behavior slowly became among Protestants the outward sign of a Christian life and in many circles equaled or surpassed the confession of a creed in importance. Human reason and experience at the same time rivaled traditional doctrine as sources of authority. Particularly among Puritan Congregationalists and Christians, confession of a common creed or belief by itself did not signify that one belonged at the table.

By the end of the nineteenth century, a thoroughly pragmatic approach to church membership pertained in most American Protestant circles and creeds were easily recited formally and dismissed as having any binding claim on the Christian conscience. Nevertheless, new creedal forms, for instance "The Fundamentals"[2] introduced in the early twentieth century brought new conflicts into American Protestant life. The traditions of the United Church of Christ did not become fundamentalist, neither did they reject conservative formulations altogether. They continued to focus on the Christian life rather than statements of belief as the identifying marks of Christian character and church membership. A liberal theological style developed in these traditions (to be discussed more fully in the next chapter), but one cannot simply find a single United Church of Christ theology much less simply label it liberal. The United Church of Christ has on the one hand remained ecumenically responsible, maintaining a recognizably orthodox[3] theological stance while remaining theologically open to engagement with the world around it. This essentially liberal style rested in the desire to remain in conversation both ways—with Christianity's apologists and Christianity's critics. Whether the United Church of Christ was critic or apologist was not always clear. In many cases it was both at the same time. Amanda Porterfield, a historian of American Religion suggests that the mid-twentieth century period into which the UCC was born, was characterized by declining interest in definitions of religious difference.

> Some commentators interpreted the general decline in the importance of religious difference in American culture as a sign of religion's lamentable retreat into a sphere of private life and, consequently, as an indication of its waning influence on public life. But this decline in the social importance of religious difference was also a sign of the lowering of barriers between religious groups in the United States and a reflection of religion's increasingly benign role in public life. In this regard, religion came to function less as an agent of ethnic identity and tribal solidarity and more as a catalyst for individual concern about social issues.[4]

Over the course of the twentieth century the traditions of the UCC and later the UCC itself sought to define themselves more in terms of an open engagement with others rather than in terms of an outside opponent. They did not even fully engage fundamentalism as an opponent. Martin Marty in a recent column in *The Christian Century* noted that mass religious movements usually grow because they have identified an enemy against which they organize and mobilize. In the nineteenth century, when our traditions were growing, the enemies were Roman Catholicism, slavery, and saloons. In the twentieth century we took a more complex and ambiguous view of evil, perhaps because we were able, for once, to see the log in our own eye. In any case, we no longer identify the Other as the enemy. Marty hopes that we do not become so anxious to grow that we go back to the old way.[5]

In this chapter, I would like to focus attention on three theological crucibles from which theologies in the United Church of Christ derive their native shapes, the Reformation, the Enlightenment, and Pietism. In addition, I would like to show how these traditional theological streams, in their encounters with modern life issues, have created a spectrum of theology in the denomination, rather than a single characteristic theological response.

How the Reformers Thought about Theological Diversity

The United Church of Christ attempts to hold together in one communion almost the entire Reformation. The German Reformed and Puritan theologians shared a basic Calvinist theology and responded positively to the growing Pietist movements in seventeenth and eighteenth century European Christianity. The Evangelical Synod came to the United States from the Church of the Union in Prussia, a grand nineteenth-century experiment in uniting Lutheran and Reformed Protestants in one Church. The more radical, sometimes Unitarian, Christian Connection nevertheless desired unity across confessional lines and, along with the Congregationalists whom they later joined, preserved a place for the historical creeds as testimonies though not tests of faith. In addition to Lutheran, Reformed, and Radical Reformation traditions, most of the Puritans also preserved their relationship to the Church of England and the principles of the English Reformation, particularly the unitive power of forms of church life where uniform theological confession proved impossible or undesirable.

The psychological distance is enormous between the Reformation, an age in which people regarded intolerance as a duty[6] and were primarily interested in discerning the one truth about God's will for society as necessary for its stability, and the Modern age in which people regard religious toleration as a virtue necessary to a stable society.[7] This distance makes it difficult for us to understand how adamantly opposed to theological diversity our forebears were. Understanding the difference between that time and our own makes it also understandable why one on-going position in the traditions of United Church of Christ does not favor theological diversity, arguing rather that the Reformation concern for witness to the single truth of the Gospel should be preserved. The Reformers assumed the truth was one and they assumed that they could discern it from a correct reading of Scripture. They also assumed that the church was coterminous with society. Church and state contained the same people. There could no more be two churches in one state than there could be two truths. In addition, they assumed the end of the world was near and that it was unconscionable to allow souls to be lost because they did not recognize the truth. Church and state cooperated to ensure correct teaching for the salvation of souls and an ordered society for the protection of the truth. Protestants and Catholics alike believed in only one truth and were willing to kill and be killed for it. They believed the survival of humanity, here and in the hereafter, depended on their passion.

In our time, I think, we ordinarily still assume the truth is one,[8] but at least most in the UCC no longer assume it is easy to discern a correct reading of it, from whatever authority. Most of us no longer assume that Scripture has the same kind of authority our ancestors assumed it had, though we still argue that it is our most important inspiration and guide for Christian faith and practice. Human experience as a source of authority was only beginning to be suggested by the Renaissance Humanists; its authority became indisputable after the Enlightenment. Is our theological diversity rooted in the finitude of human languages in the face of a divine truth we all recognize? Is our theological diversity rooted in indifference to the importance of true ideas about God? Is our theological diversity rooted in perverse individualism? When we, in the United Church of Christ, come to publicly celebrate theological diversity out of traditions that would have had nothing to do with it, what has happened? These questions remain open and may not be fully answered here.

In order to look further into these questions, I wish to organize the rest of this chapter into three parts, first a discussion of the initial inklings of tolerance among our beloved traditions, second a discussion of how the idea of theological tolerance developed in the American context, and finally how the idea of theological diversity, as having positive value, emerged among us. Along the way, I would also like to point out some of the consequences of this development, both positive and negative. I want to go on record as a United Church of Christ member in favor of theological diversity, not because I think truth does not matter, but because human understanding of God is subject to the complexity of human experience. I also think that there are basic elements of the Christian confession we do well to share with other Christians for the sake of Christian unity, whether we are completely comfortable with their expressions or not, as long as we do not abandon the conversations leading to larger understanding among all parties. In discussing the history of theological diversity as something with positive value, the idea of freedom of conscience plays an important role.

The primary Reformation ancestors of the United Church of Christ, Luther and Calvin, were interested in correct doctrine rather than diversity of theological opinion, though both acknowledged an area of Christian thought where diversity was acceptable because those matters were not clearly delineated in Scripture. Luther's idea of freedom entailed first of all freedom from the law, or freedom from works as the means to salvation. But, he reminded his readers, this freedom from the law is not freedom to do whatever we please, but freedom to love, freedom to live according to God's will. There was even a hint of insubordination toward any earthly or human authority in his concept of freedom.

> Take care not to use your freedom in the sight of the weak. On the other hand, use your freedom constantly and consistently in the sight of and despite the tyrants and the stubborn so that they also may learn that they are impious, that their laws are of no avail for righteousness, and that they had no right to set them up.[9]

This short passage from Luther's treatise on "The Freedom of a Christian" written early in his career as a reformer, is daring compared with his later insistence on obedience to governing authority in his "Small Catechism" written after the Peasant's War (1524–25).

Luther's theology rested on Paul's thought interpreted by Augustine of Hippo. In "The Freedom of a Christian" Luther simply elaborated the Pauline themes of freedom from the law because the

Christian is justified by faith alone, and that freedom is given for the purpose of loving service to God and neighbor. Luther also entertained tolerance for diversity in the church's celebration of the Eucharist, though he did not go so far as to tolerate additions that he regarded as going against the Gospel. The form of the liturgy, Luther wrote, was not to be bound by laws. "Even if different people make use of different rites, let no one either judge or despise the other . . . let them understand and know even if they do differently; and let each one's rite be agreeable to the other, lest diverse opinions and sects yield diverse uses."[10] Later in his work on the Eucharist, Luther expanded on his sense of freedom in shaping the liturgy in accordance with the Gospel outlines.

> Let these things said concerning the mass and communion suffice for the time being; other matters, use and the thing itself will teach; only let the Word of God be announced in the church actively and faithfully. For that which some require so strongly, namely, that all these things be proved by the Scriptures and the example of the fathers,[11] does not disturb us greatly; because we have said above, that in these matters liberty ought to rule, and it is not allowable to captivate Christian consciences either by laws or orders. For this reason the Scriptures define nothing of these things but permit the liberty of the spirit to abound according to its own perception in the matter, according to the fitness of places, times, and persons. Indeed the examples of the fathers are in part unknown; those which really are known are so varied that nothing definite can be established about them, evidently because they themselves used their own liberty. And even if they would be altogether definite and simple, nevertheless they could not impose upon us either law or necessity of imitating them.[12]

Luther never advocated complete liberty in Christian theology. His boundaries were the Creed, the Ten Commandments, and the Lord's Prayer, knowledge of which would keep ordinary Christians from abusing their liberty.[13] He focused on these three symbols of the faith in his Small Catechism. For Luther, Christian freedom was real. As he thought about the Eucharist, he allowed for differing forms if they did not violate the Gospel. For instance, he thought Zwingli's reformed view of the presence of Christ in the Eucharist as spiritual and remembrance only, violated the gospel.[14] Christian freedom, for Luther, did not mean one believes and does just anything. Christians are free to love their neighbors. "We conclude, therefore, that [Christians live not in themselves], but in Christ and in [their] [neighbors]. Otherwise [they are] not Christian. [They live] in Christ through faith, in [their] neighbor through love."[15]

Ulrich Zwingli, Luther's contemporary and the reformer of the church in Zurich, also did not allow much room for theological diversity, though he opened the door for some diversity of expression of the faith. He firmly limited Christian thought to the substance of the Gospel. In 1523 he formulated a list of his opinions, and those things he preached in Zurich, arguing that they are based upon the Scriptures that are themselves inspired by God.

> The sum and substance of the Gospel is that our Lord Jesus Christ, the true Son of God, has made known to us the will of his heavenly Father, and has with his innocence released us from death and reconciled us to God. Hence Christ is the only way to salvation for all who ever were, are and shall be. Who seeks or points out another door errs, yea, he is a murderer of souls and a thief.[16]

However, Zwingli discarded the layers of Medieval regulations of piety by writing "That no Christian is bound to do those things which God has not decreed."[17] Christian freedom, for Zwingli, lay in the freedom *not* to do the myriad of things that had become customary for the pious Christian of the time. Zwingli's principle regarding Christian practice was the congregation's judgement that any given practice was "beneficial and appropriate to enhance in some degree the spiritual memorial of the death of Christ, the increase of faith and [neighborly] love, the reformation of life, and the prevention of the vices of the human heart."[18] Like Luther, Zwingli discussed Christian freedom in terms of practice rather than belief. Both continued to affirm a basically Pauline theology and both retained the traditional ecumenical creeds. In their theological difference over the Eucharist, discovered in the Colloquy of Marburg,[19] both were adamant that theirs was the only truth. The idea of unity in diversity, theologically, was untenable because it would violate the unity of truth. Only one of them could be right, and souls were at stake. Each accused the other of blasphemy, a serious sin. They never met again and their traditions diverged only to begin to be reconciled in the nineteenth and twentieth centuries.[20]

John Calvin converted to Protestantism as it was becoming divided within itself. He followed Zwingli's Swiss Reformed tradition, working out its implementation in the city of Geneva. He shared with Luther's colleague Melanchthon a desire to unify the Protestant movement, and to at least leave the door open to reunion with the Roman Catholics. He continued the Pauline/Augustinian emphasis of Luther and Zwingli on Christian freedom as freedom for the service of God and love of neighbor. Calvin also distinguished between those things expressly commanded by God, the law that Christians as recipients of grace nonetheless work to follow out of love for God, and those things that are "indifferent" things Scripture records as God's commands to particular people at particular times, but not binding on all people in all times. Similarly to Luther's criteria of love, Calvin's criterion of service to one's neighbor helped the Christian discern what to do. Jane Dempsey Douglass in her discussion of Calvin's thought about Christian freedom points out a tension in Calvin's thought between the Christian's freedom to serve and the Christian's freedom of conscience in indifferent things.[21]

In his *Institutes of the Christian Religion* in the chapter on Christian Freedom, Calvin wrote. "Our freedom is not given against our feeble neighbors, for love makes us their servants in all things; rather it is given that, having peace with God in our hearts, we may also live at peace with [human beings.]"[22] Calvin's concern for freedom is not the freedom of the individual per se, but the freedom of the individual to participate in God's work of love in the world.

German Reformed people for the most part followed Zwingli and Calvin on the matter of freedom and toleration. They argued for the freedom of the Christian conscience for love and service to one's neighbor, but they agreed that society was best served by uniformity in Christian theology and practice, that the truth was one, and knowing it was important for the fate of the soul. The German Reformed tradition in the Americas was heavily influenced by the stricter Dutch Reformed views. The Dutch Reformed church particularly desired to distance itself from the ideas of Arminius.[23]

The English Reformation began as a reformation of church structure only, Henry VIII's separation of the Church of England from the jurisdiction of the Pope. Motivated by Lutheran theology, Henry's son Edward VI and the ecclesiastical leaders of his administration attempted to further reform the English church along Lutheran lines. The attempt was short-lived and the Church of England reverted to Catholicism under Mary. In the final stages of the English Reformation, Elizabeth I, again removing the Church of England from the authority of the Pope, opted for a liturgical uniformity without requiring theological uniformity, attempting to make room for a diversity of theological view in a single church. The church still served in her mind to unify society. As long as those clergy with diverse opinions did not change the liturgy or preach their dissenting opinions openly, they and their parishioners were free to believe what they would. This seemed well in theory, though it inspired significant opposition. The Book of Common Prayer of 1559 was not reformed enough for many English Protestants, particularly those who had spent Mary's reign in exile in Calvin's Geneva. They did not disagree with the principle of allowing private difference of opinion within the context of public uniformity, they simply wanted that uniformity to be based on what they considered to be a more complete truth.

The Radical wing of the Reformation diverged considerably from the rest of Western theological orthodoxy. While they created diversity in their times, they did not tolerate diversity of opinion among themselves. Had they had the upper hand, it is not clear that they would have been any more tolerant than their more mainstream fellow reformers. Radical reformers introduced two principles that shaped portions of the history of the United Church of Christ. One was the separatist principle. The earliest of the radical reformers, the Anabaptists Thomas Muntzer and Menno Simons, argued for the separation of church and state. The same theme is echoed in Robert Browne's 1582 "Treatise of Reformation without Tarying for Anie." "Let us not therefore tarie for the Magistrates: For if they be christians thei give leave & gladly suffer & submit them selves to the church government. . . . If they be not christians, should the welfare of the church or the slavation of mens [and womens] soules, hang on their courtesie?"[24] The second principle was the moderate biblical Unitarian principle derived from the communities sharing the ideas of the sixteenth century Anabaptists such as Adam Pastor and the Italian humanist Socinus, and influencing later English and American thinkers. In essence this group of Unitarians followed biblical ideas about God,

Christ and the Holy Spirit, but rejected the later philosophical formulations of the ecumenical creeds.Their own experience of persecution as minority traditions later sparked their desire simply to be left alone, paving the way in the American context for legalization of religious toleration, and finally complete disestablishment of religion.The Christian movement took up some of these ideas from the radical reformation. Some Christians adopted the Anabaptist practice of adult (believers) baptism and some the Unitarian theological principles.

The Protestant tradition continued to diverge because the appeal to Scripture alone and the priesthood of all believers allowed varied theological positions to emerge, each claiming to be the one truth, each carefully excluding the others. In the late sixteenth and seventeenth centuries Protestantism disintegrated into sectarian violence, with various forms of Protestant Christianity allowing themselves to be identified with rising nation states, all continuing to assume that theological unity fostered social stability and prosperity.

The Enlightenment and Pietism

One immediate effect of the Reformation was the proliferation of theologies but also a strengthening of the impulse to enforce uniformity of both belief and practice. The end result was violence and as many began to recognize this was a violation of the Gospel itself. By the end of the seventeenth century two movements arose both fostered by the weariness of the social dislocations of Christianity in their time and desiring to recover stability and meaning. Historians have named one movement the Enlightenment, and the other Pietism. Both share similarities. They had a high regard for human experience as a source of truth and authority. They both rejected unexamined claims for the authority of dogma. Both rejected or at least critiqued the connection of church and state. And both saw Christian character rather than creedal confession as the measure of one's faithfulness to the Gospel. They differed though, and to put it simply, the Enlightenment centered in human reason, in the brain if you will, and Pietism centered in human feeling, or the heart. Both movements influenced the traditions of the United Church of Christ, indeed in many important cases single individuals partook of both movements as they developed their theologies. Both movements contributed different theological emphases though, and many times seem to diverge from each other irreconcilably.

First let us examine the Enlightenment and its contributions to our traditions. The term Enlightenment usually refers to the eighteenth century, but it rests in previous developments in Western European thinking, particularly in the recovery of Greek and Arabic science beginning in the Middle Ages, the rise of Christian Humanism[25] in the Renaissance, and most especially by the rediscovery of the experimental method[26] in investigating the physical world. Enlightenment thinkers such as Isaac Newton, John Locke, Rene Descartes, Adam Smith, Mary Wollstonecraft, and Immanuel Kant are well known figures in the history of philosophy and they inevitably influenced religious thought in their time. Newton's "Optics" and "Principia Mathematica" (1687) were part of Jonathan Edwards' reading list. Locke's "The Reasonableness of Christianity" (1695) stood beside his works on civil government and his inquiries into how people know things. All of these works influenced not only the development of religious life but also the political structure of the United States and many Protestant denominations within it. The key contribution of the Enlightenment, besides centering authority in the systematic rational investigation of the world, was the idea of progress, that human beings, by applying their reason to the problems of life can by themselves bring about positive changes in the human condition. They placed a high value on education as a tool for progress and reform. Their critique of the churches rested not so much in skepticism or unbelief, but in the way the churches appealed to authority in the face of the conclusions of human reason, denying aid to human suffering for the sake of preserving the dogmas upholding their institutional power.

Within the churches, Enlightenment thinkers brought reason and experimental method to bear on moral and religious questions. Jonathan Edwards, one of the people in the Congregational tradition who combined interest in Enlightenment ideas with Pietism though he did not explicitly identify himself with either movement, undertook an experimental investigation of religious experience, his "Treatise Concerning Religious Affections" being the results of his work. The Puritan ecclesiology from which Edwards worked, identified the church as the visible company of the elect. In order for a person to join the church she or he had to give an account of a saving experience of grace. Knowing that either the candidate or the church could be mistaken in judging such experience, Edwards sought to understand the phenomena more completely. In his investigation he sought a reliable way to distinguish between true and false religious feelings or experience by observing the outward lives of those converted in the revivals of the first Great Awakening. While he did not presume to investigate the working of God, he did presume that the effects of a religious experience would be reliably similar to the human eye. Among the twelve signs of "Gracious Affections" he identified the following: the Spirit brings about a change in the person as a whole, they display integrity of action and affections; they have an immediate certainty of the truth of religion; they voluntarily acknowledge God's sovereignty; they exhibit love, meekness, tenderness, and quietness of spirit; and they practice these to the end of their days.[27] Though he recognized that an outwardly moral life was not enough, that it could be just for show, he believed that ultimately the selfishness of such a show would be discernable. His interest in this problem lay in his understanding of his duty as a pastor to exhort his people not to put barriers between themselves and whatever God desired to work in their hearts.

At its extreme, the Enlightenment approach to religion resulted in a completely rational faith, simply disavowing any religious claim that could not be verified by human reason. Miracles made such thinkers especially uneasy. The accounts of miracles in the Bible raised not only questions about the reliability of the physical universe, but also the reliability of moral law. If God can simply set aside the laws of nature and act unilaterally in opposition to such laws, how can the truth really be discerned? How can the human Christian argue for a moral law that God appears to violate—for instance in the unjust treatment of Job? While most Christian theologians undertook the task of defending God from such accusations, others rejected much of traditional Christian teaching in order to maintain their faith. While they preserved the idea of God, especially as Creator, they dismissed as untrue, as "myth" or "legend,"[28] whatever in the Scriptures seemed supernatural, or in their eyes, unnatural, or whatever could not be historically verified as factual. Thomas Jefferson's famous, or infamous, Bible is an example of such rational approaches to religion. Though he is not part of the UCC tradition, he illustrates the rationalist or Deist mode of thought very well. Jefferson expressed his understanding of Christian truth by taking two copies of the Bible and snipping out all those passages which he judged to contain legendary, mythical, or supernatural material and kept only the ethical precepts and those parts he accepted as historical fact. The parts he kept he then pasted back together to form a Bible without any elements that would defy human reason.

The Enlightenment shaped both the Congregational tradition and the German Reformed tradition in the colonial era. The Congregationalists in particular found a Lockean, Enlightenment understanding of government congruent with their Congregational ecclesiology and combined the Protestant idea of the priesthood of all believers with Locke's idea of the source of government authority lying in the consent of the governed. The subsequent theological developments in all the traditions of the UCC are shaped in response to the Enlightenment. In the next chapter we will look more closely into the ways that conversation is shaped in the nineteenth century. At this point we shall turn to the eighteenth-century Pietist movement.

Pietism

Whereas the Enlightenment was a movement primarily of the mind, Pietism was a movement of the heart. The Enlightenment was centered among the intellectuals and clergy, Pietism originated as a lay movement though clergy were active in it. The Pietists did not dismiss human reason, but they were not so interested in proving or disproving the truth of matters of doctrine. Their main concern was living a Christian life based on scriptural premises with the practical effect of increasing love. They emphasized feeling, not just as emotion, but as embodied experience, and stressed the human element in Christ's life. They were suspicious of a science without compassion, though they did not simply dismiss scientific investigations of the world. They were hesitant to make pronouncements about nature and history, but did not oppose the effort to understand both science and history. In common with the Enlightenment thinkers, they elevated education as a tool for improving society, though they laid more stress on the moral life than on the experimental method as the vehicle for improving the human lot. Dismayed by wars justified as fights over the differences in Christian creeds and the shallow religious life of the state churches, the Pietists sought in the Bible a sense of the voice of God addressed to human society. The movement was widespread and influenced both Protestants and Catholics.

The most important early figure in the Pietist movement was the Lutheran Philip Jakob Spener. Though he was not the only thinker of the movement, his work serves as an example of the general approach of the Pietists. His Pietism grew out of discontent with both the shallow religious life of the state church and the pedantic theology of the "Protestant Scholastics."[29] In 1675, Spener published his *Pia Desideria,* a work containing six proposals for restoring Christianity. His proposals presupposed small groups of Christian people meeting together for mutual prayer and spiritual direction, not separated from the Church (in his Lutheran context, a state church) but forming the spiritual heart of the church, its centers of vitality. His proposals called for intensive Bible study; exercise of the priesthood of all believers by the laity, including mutual pastoral care; the manifestation of charity in religious controversy, seeking to win the heart not the argument; establishing higher standards of religious life among theological students and faculty; and reforming preaching in order to revive the Christian life with sense of the voice of the living God in Scripture.[30] Pietists characteristically emphasized the emotional aspects of faith and a life style based on scripture. They stressed the human nature of Christ and Christ's identification with the human condition.

Pietists were not anti-intellectual however. They, like the Enlightenment thinkers, thought education in matters of philosophy, theology, history, and science was important. The heart as well as the brain had a role in human life, both spiritually and physically. Particularly important for understanding the emergence of the United Church of Christ is the Pietists' ecumenical spirit. They sought unity with Christians of other creeds through common religious experience of God and through study of the scriptures, the source of Christian practice for all those who claimed faith in Christ.

Many important theologians united Enlightenment and Pietism in their thinking. Two who are important in United Church of Christ tradition are Jonathan Edwards and later, Friedrich Schleiermacher. Neither of these two theologians would have used either term to describe his thinking. Both show signs of the influence of these two movements in their thought. Both Edwards and Schleiermacher were exceptionally creative and were themselves founders of new movements in theology. Edwards provided the foundation for the first identifiably American movement in Protestant thought. Schleiermacher was the catalyst for developing liberal theology.

Jonathan Edwards (1703–1758), a graduate of Yale, was for most of his career pastor of the church in Northampton, Massachusetts. He became one of the most important figures in the First Great Awakening, a period of religious revival that swept through the New England Colonies in the 1740s. The revival was one of the expressions of the Pietist movement, encompassing the Methodist movement of John Wesley and in the Reformed and Congregational communities, the work of George Whitefield and Jonathan Edwards. Other participants included Count Zinzendorf, a Moravian who influenced both Wesley and some of the German Reformed people of Pennsylvania; Gilbert Tennent, a Presbyterian; and opponents of the awakening, such as Charles Chauncy, a thoroughgoing Enlightenment rationalist. In general, Pietists tended to favor the revivals but those of Enlightenment stamp tended to oppose them. Jonathan Edwards is unusual in his rational inquiry into the religious experience and results of the revivals, taking seriously the working of God on human religious affections as well as being a dispassionate critic of both those who dismissed the revivals as false and those who enthusiastically embraced them without considering whether the results justified the claims of those converted.

Friedrich Schleiermacher (1768–1834) lived a century later than Edwards in Germany. He was educated in the Pietist University of Halle under the influence of Immanuel Kant, and was later a hospital chaplain and pastor in Berlin, teaching theology at the University of Berlin. Schleiermacher was at the height of his career when Frederick Wilhelm III of Prussia acted to unite the Reformed and Lutheran churches in his realm in 1817.[31] The action coincided with the 300th anniversary of Luther's Ninety-Five Theses. Those members of this union church, The Church of the Union in Prussia (now part of the UEK), who came to the United States, eventually formed the Evangelical Synod of North America. Edwards represented the first generation of theologians to grapple with the issues posed to Protestantism by the Pietist movements and the Enlightenment. Schleiermacher represented the second generation to do so.

Edwards' main contribution to the understanding of religious experience as he participated in and witnessed the revivals, was to apply the principles of experimental method such as they are used in science, to the observation of the revivals as a phenomenon. In the "Treatise Concerning Religious Affections,"[32] his analytical treatment of the phenomena of religious experience, Edwards divided the work into three parts, first an introduction and then two extended lists, one of those signs commonly used to claim that someone has had a religious experience or affection which on investigation turn out not to be reliable, and secondly a list of signs that can reasonably be supposed to characterize a true religious experience or affection. These signs of true religious affection include a noticeable change in the person as a whole integrity of actions and affections; a love for God that is for God's excellence in itself and not because of God's forgiveness or anything else God has done for the person; affection arising out of the beauty of holiness; having spiritual understanding or sense; voluntary acknowledgment of God's sovereignty; love, meekness, tenderness, and quietness of spirit attended by increased appetite for God; and lasting influence of these signs on one's Christian practice, lasting in fact until the end of one's days.[33] Edwards applied those principles, not without compassion, but with a pastor's concern for the souls of the people.

His observations about the revivals focused on people's changed behavior. In discussing the revival of Religion in Northampton, he seemed unconcerned about creedal doctrine but concerned especially about true and false conversions, or true and false understandings of the experience of God's grace as they manifested themselves by people's habits of life.

> 'Tis evident that there may be great religious affections, that may in shew and appearance imitate gracious affections, and have the same effects on their bodies, but are far from having the same effect in the temper of their minds, and course of their lives. And likewise there is nothing more manifest by what appears amongst us, than that the goodness of [a] person's state is not chiefly to be judged by any exactness of steps, and methods of experiences, in what is supposed to be the first conversion; but that we must judge more by the spirit that breathes, the effect wrought on the temper of the soul, in the time of the work, and remaining afterwards.[34]

He included in his treatise, "The State of Religion in the Church in Northampton," the covenant by which the people renewed their relationship with God. It put forward a way of life rather than a creed and particularly a way of life that increases community rather than destroying it. It calls for strict regard for honesty, justice, and uprightness, for rendering everyone his or her due, for repaying any injuries one does to one's neighbor, for carefully avoiding slander or doing or saying anything out of bitterness or revenge, and particularly if one is a leader or managing public affairs, for putting public interest and concern before one's own. Edwards then assessed the results. The covenant concluded with a reaffirmation of attention to public and private religious duties, worship and prayer.[35]

> Notwithstanding all the corrupt mixtures that have been in the late work, here: there are not only many blessed fruits of it in particular persons, that yet remain, but some good effects of it upon the town in general. A party spirit has more ceased: I suppose there has been less appearance these three or four years past, of that division of the town into two parties, that has long been our bane, than has been these thirty years; and the people have apparently had much more caution, and a greater guard on their spirit and their tongues, to avoid contention and unchristian heats, in town meetings and on other occasions. And 'tis a thing greatly to be rejoiced in, that the people very lately have come to an agreement and final issue, with respect to their grand controversy relating to their common lands; which has been above any other particular thing, a source of mutual prejudices, jealousies, and debates, for fifteen or sixteen years past. . . .[36]

In his work, Edwards never subordinated faith to reason, but he did stress that feelings alone are misleading and we require the use of our reason to check or corroborate what we think we learn from our affections. The fifth distinguishing sign of a true or gracious affection, as he stated it in his "Treatise," is this: "Truly gracious affections are attended with a reasonable and spiritual conviction of the judgement, of the reality and certainty of divine things."[37] Of course, Edwards did not claim to know the actual state of any individual soul, especially not his own, but he did focus on the outward evidence of one's inward state, given in one's behavior toward others. "Thus it is plain that Christian practice is the best sign or manifestation of the true godliness of a professing Christian, to the eye of his neighbors."[38]

On the other hand, reason also prevents the thoughtful person from simply equating goodness with outwardly observed behavior. In the second part of the "Treatise on Religious Affections" Edwards systematically pointed out that one's claim to have had an experience of conversion can be merely for show, or it can be genuine at the moment but not long lasting, or that a person can behave in one way publicly and another when not under scrutiny. In both cases reason plays a role in distinguishing true from false religious experiences and claims. Edwards' reliance on experience and reason shows him to be the child of both the Pietists and the religious thinkers of the Enlightenment.

Edwards also took seriously the experience we might characterize as mystical, arguing that people can have both direct and indirect experience of the divine. "Thus a soul may have a kind of intuitive knowledge of the divinity of the things exhibited in the gospel; not that he judges the doctrines of the gospel to be from God, without any argument or deduction at all; but . . . the mind ascends to the truth of the gospel by one step, and that is its divine glory."[39] Edwards has remained among the most important American Protestant theologians, his insistence on the value of both reason and experience helped to shape an openness to diversity in theological thinking in subsequent generations. Edwards' concern for Christian behavior and the Christian shape of society rather than concern for confessional orthodoxy showed the direct challenge of both Pietism and the Enlightenment to doctrinal formulations based on the authority of tradition alone, either by dismissing the claims as unreasonable or by de-emphasizing them. Edwards held to the basic Augustinian theology of Calvin and the Reformed tradition in general, he regarded Scripture as the revelation of God, but he was most interested in the way in which Christian belief led to visible Christian life.[40]

With Edwards' openness to the Enlightenment and his avid reading of Newton's work, the historian William Clebsch asked, "If more than two centuries ago Edwards brought together the noumenal and the phenomenal, if he unified divine revelation and empirical experience, how did he escape the conflict of science with religion?"[41] From the Enlightenment he took the idea that both the new physics of Newton and the psychology of Locke "reinforced the reliability of both Creator and creation."[42] From the Pietists he took the idea that Christian faith should result in a changed society. He turned his attention away from the sources to the effects of Christian faith.[43] We tend to say the Enlightenment religion was a "head" religion and Pietism a religion of the "heart." But here we have a theologian who respected both.

> Edwards and [Ralph Waldo] Emerson and [William] James form a stream of religious thought in America intent on distinguishing the head from the heart in order to use the head for learning what goes on both in the head and in the heart, as well as to hear what the heart may have to say about the limits of the head.[44]

Acceptance of both head and heart, reason and faith, science and religion, provides a particular kind of diversity in the traditional theologies of the United Church of Christ. The effort to unify them provides yet another kind of theology. Edwards was not the only theologian to bring the two together within the UCC traditions. Returning to Schleiermacher we can see another approach to the same problem and another approach to theological diversity.

While Edwards lived at the beginning of the Enlightenment and at the height of the Pietist movement, Schleiermacher lived as both movements were fading. He synthesized them and founded a new theological movement often labeled "liberal" or "romantic." However, he worked with the same questions as did Edwards. Between Edwards and Schleiermacher lies the important philosopher Immanuel Kant (1724–1804). Though Kant was already over thirty years old when Edwards died, his major philosophical works were published later. Edwards did not know of him, and it is doubtful if Kant had ever heard of Edwards. Kant, like Edwards, addressed both the Pietist concerns about a religion that moved the heart as well as Enlightenment concerns that religious truth be rational. He leaned toward the Enlightenment. In his major work on religion, *Religion within the Bounds of Mere Reason* (1793), he regarded religion as purity of heart, arguing that the essence of religious truth lay in moral reason. Belief results in moral endeavor and the reliability of belief, Kant thought, should be tested by the kind of morality it inspired. Moral duty was, for Kant, the heart of religious life. Moral principles, understood as having their source in God, served to unify humanity across religious lines. Kant's religion of morality required no other doctrines than simply belief in God and a future life.[45] Essentially, morality rested on duty and will. The human being, using practical reason and experience knows his or her duty and uses will to accomplish it. A good will is necessary for human happiness.[46] But, Kant acknowledged, it was not a simple matter. Human reason does not always guide the will reliably, nor can the will be commanded, though one's actions might be.

> It is in this way, undoubtedly, that we should understand those passages of Scripture which command us to love our neighbor and even our enemy, for love as an inclination cannot be commanded. But beneficence from duty, when no inclination impels it and even when it is opposed by a natural and unconquerable aversion, is practical love, not pathological love; it resides in the will and not in the propensities of feeling, in principles of action and not in tender sympathy; and it alone can be commanded.[47]

Whatever we claim to be true in religious thought we must show it to be morally reasonable. The historian W. H. Walsh summed up Kant's philosophical project this way. "He wished to insist on the authority of science and yet preserve the autonomy of morals."[48]

While morality, for Kant, rested on belief in God, the important element for knowing the truth about anything lay in human freedom to use reason. Kant warned, however, that it was not the individual using his or her reason privately who found the truth, but it is rather the exercise of reason in public, where the results of one person's reason may encounter the results of others' free use of reason, that promotes truth.[49] Here it is not simply the truth as a stable, unchangeable thing revealed in the past that makes one free. Free use of one's reason reveals the truth that will finally free humanity from slavery and superstition. This has not, of course, produced the perfect world any more than religious dogma enforced by secular authority produced such a world. Kant's principle runs through the UCC traditions, and we value free discussion of alternative ideas as a good way to understand the mind of God on any matter.

However, Kant left an unanswered question regarding the relationship between thinking and feeling, science and the heart, or the mind and the physical world.[50] Friedrich Schleiermacher (1768–1834) attempted to bring the two together, to find a link. Schleiermacher thought that we encounter God at the point between thinking and being, physical being. God is the "being of things," upon which everything depends. Our certainty about God rests in our "certainty of life," and that certainty is grounded in our feeling, or immediate awareness.[51] Like Edwards, Schleiermacher took both religious experience and reason seriously. As will be clear in the next chapter, Schleiermacher has been dismissed by many theologians lately on the mistaken idea that he simply equated Christian faith with feeling or emotion, particularly the human feeling of absolute dependence or contingency. He thus came to be identified as the founder of the "feel good" theology, that whatever feels good must be true. However his thought is much more complicated than that, and he deserves renewed attention by Christian theologians, and especially by United Church of Christ people interested in the issues arising from theological plurality in our church. The particular issue Schleiermacher could help us resolve is the seeming separation of theologies that have their origins in human reason and intellectual work and those that arise from human religious experience. Too often, still, we separate the two realms of human religious activity and give one or the other the privilege of more authenticity than the other. Or worse, we discount one or the other all together.

Schleiermacher, relying on the capacity of human reason to help sort out competing truth claims, argued for a diversity of theological approaches. In his set of speeches *On Religion*, he states,

> The whole of religion is nothing but the sum of all relations of [humanity] to God, apprehended in all the possible ways in which any [one] can be immediately conscious in . . . life. In this sense there is but one religion, for it would be but a poverty-stricken and halting life, if all these relations did not exist wherever religion ought to be.[52]

However, though he recognized the multiple manifestations of religion, and recognized the validity of religions outside of Christianity, he argued for the unity of the Church. In fact there were boundaries to his plurality of religion. He continues in the speeches,

> Above all I beg you not to be misled by the two hostile principles that everywhere, and almost from the earliest times, have sought to distort and obscure the spirit of religion. Some would circumscribe it to a single dogma, and exclude every-

> thing not fashioned in agreement with it, others, from hatred or polemics, or to make religion more agreeable to the irreligious, or from misunderstanding and ignorance of the matter, or from lack of religious sense, decry everything characteristic as dead letter. Guard yourselves from both. With rigid systematizers or shallow indifferentists you will not find the spirit of a religion. It is found only among those who live in it as their element, and ever advance in it without cherishing the folly that they embrace it all.[53]

He went so far as to define Christian heresy, the boundary between a true and false understanding of the faith. Defining the essence of Christianity to be related to the redemption wrought by Jesus of Nazareth, he pointed to two kinds of heresies, "*either* human nature will be so defined that a redemption in the strict sense cannot be accomplished, *or* the Redeemer will be defined in such a way that He cannot accomplish redemption."[54] Schleiermacher walked a middle line, acknowledging the importance of a plurality of understandings of the Christian faith within an ideal One Church, not dogmatically systematized but also not indifferently inclusive.

In the Puritan Congregational and Reformed traditions, the eighteenth and nineteenth centuries were characterized primarily by systematized Calvinist orthodoxy. Though Edwards and Schleiermacher and others had begun to suggest that theological diversity had a place, for the most part people were more satisfied with clear doctrinal positions. The councils and statements of both traditions, the Heidelberg Catechism (1563); the Canons of Dort (1619); the Westminster Confession (1646); and the Cambridge Platform (1648)[55] all affirmed a conventional Pauline, Augustinian, Calvinist theology though they differed on matters of church polity. They all represented a concern for Christian unity amid the growing diversity of the Protestant tradition. The Reformed writers of the Heidelberg Catechism carefully worded it so that it would be recognizable to the Lutherans. The Synod of Dort held by the Dutch Reformed Churches had two representatives from the English Separatist Congregationalists. The Cambridge Synod met to affirm the Westminster Confession, Congregationalists differing from the Presbyterians only on the matter of church governance.

Throughout the history of the Reformed, Congregational and Evangelical traditions of the United Church of Christ they reaffirm these foundational Reformed Protestant statements of belief, however, they have rarely used them as tests of faith. Instead all four major traditions of the UCC came to emphasize Christian practice. The Enlightenment and Pietist respect for human experience and reason shaped in all of these traditions an allowance for many interpretations of traditional formulations of the faith, and allowed individual theological dissent from beliefs even as central as the Trinity, when people's own searching of the Scripture failed to convince them of its central truth. Far more characteristic of the traditions of the United Church of Christ has been a Christian activism and high regard for the application of individual Christian experience to the betterment of society.

Shaping Theological Inclusivity in the United Church of Christ

In the final section of this chapter, I want to explore how the tensions and complementarity of the two movements, Pietism and Enlightenment, play out in the nineteenth and twentieth centuries. First, I want to consider the case of the Christians, their idea of the church and the place of theological thought and formulation within it. Then I want to consider the issues of the Mercersburg Movement within the German Reformed Church and its call for Protestant and Catholic unity. Thirdly, I want to look at the issues of theological openness in the liberal tradition (which I will discuss in depth in the next chapter). Finally, I want to consider the case of the feminist theological critique of the traditional creedal language of the United Church of Christ Statement of Faith and the questions it raises for our contemporary understanding of the nature of the Church.

"No creed but Christ," was a rallying point among the various Christian traditions of the early nineteenth century. Among them the Christian Connection represented people from the Pietist Methodist tradition, the Anabaptist tradition of the Baptist churches in America, the Reformed—both Presbyterian and Congregational, and the radical and rational Unitarians. The Christian tradition might be said to be the earliest example of the kind of coalition of churches represented later in the twentieth century ecumenical movements of the United and Uniting Church traditions. As Reinhard Groscurth, a leading historian of these churches, has pointed out, characteristically such movements must do without doctrinal clarity.[56] This of course does not preclude their developing such clarity in the future, but it is a difficult matter and takes many generations. The Christians were not able to hold their entire movement within one church, but each of the different groups of Christians did share a simple, yet powerful set of common thoughts on what is essential for the theological definition of the church. One example is the recitation of the principles of the Christian "denomination" by George Dunn, a pastor of the African American Christian Churches, who used them in 1880 in an appeal for funds for establishing the Franklinton Christian College.

> Let me give you our creed: 1. The Lord Jesus Christ is the only head of the church. 2. The name Christian is the only appellation by which we will be known to the exclusion of all party or sectarian names. 3. The holy Bible or the Scriptures of the Old and New Testament are our only creed or confession of faith. 4. Christian character or vital piety is the one scriptural test of fellowship and church membership. Space will not allow me to say any more about the rules.[57]

Christians did not attempt to agree on a single formulation of this "creed" but most Christian statements contain a similar list of four to six principles.[58] They exhibited the same desire to unite Enlightenment respect for human reason and the Pietist emphasis on religious experience and Christian life. Joseph Badger in the *Christian Palladium* 1 May 1834, wrote specifically "We shall use every exertion in our power, to persuade our readers to be *enlightened, rational, liberal, charitable, kind, experimental* and *practical* Christians."[59] Christian aversion to creeds could be strenuous. For example Elder Simon Clough's "Creeds Rejected," in the *Christian Palladium* 15 March 1838 reads,

> We object, then, to creeds and confessions of faith, as bonds of Christian union, as conditions of Christian fellowship, as means of fastening chains on men's [and women's] minds, because they are unauthorized by Scripture—because they're contrary to the Scriptures—because they infringe the right of private judgement—because Christianity as incorporated into them presents a very defective and distorted character—because they have a tendency to lessen the authority of Christ

> and a sense of obligation to him—because they lead to oppression and hold out temptations and allurements to practice hypocrisy and deception—because they destroy that perfect equality in matters of faith and conscience which Jesus Christ has instituted among his disciples—because the end proposed by them can never be obtained—because they carry upon the very front of them a direct falsehood—because they have a tendency to perpetuate error—because they shut the door against free inquiry—because they are a fruitful source of strife and contention—because they separate us from Jesus Christ our spiritual guide— . . . because they favor unbelief. Such are the reasons which have induced us to reject creeds as confessions of faith, as terms of Christian communion.[60]

The objection of some Christians to creeds also entailed an objection to the doctrine of the Trinity. "Now if the doctrine of three persons in one God is true, what a pity it is that it had not received its *finishing touch* in the sacred oracles!" wrote David Millard in the *Christian Palladium* in 1834. Participating both in the revivals with Baptists and Methodists and in conversation with the Unitarians, the Christians were struggling to hold together both head and heart, Enlightenment reason and Pietist experiential religion. While theirs has not proved to be the great road to Christian unity they had hoped, neither has it proved to be completely unsuccessful.

So far, we have considered the ways the traditions of the United Church of Christ dealt with the theological diversity issues from the Reformation and from the Enlightenment and Pietist movements. Toward the end of the nineteenth century, another movement emerged in the Reformed tradition that attempted to address the issues of Protestant and Catholic difference in an effort to unify the two major streams of the Western Christian tradition. This was the Mercersburg Movement. The movement began in 1844,[61] the year Philip Schaff arrived at the Mercersburg Theological Seminary of the German Reformed Church, where he and John Williamson Nevin formed the heart of the faculty. Nevin and Schaff's ideas proved controversial in the German Reformed Church, involved them both in heresy trials, and failed to dominate the direction of that denomination in their own times. The movement continued until nearly the end of the century when its ideas died out except among ecumenists. The principle person responsible for carrying the Mercersburg vision of Christian unity forward into the twentieth century was George Warren Richards, President of Lancaster Seminary and later President of the Evangelical and Reformed Church. He was one of the theologians active in the formation of both the Evangelical and Reformed Church and the United Church of Christ. The Mercersburg theology regained influence in the middle and late twentieth century as its ideas proved particularly useful in the growing ecumenical movement and renewed Protestant interest in liturgy.[62]

The Mercersburg theology was characterized by a particular understanding of history, an emphasis on the Eucharist as central to Christian life and thought, and a passionate belief that unity was the nature of the Church. Nevin described the movement as having as its cardinal principle "the fact of the Incarnation" and its distinguishing characteristic "Christological interest."[63] The theology answered two concerns Nevin and Schaff noted in American Protestantism, increasing sectarianism and the Arminian ideas about grace prevalent in the revival movement.

Regarding Christian sectarianism the Mercersburg theologians were concerned about the way in which it put the principle of individual freedom above the responsibility to be true to the Gospel. They included in this anxiety, concern about the effects of official toleration by the state of a variety of forms of Christianity. Nevin wrote,

> But there is a vast chasm also in the political or outward toleration itself, as it may be called, to which the sect system affects in general to be so favorable. It is full of zeal, apparently, for human freedom in every shape, the rights of man, liberty of conscience, and the privilege of every man to worship God in his own way. The Independents [the Congregationalists] claim the merit of opening, in regard to these great interests, a new era in the history of the human race; but they had no toleration originally for the Quakers and Baptists; . . . The "Christians" sprang from the same idea of independence. One portion of them styled themselves at first characteristically "Republican Methodists"; another grew out of "a peculiar travel [sic] of mind in relation to sectarian names and human

> creeds," on the part of one Dr. Abner Jones, . . . As a general thing, sects are loud for liberty, in the more outward sense, and seem to be raised up in their own imagination for the express purpose of asserting in some new way what they call liberty of conscience.. . . All sects, in proportion as they deserve the name, are narrow, bigoted, and intolerant. They know not what liberty means. They put out men's eyes, gag their mouths, and manacle their hands and feet. They are intrinsically, constitutionally, incurably popish, enslaved by tradition and prone to persecution [of others].[64]

Against the individualistic sect ecclesiology, Nevin and Schaff argued that the churches all share a common history that has authoritative weight. The revelation of the Incarnation took place in history and the church has participated in that revelation in all of its history. The Protestant movement itself was, Schaff argued, a product of the very Medieval Catholicism that the Protestants now deny.

> The Reformation is the legitimate offspring, the greatest act of the Catholic Church; and on this account of true catholic nature itself, in its genuine conception: whereas the Church of Rome, instead of following the divine conduct of history has continued to stick in the old law of commands, the garb of childhood, like the Jewish hierarchy in the time of Christ, and thus by its fixation as Romanism has parted with the character of catholicity in exchange for that of particularity.[65]

The Mercersburg theologians sought to restore a sense of the church as catholic to the American Protestant ethos. Here Nevin challenged the common Protestant identification of the Papacy with the antichrist, and charged Protestant sectarianism itself with that identity. Protestants also take on the particular sin the Mercersburg theologians laid at the feet of the Roman church, namely thinking of themselves as the perfect expression of Christianity.[66]

Schaff approached the problem as a historian and urged the authority of history against the individualism of American Christianity. Nevin approached the matter by urging a Christological return to the Eucharist as the central moment of Church life. His major work *The Mystical Presence* contains his main argument. Whatever diversity there was in Christianity, and diversity was to be expected, Catholics, Reformed and Lutheran Protestants, and all the other Christian sects needed to recognize their unity in Christ around whose table they all gathered.

As a result of their biblical and historical investigations, the two theologians proposed the Mercersburg Liturgy to the German Reformed Church. The liturgy was based on Schaff's study of early Christian worship and Nevin's investigations into Eucharistic theology. In the liturgy they sought to recover ground upon which Christians of whatever culture or sect could unite in a historically grounded common sacrament. Instead the liturgy created such controversy within the German Reformed church that the Mercersburg movement came to an end for all practical purposes. Its liturgy proved to be too close to the form of the Roman Catholic Mass for the taste of most in the Reformed Church. Nevertheless, the historical investigations of Schaff and the theological reflection of Nevin on the Eucharist began to bear fruit in the twentieth century when the Protestant churches became more open to understanding themselves as sharing a common history and tradition predating their splintering in the Reformation.

While, neither Nevin nor Schaff favored unlimited Christian freedom, both of them shared the Enlightenment and Pietist impulses toward human reason as a tool for overcoming blind adherence to limited sectarian understandings of the faith and a deeply felt kinship, through Christian experience and way of life, with the Roman Catholics. The Mercersburg theologians rejected the inclusion of any theological argument that did not take into account the weight of the whole history of Christianity.

The final case in our consideration of the theological roots of theological diversity in the UCC comes from more recent times, but provides a lens through which to view some developments in nineteenth century Congregational theology. The Congregational Christian tradition included within it a traditional kind of theological diversity born in the nineteenth century and colored by the Fundamentalist/Modernist controversies of the early twentieth century although the Congregational Christian Churches were not affected as much by these debates since they regarded dogma as something each congregation was free to decide for itself. In these churches we find three kinds of theology, orthodox evangelical Calvinism; Unitarian views of either the Christian kind which simply viewed the Trinitarian creeds as unscriptural or the more transcendental kind open to many religious voices outside Christianity if they seemed in accord with the Gospel; and the large group of liberals in the middle, including the Social Gospel stream and Neo-orthodoxy.[67] In the formation of the United Church of Christ Statement of Faith these three kinds of theology came into play, as well as similar diversity within the more centered doctrinal orthodoxy of the Evangelical Synod and the Reformed Church.

The Statement of Faith and the *United Church of Christ Hymnal* appeared within a decade after the formation of the United Church of Christ, and prepared the church neither for the sudden storm raised by the second wave of the modern feminist movement, nor for the rise of new theological questions from the racial and cultural margins of the church. Nor was the response of the United Church of Christ initially able to fully integrate all the questions arising from these two movements. UCC theologians were more concerned in the 1960s with the European confessional questions raised by Barth and Bonhoeffer and the existentialist theological issues arising from modernism including the works of Paul Tillich, John Robinson's *Honest to God,* the death of God and theology of hope.

The case of feminist critique of the United Church of Christ Statement of Faith generated as much, or perhaps more, controversy than the Mercersburg liturgy. The ink was hardly dry on the Statement of Faith, and the new *United Church of Christ Hymnal* had not left the presses when the second wave of the Feminist movement swept over the church. Sparked in the secular world by Betty Friedan's book *The Feminine Mystique* and in Christian circles by Mary Daly's *The Church and the Second Sex,* the women of the early 1970s confronted the power of human language to shape human self-identity and society. Far from being a neutral instrument of human conduct, language played a role in the oppression or liberation of everyone. The women quickly called into question the way in which positing God as male, as had been the custom from before the origins of Christianity, had the effect of making the male divine. As Mary Daly published her second and more radical book, *Beyond God the Father,* a few women within the church began to ask the question of whether Christianity, with its motif of the reconciliation of sons to Father through the self sacrifice of one of them, was a religion for women at all, or was it essentially about male experience and male salvation. Many more women, who found in Christianity a sustaining religious tradition, asked whether the exclusion of women from leadership in church and society, and the persistent identification of the female with sin, temptation, weakness and evil was consistent with the message of Jesus Christ and the continuing revelation of God as just and compassionate.

Society had assumed, since the nineteenth century particularly, that masculine words could generically include the female as well.[68] However women knew that one always had to wonder. The Declaration of Independence stated that "all men are created equal," but everyone knew that historically those "men" were white, free, adult and male. In some cases such equality extended only to property owners. It was not until later that equality widened to include first those who did not own property, then males who were not white, and only in the twentieth century did it include women. So when the Church claimed that generic language included women, what did that mean? In the early 1970s women from several settings of the United Church of Christ raised the question of sexist language in the Statement of Faith. One proposal in particular came in 1972 from the Task Force on Women in Society to Robert Moss, the President of the United Church of Christ, and to the Executive Council requesting that the Statement of Faith be changed to use inclusive language in time for the anticipated 1974 printing of the United Church of Christ Hymnal. Moss in turn consulted the group that had prepared the Statement of Faith, as well as a number of women theologians in the church. One of them Bernice Buehler replied:

> The request to review the "sexist language" in the Statement of Faith brought forth my WOW! First reaction surprise, then resistance almost disgust with an overemphasis. . . My first thought on eliminating "he" etc. was: Everyone knows "man" symbolizes mankind; Jesus was not a woman! . . . THEN: . . . I went to a meeting of Christian Educators including males as well as females, where I shared the concern and the letter. Surprise! The men were more willing to consider change of language than women. One said; "We know that racist language influences racial attitudes." No doubt our male dominated religious language and witness needs rethinking.[69]

Others objected to changing the Statement of Faith. Moss replied to one man,

> You argue that the issue is contrived and suggest that language can be changed to manipulate and persuade in a hidden way. I would argue that in its present use of sexist language our "mother" tongue contributes to manipulation and hidden persuasion. What is involved here is not an attempt to propagandize but rather to clarify. In the past, as you know, the indefinite pronoun "he" was interpreted to mean " he or she." Why not make that explicit since women and men alike are saying that the use of "he" to mean both sexes has had an unconscious or subliminal effect on their thinking about the equality of the sexes?[70]

Two revised versions of the Statement of Faith emerged from the controversy. Neither version, however, was ever put to a vote of the Synod or the Conferences and Churches. They are both in common use in the UCC, particularly the version proposed by Robert Moss himself in the form of a Doxology. "We believe in you, O God, Eternal Spirit, God of our Savior Jesus Christ and our God, and to your deeds we testify. . . ."[71]

Beginning in the early seventies and continuing to this day, the church has engaged in a process of rethinking the meaning of long-held ideas about language and Christian truth. The approach of the United Church of Christ mirrors the way in which Congregationalists in the nineteenth century came to call themselves liberal in their theology.[72] They sought a middle way between strict authoritarian dogma on the one hand and either unbelief or indifference on the other hand. Liberal theology sought the truth in the middle, bringing human reason to bear on long-standing dogmas but affirming that religious truth went beyond or deeper than that reality human beings could understand using their reason alone.

The feminist question about God has raised the most fundamental questions about the way Christians include or exclude diverse theologies. Recently, new work on the effect of religious language on concepts of race and ethnicity strengthens this point.[73] In some ways the question of language regarding human beings was easy to resolve. Wherever generic masculine language is used, we choose a term that is inclusive but not generic,[74] and masculine language is reserved for times when one is referring to males. But words for "God" are another problem. To some the solution seemed obvious - to take an essentially Unitarian view and thus remove the most obviously masculine vocabulary for God to the side, particularly avoiding the classical father and son vocabulary in Trinitarian creedal formulations.[75] However, the United Church of Christ has been a Trinitarian church body and its own Statement of Faith is indeed Trinitarian. Another solution seemed to be to adopt a functional view of the Trinity, naming the persons by the functions they serve rather than by the relationships they share, for instance, Creator, Redeemer, and Sustainer. This, however, removed one of the most powerful ideas about God, particularly the relational nature of God as the basis of the beloved community. For the most part the official decisions regarding theological language used at national and many conference settings opt for a neutral style, using words neither masculine nor feminine, though a few have experimented with the equal inclusion of both masculine and feminine language. In individual congregations, many pastors and church members continue to use traditional language.

The case for theological diversity became complicated for the United Church of Christ because its response to this issue affected its ecumenical assumptions. In the Christian tradition and to some degree in the Congregational tradition there was some room in modern times for a unitarian point of view given the theological view of creeds as testimonies of and not tests of faith. This at least avoided the familial language of father and son. But the Evangelical and Reformed tradition did not so readily accommodate a Unitarian view. In addition, one stream of feminist thought sought to reincorporate specifically female understandings of deity and introduced not only biblical language of Sophia, the Wisdom of God from Proverbs, and female pronouns referring to the Holy Spirit following the feminine gendered words in both Greek and Hebrew, but they also introduced more general terms such as Goddess which struck some as unchristian or frankly pagan. Whether Christianity can accommodate translation into female language remains to be seen.[76] The United Church of Christ has undertaken to incorporate female symbols into its Christian theology and life and into its everyday language.

The United Church of Christ has also undertaken to incorporate theological language and image from the multiplicity of racial and ethnic groups within it. These groups have not always been open to the experiment in language including the feminine. "White women's Christ, Black women's Jesus," a phrase from a title of a book by Jacquelyn Grant,[77] illustrates the cultural difference even among women in the United Church of Christ about how to symbolize the divine and the figure of Jesus Christ in the church's teaching.

The discussion of inclusive language was one circumstance galvanizing the organization of the Biblical Witness Fellowship of the UCC, and later the Confessing Christ group. Both are concerned to preserve a traditional orthodox theology and language in the United Church of Christ, but the Biblical Witness Fellowship also wishes to create a more conservative ethos on issues of social justice particularly with regard to women, the family, and matters of sexual orientation. The Confessing Christ movement is concerned about the effects of UCC theological language diversity on our ability to participate in the ecumenical conversations as a reliably and recognizably Christian church. Moss was right that language does shape our self-identity and our views of others. With regard to the language defining the beloved community of the Church and our covenant to give witness to its unity, and the common confession we are called to give before the world, the United Church of Christ retains classical Biblical and creedal language in its officially voted Statement of Faith. We have never voted to discard it. However, true to our Reformation roots, we find it necessary to attempt to retranslate the faith for a new generation with new concerns.

How do we come to know God except through the vehicle of human language and our experience of community? Both language and experience suffer from the finitude of human nature. Many of the sixteenth-century Reformers were influenced by Nominalism, as was the developing scientific method. This theology developed in the thirteenth century. It aroused suspicion in theological circles because one argument nominalists could make was that the Trinity as an idea had no reality, only the individual members or persons of it, or simply God as a single entity, could be thought to have reality. Nominalism also fostered a tendency either to place faith in the Scriptures, a kind of literalism that gave reality only to the particular revelation contained there, or to place faith in the mystical experience of a particular individual.[78] On the other hand, specific experience shared by a body of people, had weight. The community's understanding of the truth was based in the specific experience of each member.

As we will see in the next chapter, the UCC understands itself to be called by God to doubt the adequacy of individual human containers of the faith, to rethink them over and over as a community, and to deepen our understanding. The temptation may be to say we cannot hope to share a common confession. I think we simply do not know each other well enough. Until we take life as the Beloved Community in all its diversity more seriously, we will have difficulty making a common confession of the faith. The early twenty-first century is an unsettled time for the expression of the faith as well as the discernment of the mission of God among such a diverse people. Only in community can we come to an adequate vocabulary to convey the saving power of the love of God and what that love requires of us.

The theological diversity of the United Church of Christ remains. It still encompasses the traditional Reformed or Calvinist orthodoxy, particularly in its American evangelical form. It contains a small strand of Unitarianism as well, both of the Biblical kind and of the more rationalist kind. It remains largely liberal, but within that liberalism the UCC contains liberation theologies, feminist theologies, neo-orthodoxy, and the social gospel. The United Church of Christ is hardly a monolithic theological body.

Four

The Entertainment of Doubt

One cannot define a UCC theology. In spite of this, in their study of churches in America,[1] Wade Clark Roof and William McKinney, two sociologists of American religion, place the United Church of Christ in the liberal theological category. And as we saw in the previous chapter, the UCC emerges as an expression of liberal aspects of older Reformation traditions. The word "liberal" has a variety of meanings in the context of American culture and Christianity. Observers of American religious life recognize certain forms of Christian belief as liberal, but that characterization can mean theological position, approach to ethics and social mores, or political commitments. In this chapter, my intention is to work with the characterization of the UCC as a liberal church, and to explore further its roots and its complex contemporary expressions.

How did the UCC come to be in the liberal category? I will argue in this chapter first, that since the Reformation, the traditions of the United Church of Christ have shared fundamental aspects that can be termed "liberal;" second, that the meaning of the word "liberal" in the context of the United Church of Christ has changed over time; and finally, that what can be termed liberal in the United Church of Christ traditions is primarily a style or a way of thinking theologically, a theological culture whose essential element is a willingness to entertain doubt, even at times a willingness to entertain doubt about liberalism[2] itself. Generations of theological thinking in this style, I argue, have produced a supple body of theology engaging changing cultural, political, economic, and intellectual contexts of the last five hundred years, though not necessarily with complete success.

Approaching the question of a liberal theological culture in the UCC

Perhaps my interest in things liberal is related to my location in Berkeley, California. From Berkeley, I sometimes think that what United Church of Christ people think of as liberal is somewhat tame. On the other hand, there is a dogmatic edge to Berkeley liberalism that emphasizes its ideological character to the weakening of its converting power. The paradox of liberal dogmatics is all around me. For this reason, I want to begin by explaining why I prefer the phrase "liberal style" rather than "liberal theology." In the nineteenth century, the Reformation principle that Scripture alone should guide the Church in both its faith and practice was tested by the findings of scientists and historians most notably in biblical archeology, geology, and biology. At the same time the churches struggled to address a new industrial economy with a social ethics shaped by Protestant emphasis on individual responsibility. In the twentieth century, the initial and sometimes simplistic and overly optimistic early expressions of modern theological liberalism invited serious challenge. Twentieth century Neo-Orthodoxy, liberation theologies, existential and process theologies all represented more complex reframing of a persistent liberal impulse. I argue that what persists more strongly in these theologies is a way of thinking that does not necessarily lead immediately to particular theological formulations. It is a style rather than a teaching, and I find it more often formulated in ethical norms or social advocacy than in systematic theological works. One of the open questions in the United Church of Christ remains how to clarify the relationship between this liberal style and the great variety of theological traditions represented among us. The majority of the traditions in Christianity express their unity in a common theological confession. The United Church of Christ shares these historical expressions of Christian unity, while our ecclesiology requires that we continually honor our covenant as a diverse people in community together. Though we did not deliberately seek cultural and theological diversity, it has been given to us. The vocabulary of the faith has to become elastic enough to express and re-express the meaning of the essential unifying love of God present in the ministry and resurrection of Jesus Christ, and the mission that love requires us to undertake as a people of deeply diverse histories, cultures, and social contexts. We are pushed into our liberal style by our commitments to one another.

According to Roof and McKinney, the United Church of Christ, along with the Episcopal Church and the Presbyterian Church, comprise the heart of what until recently was the main stream of American Protestantism. All three churches are rooted in the British North American colonial experience and, though their collective numbers have declined lately (presently they are slightly less than ten percent of the American population), they still enjoy a disproportionate cultural influence.[3] Roof and McKinney characterize them as liberal churches.[4] By liberal they mean the three churches share a Protestant theology rooted in the Reformation with an emphasis on nurture and education rather than conversion, a positive engagement with modernity including science and historical-critical approach to the Bible, ecumenical vision and strong social conscience. Most particularly for our purposes here, Roof and McKinney point out that in these communions "levels of orthodox belief are low, doubt and uncertainty in matters of faith common, knowledge of the Scriptures exceedingly low."[5] All three are characterized by a willingness to entertain doubt.

The identity of the UCC as well as its future as a liberal denomination lies, I believe, in the way we approach the doubts of our time. The questions of our future rest in our ability to continue to think through these doubts in community with each other. American Christians approach doubt in three basic ways. The first two ways I want to mention are not at all characteristic of the UCC, and they are at opposite ends of a spectrum. The first way dismisses doubt altogether, or regards it as a test of faith. The basic certainties of the faith are available to every believer and the believer can quickly eliminate any doubt that arises remembering these certainties. If doubt persists, these believers continue to regard it as sent from or allowed by God as a test of their faith. The faithful response to doubt in this view is defense of the faith. The second approach regards doubt as unappeasable. This unappeasable doubt eventually leads most of its sufferers to unbelief. The cynic or agnostic dismisses religion as not having any reliable truth.

A third approach is, I think, quintessentially liberal. This approach to doubt was described best by the American philosopher Charles Sanders Pierce in a 1878 article in *Popular Science Monthly* entitled "How to Make Our Ideas Clear."[6] Pierce regarded doubt and belief as part of a single process, not as opposites. He also described thought as having two aspects, active thought and thought at rest. Belief, for Peirce, is thought at rest. In the evolution of human thinking, people developed beliefs, useable answers to questions that they sorted out in a particular environment, so that the questions no longer needed to take up their energy. We base our habits of life on our beliefs. In other words, because we think actively in order to come to terms successfully with our environment, beliefs lead us to habits of life representing a successful negotiation of the problems an environment presents to us. But as we go about living our lives according to our habits, Pierce observed that we encounter situations for which our belief provides no understanding and no guidance. This creates the irritation of doubt about our belief. The irritation of doubt stimulates thought in action. Thought in action exists both in our minds as we think out possible ways of coming to terms with the new situation, and in our actual experimental activity or trying new ways. In the process of this active thought both in mind and body, we come to a new or deeper understanding or belief that takes into account the new situation. This new or deeper or more complex belief then becomes the foundation of new habits. But we continue to encounter new environments and new situations and doubt arises again. The situation of active thought is normal, though we long for the pleasant rest of belief. In the Church, belief originates as testimony to our understanding of God's presence and action in the history of the people. Habits of confession, worship, and practice in turn shape our relationships and mission. Theologians will recognize this also as Paul Tillich's "method of correlation." But in that mission we encounter a world that does not fit our beliefs. We either defend the faith, give up our belief altogether, or engage in active theological and ethical thought that may reshape both our confession and worship as well as our ethical practice and mission. This active thought is characteristic of liberal Christianity though not unique to it.

The word "liberal" has a long history from the Middle Ages to the present. I argue that in each era the liberal spirit is characterized by an engagement with doubt. Sometimes it is doubt about social structures, other times doubt about received truth or tradition, and at still other times doubt about the effectiveness of theological constructs. There has never been a satisfactory characterization of the liberal shared across all times. One must always ask "which liberalism?" I will summarize here the main turning points in understanding the term "liberal" and then look more closely at the key times. In the Medieval Era, liberal referred to those who were free in the sense of not being bound to the land or service of a particular ruler. In education, the liberal arts represented those forms of knowledge necessary to live as a liberal or free person. This Medieval liberalism, culminating in the Reformation, entertained doubts about the traditional authority of both Church and State based upon the expanding consciousness of other cultures outside their own, particularly that of the Islamic Arabs and their Aristotelian science.[7] The engagement of these doubts about authority resulted finally in new structures for the Church, and a new claim, among Protestants, for the authority of Scripture alone. The displacement of authority from traditional ecclesiastical structures to the Scripture and individual conscience in the Calvinist tradition began to shape a high view of individual or local responsibility and autonomy and a correspondingly weaker sense of communal accountability.

This trend solidified in the eighteenth century. The Enlightenment further explored the doubts about received authority and the divine right of human rulers raised in the sixteenth century and developed new doctrines of human rights, popular or representative democracy, and above all a celebration of the powers of human reason to alleviate the suffering of humanity. At the same time the Pietists continued to entertain doubts about received authority of the state church and the formalized creeds of orthodoxy to shape a reliably Christian community. They developed new more active forms of Christian faith, honoring individual conscience, but calling each individual conscience into a life that was recognizably Christian in its outward form.

Christian engagement with doubts increased in the nineteenth century as geological, biological, and historical findings, based in the work of the Enlightenment's new-found confidence in human reason, challenged the Protestant belief in the authority of Scripture alone. As in each previous era, a few Protestants chose to entertain these doubts, most resisted them, and growing numbers abandoned belief when Protestant theologians sought to defend orthodox creedal formulations by seemingly scientific reasoning that only served to make belief seem ridiculous.[8] Those who engaged these new doubts about the historical and scientific reliability of Christian scriptures fell into several groups depending on the ways in which they resolved the problems these doubts posed, and among them we can find the ancestors of the United Church of Christ, Reformed, Congregational, Evangelical, and Christian.

In the twentieth century the nature of the doubts shifted again. The authority of dominant cultural forms and ethical principles came increasingly under fire in the violence, social change, and increasingly global environmental effects of Western economic orthodoxy. The United Church of Christ did not emerge from the twentieth century with a unified new sense of authority. It has participated fully and continues to participate in the entertainment of the doubts of our time and the struggle to rethink and represent the Christian faith in this new generation.

The Middle Ages and Reformation: Entertaining Doubt about Traditional Authority

From the fourth to the thirteenth century, Western Christianity forged a strong understanding of ecclesiastical authority centered in the papacy and the bishops. According to this understanding of the Church, God authorized this hierarchy through Christ's appointment of the apostles, and their appointment of their successors. The Western church had also negotiated a tenuous shared power with the feudal political order. God appointed each person to a station in life for the good of the whole social order. The bishops had oversight over the souls entrusted to them, the secular rulers had oversight over the safety and well-being of those under their protection; the peasants and artisans had responsibility for producing what their community needed to eat, wear, and use; and the knight and soldier protected the community from enemies. It was a workable and stable arrangement and few questioned it for many centuries.[9]

After the thirteenth century however, doubts began to arise. To begin with, the bishops and the secular rulers lived in considerable tension under this seemingly settled arrangement. Neither really wanted to share power. They did so only because neither could quite overcome the other. Yet the bishops and rulers were inseparable. The bishops agreed that God appointed the rulers and verified that appointment by investing in them some authority over church affairs in their territories, such as the ability to ratify episcopal appointments. The rulers on the other hand invested the bishops with secular authority over certain lands and thus gave the bishops not only religious but also political power over some of their subjects as well as the economic benefits of the land. Both bishops and secular rulers shared the theological authority of community oversight (*episcopé*).[10] The ecclesiological aspects of this community function were inevitably superceded by political aspects wherever the church, as it certainly had in the West, aligned itself with empire or its rulers.

The complex relationships between sacred and secular power in the Western church proved in many places to be conducive to corruption. Many bishops became wealthy and ceased to care for the poor. They sought the favor of the secular rulers rather than the favor of God. The secular rulers exercised power over the church shaping it to suit their own ends. These situations of greed and abused power raised doubts about the authority of the age old power structures. At first engagements with this doubt were tolerated within the church, for instance, by the formation of the Franciscan order, or the veneration of mystics who taught a different way of life. But by the end of the fourteenth century, those who challenged the church status quo were too many to contain. Jon Hus, John Wycliffe, Copernicus, and others were silenced or killed. However, their doubts about the authority of the church, its Pope, and bishops did not die with them.

Eventually, in the Reformation of the sixteenth century, a new theology of authority gained widespread credence and virtually replaced the belief in divine appointment of religious and secular rulers that had preceded it. That doctrine was the authority of Scripture alone. At least four generations of theologians from Wycliffe and Hus to Luther and finally Calvin entertained doubt of the authority of the church and developed the new teaching of the authority of scripture. *Sola Scriptura* (Scripture alone) along with *solo fides* (faith alone) became the watchwords of the Reformers. Disregarding the fact that the church existed before the New Testament was written, and that the New Testament was itself a creation of the church, the Reformers elevated the Scripture to the place of supreme authority as the Word of God. They located the recipient of divine inspiration in the individuals who wrote the text rather than in the church as a community.

I note with interest that in none of the major documents defining the Reformation, Luther's Small Catechism, the Augsburg Confession, the Schleitheim Confession or Huldrich Zwingli's Sixty-seven Articles, is the principle of the sole authority of Scripture stated explicitly.[11] In several of them, references from the Bible permeate the text, but the authors simply assumed biblical authority. In Zwingli's Articles, at the beginning, he confesses that what he writes is based upon the Scriptures "which are called inspired by God."[12] In addition, in the course of the Marburg Colloquy it became clear that the two Reformation leaders, Luther and Zwingli each meant something different by that authority and their interpretations of scripture differed significantly. For Luther the church and even individual believers were free to decide for themselves those things that were not specifically mentioned in Scripture. Thus for instance Luther admitted musical instruments in Christian worship. However, on those things found in the Bible, Luther took a more literal view, insisting that Christ's declaration at the Last Supper, "This is my body broken for you" meant that Christ was physically present in the celebration of Communion. Zwingli on the other hand interpreted Scripture more strictly, and argued that unless something was specifically stated in the Bible as permitted, Christians should not do it. Therefore, in Zwingli's church there were no musical instruments. However, he interpreted the Scripture more metaphorically, taking "This is my body" to be symbolic and emphasizing instead, "Do this in memory of me" to be the more important text for interpreting the Church's actions in the celebration of the sacrament.[13]

It was not until Farel and Calvin published the Geneva Confession in 1536 that a doctrine of the Word of God appeared in a definitive Reformation church document.

> First we affirm that we desire to follow Scripture alone as rule of faith and religion, without mixing with it any other thing which might be devised by the opinion of men apart from the Word of God, and without wishing to accept for our spiritual government any other doctrine than what is conveyed to us by the same Word without addition or diminution, according to the command of our Lord.[14]

Just as one can read the Bible from a strictly literal view or a more metaphorical and interpretive one, so too did Calvin himself have variant interpretations of this doctrine. Though Calvin's theological emphasis may have been on Church order rather than law, his followers did not always distinguish the two. The Reformation doubt about ecclesiastical authority was solved for a time by the doctrine of the sole authority of Scripture for Christian faith and practice.

Indeed, Calvin was uneasy about the entertainment of doubt. Christian doubt of God's faithfulness, a doubt likely to come upon those who suffer unmanageable pain or trouble, was for Calvin evidence of the work of Satan trying to draw the Christian away from faith. But, Calvin did not deny the reality of doubt and he suffered doubt himself from time to time. Writing to his friend Viret, Calvin reports his overwhelming grief at the death of his wife Idelette. "You will have perhaps heard of the death of my wife. I struggle as best I can to overcome my grief. Friends do everything in their power. Nothing altogether avails but I cannot tell you how grateful I am for everything. You know how sensitive I am or rather how weak. If I did not take myself severely in hand I could not stand up. . . . I am now plunging into work to drown my sorrow."[15] Years later in his Commentary on the Psalms, Calvin shed light on this kind of profound spiritual doubt. "If God lets us remain long in grief and be almost consumed by it, we cannot but feel, humanly speaking, as if he had forgotten us. . . Faith does not obtain the victory at the first encounter, but exercised by many trials, [only] finally emerges the victor."[16]

The doubt Calvin was willing to entertain more fully was that Christian life could ever be settled and comfortable. The Christian life was a pilgrimage, a journey, where the faithful do not know much rest. Calvin's legacy to the liberal theological style of the United Church of Christ is not found in his doctrinal formulations, but in his persistent engagement with his times. Though his thought has been used legalistically by many since, he himself revised his *Institutes of the Christian Religion* again and again because he doubted the adequacy of his own formulations. But he never doubted the faithfulness of God, or the freedom of God to bring redemption to a world that seemed to him hopelessly bound by human sin. For Calvin, God was the liberal. Our freedom (real though used most often as freedom to sin) is a gift from a generous God. God's generosity undergirds our well being, indeed our very existence.

The constellation of Reformed Protestant churches centered in the theology and practice of Zwingli and Calvin contained increasing myriads of groups applying this "reformed" theology and structure to new cultural settings. First in France, Germany, and the Netherlands, then as the Genevan refugees from England and Scotland returned to their homeland it blossomed into the Puritan movement and finally spread into the whole world. Not long after that, the more radical reformed Protestants and the English Separatist Pilgrims, moved to North America in search of a space to create their ideal society. A few years later their more conventional brothers and sisters, the Puritans, Presbyterians, and the German Reformed followed. Much of our inheritance in the United Church of Christ stems from this Reformed movement to Massachusetts Bay Colony, Pennsylvania, and other nearby British colonies.

These British and German Reformed people focused their doubts on their culture's assumptions about the magisterial reform,[17] namely that the state provided the most effective means for reforming the church. This is not to say that they did not, especially on the Puritan side, attempt to create their own version of the state church. But in moving out of their accustomed cultural geography into an entirely new place they expressed a fundamental doubt about their original society's ability to embrace them and what they understood to be the truth. It took one hundred and fifty years (from the 1620s to the 1770s), but the irritant of doubt about the state church resulted finally in Protestant ability to entertain the idea of separation of church and state and new applications of Reformed polity to a church unsupported by secular power and resources. The resulting covenant theology and the church polities that grew from it, represented by the Mayflower Compact and the Salem Church Covenant, provided a foundation for the development of a democratic civil polity under the idea that a government exists as a contract with its subjects, obligated to preserve certain individual natural rights, and holding the will of the majority in highest regard. In the next chapter I will discuss this matter of the covenant more fully, but here it is important to note that this covenant theology contributed to the development of political liberalism leading to the American War for Independence in the eighteenth century.

Seventeenth-Century Issues Leading to Theological Liberalism

Political liberalism and the ultimate disestablishment of the church in the United States were not the only liberalizing developments in colonial Reformed traditions related to the United Church of Christ. Issues of doubt arose regarding theological and hermeneutical (interpretive) principles as well. The Antinomian controversy in Massachusetts Bay Colony in the 1630s serves as an initial example. Calvin's theology rested on a hermeneutical principle regarding the nature of the relation of the scriptures to the Word of God, namely that while the Word of God is incarnate in Jesus Christ and contained in the scriptures, the scriptures are not exactly identical with the Word. God accommodated to finite human understanding and changeableness, so that for instance, God's decrees recorded in the scripture change over time according to the cultural circumstances of the people. In answering the question of why there are differences in the presentation of God's justice in the Bible, Calvin wrote:

> . . . I reply that God ought not to be considered changeable merely because he accommodated diverse forms to different ages, as he knew would be expedient for each. . . . Why, then, do we brand God with the mark of inconstancy because he has with apt and fitting marks distinguished a diversity of times?[18]

This complication did not, for Calvin, disturb the authority of the scriptures for the church; the church can be mistaken in its interpretation either willfully or intentionally. Thus, while Calvin can be taken, and has been by many, to mean that the scriptures are literally infallible, he also destabilizes any static literal reading, opening the way for multiple interpretations as the church deliberates on new circumstances. The Antinomian controversy of 1637 in Boston tested the degree to which individual interpretation could claim authority within the emerging Congregational system.

This controversy also served as a public occasion for raising doubts about the authority of the clergy in the Puritan understanding of the Church. The main protagonist in this controversy was Ann Hutchinson, a lay woman, midwife, and leader of a Tuesday bible study for women that drew large numbers of men as well. Her foundational position was that God spoke directly to her in her reading of Scripture, "by an immediate revelation," the same way that God spoke to Abraham.[19] One of the characteristic teachings of the Protestant churches was the priesthood of all believers, a trust in the individual believer to have unmediated access to God. Citing such biblical passages as I Peter 2:9, "But you are a chosen race, a royal priesthood, a holy nation, God's own people," (NRSV) or the metaphor in I

Corinthians 12 that we are all one body in Christ and each member has his or her own important role, and Revelation 5:9 praising Christ saying, "saints from every tribe and language, and nation; you have made them to be a kingdom and priests serving our God, and they will reign on earth," (NRSV) Luther attacked the idea that the clergy, by their ordination, have an exclusive right to the interpretation and proclamation of the Gospel.

> To call popes, bishops, priests, monks, and nuns, the religious class, but princes, lords, artisans, and farm-workers the secular class, is a specious device invented by certain timeservers; but no one ought to be frightened by it, and for good reason. For all Christians whatsoever really and truly belong to the religious class, and there is no difference among them except in so far as they do different work. . . . This applies to us all, because we have one baptism, one gospel, one faith, and are all equally Christian. For baptism, gospel, and faith alone make [people] religious, and create a Christian people. . . the fact is our baptism consecrates us all without exception and makes us all priests.[20]

The principle could be taken to an extreme, allowing each individual believer to become in essence his or her own church. As Protestantism developed some have been inclined to attribute its propensity to splinter to this very principle. What then becomes of the authority of the clergy in this context? Luther never intended the principle of the priesthood of all believers to become justification for any individual opinion.

> Therefore everyone who knows that he [or she] is a Christian should be fully assured that all of us alike are priests, and that we all have the same authority in regard to the word and the sacraments, although no one has the right to administer them without the consent of the members of his [or her] church, or by the call of the majority (because, when something is common to all, no single person is empowered to arrogate it to himself [or herself], but should await the call of the church).[21]

In addition, Luther granted to civil magistrates a larger share of oversight of the Church than the ordinary lay person possessed, though he admonished the civil magistrates to remember that their authority also ultimately rested on the consent of the community. In general, Protestants agreed that authority in the church is granted by the whole body of the laity in the church, that all of them were qualified by baptism to assume such roles, though these roles were not to be assumed by any particular persons acting on their own desires, but that this authority of the laity did not generally extend to women.

The defensiveness of the Massachusetts clergy in the face of Hutchinson's entertainment of doubt about their authority shows in the transcript of her trial.[22] Clearly, the community was granting her some kind of authority by their presence when they attended her meetings. Her opinions had political influence in Boston. Boston clergy and civic leaders were not prepared to have to earn the respect of women. They accused her of violating the fifth commandment (You shall honor your father and mother) understanding the pastors and teachers of the church and the magistrates to serve as mother and father of the congregation and the community in general. Throughout the proceedings she asked them to show her some law in the Bible which granted them authority to prevent her from holding opinions she derived from Scripture or from holding regular meetings of women to study the Bible and discuss the Sunday sermons. In her opinion, the magistrates were not able to show her such a law. They could only claim that the law she used to justify herself had less authority than the one they used to justify themselves.[23] The Massachusetts authorities banished Ann Hutchinson and later others like her, but could not, in the end, suppress the doubts she raised.[24]

A decade after the Antinomian Controversy, the Cambridge Synod (1648) made a formal declaration of the authority of the clergy. "A church being free cannot become subject to any but by a free election. Yet when such a people do choose any to be over them in the Lord, then do they become subject and most willingly submit to their ministry in the Lord whom they have so chosen."[25] In practice however, few Congregational clergy have ever been able simply to dictate to their congregations. Their authority rests on much more than a principle. It rests above all on a relationship of trust. The Congregationalists have always entertained doubt about the authority of their ministers, probably rightly so. This doubt of clerical authority made it easier, eventually, to entertain doubt about doctrinal principles as well as including the doctrine of the infallibility or even the divine inspiration of the scriptures.

Pietism and the Enlightenment

The seventeenth and eighteenth centuries produced two movements which further contributed to the development of a liberal style in the Puritan Congregationalist and German Reformed churches in the English colonies. The Enlightenment contributed a respect for human reason, a high regard for education, optimism regarding human possibilities, and the view that an increase in human freedom tends to be a good thing. Pietism, a contemporary movement, also stressed the authority of human experience in religious matters, an equally high regard for education, optimism about human spiritual ability, though for the Pietists, human freedom had its source in God. Pietism stressed a sense of the nearness of God. In contrast, the Enlightenment tended to note the distance of God from human affairs. For the Enlightenment philosophers, especially the Deists, God was the designer and initiator of the natural order, but after that remained at a distance uninvolved further in the life of the world, whereas for the Pietist, God was available to guide each step.

Both movements, in some respects, were reactions to the intense religious conflict in Europe after the Reformation and the consequent development of strictly and narrowly defined confessional identities among the European churches, often resting on single points of small difference in doctrine. Pietism and the Enlightenment both claimed the value of human experience as a ground of truth. Both tended, therefore, to be suspicious of doctrine or belief as the mark of Christian faith and instead turned to ethics for criteria by which to judge the outward moral behavior of those who claimed to be Christian. The Enlightenment was a rational movement of the intellect, whereas Pietism emphasized the heart.

In the more extensive discussion of these movements in the previous chapter, we saw how each one contributed to the diversity of theological positions within the United Church of Christ traditions. Here I want to examine how each contributed to the characteristic liberal theological culture in these traditions, particularly the way in which both movements fostered the entertainment of doubt. Both movements entertained doubt about received doctrinal teaching in the churches. For the philosophers of the Enlightenment, truth was rational and verifiable by human experience. The supernatural did not exist as something to take seriously because individuals claiming supernatural experience could not provide a repetition of the phenomenon to be verified by others. The inexplicable events lying behind the natural world did not come under the purview of eighteenth-century enlightenment philosophy. God, the Creator, presumably designed the world rationally and its accessibility to the human mind made nature the subject of human investigation. We would understand everything eventually. Human happiness rested most reliably on the steady application of human reason to the alleviation of human suffering. In the theological realm, this application of human reason to the problem of religious conflict resulted in doubt about the ability of received doctrine and tradition to foster human happiness. Contrary to the ethical claims of the Gospel, traditional Christian doctrine appeared to the Enlightenment mind only to divide and create enmity among even well-meaning people.

Based on the moral teachings of Christianity, Enlightenment thinkers also sought the greatest possible liberty of conscience. Following John Locke, they argued that human beings had God-given rights, natural rights, which included even the right not to believe. Locke, along with other Enlightenment philosophers, argued that human social life was not a structure given authority by traditional doctrine but a contract among diverse people setting out political structures to serve the common good, but acknowledging a right of the people to depose a government that failed to promote that good. Enlightenment thinkers regarded the right to doubt as a fundamental and God-given right, and they had confidence in the capacity of human reason, also God-given, to address that doubt.

Pietists also entertained doubts about traditional religious authority. But they trusted the heart more than the head. The movement originated in German Protestantism but soon spread to most forms of Western Christianity. In an environment where small differences in points of doctrine served to justify war, the Pietists challenged both secular and religious authority with the authority of human religious experience, a change of heart that led not primarily to correct belief but to authentic Christian life. What marked a person as a Christian for the Pietists was the way one lived the Gospel, not specific beliefs about the Gospel. The Pietist could question the authority of the clergy if their mode of life did not correspond to their preaching, and likewise they challenged the authority of secular government if it violated Christian ethical principles. While the Enlightenment was disposed to doubt Christian doctrine based upon rational principles, Pietism was disposed to doubt the authenticity of a person's claim to be Christian on the basis of belief alone without a corresponding practical effort to live by that belief. Both movements influenced the development of a liberal style in the traditions of the United Church of Christ, the Enlightenment by fostering a willingness to question received tradition by virtue of human reason, and Pietism by fostering the authority of personal experience and integrity of behavior. Both movements favored education, which shaped both reason and character.

Jonathan Edwards embodied both the Enlightenment and Pietist modes of thought. In this chapter, I have no hope of doing justice to his theological contributions to both liberal and nonliberal traditions in American Protestantism. What I do hope to do is use his complex and innovative thought to illustrate the ways in which Enlightenment principles and Pietist practice combined to provide a foundation for certain central themes in the liberal style of the United Church of Christ. As a supporter of the revivals of the eighteenth-century Great Awakening, he was thoroughly Pietist. He shared their doubts about the ability of correct doctrine on the part of the traditionalists and rational reductionism on the part of the Deists to produce faith and ultimately Christian community. As an Enlightenment thinker, he entertained doubts about the pietist tendency to equate emotional experience with religious truth. His active struggle with these doubts resulted in a rich body of theological reflection and practical application of ideas to the problem of church renewal in his own day. He remains one of the most influential American theologians.

In his "Treatise on Religious Affections" (1746), as we read in the last chapter, Edwards brought together his Enlightenment and Pietist questions. In the aftermath of the revival in his congregation, one he attributed solely to God and not to his own preaching or other efforts, he became troubled by the propensity of the people to equate emotional experience with religious conversion. Many sought the emotional "high" of the revival without subsequent interest in understanding the experience or in making serious change in their moral lives. He was alarmed at their propensity to fool themselves about the difficulties of conversion thus endangering their souls, or their excessive pride in their spiritual accomplishments and disdain for their more modest neighbors. Yet he was equally troubled by those who used rational critique of revival excesses to dismiss the need for conversion. Those who understood Christianity intellectually, but were unable to cultivate the ability to love, also participated in what Edwards termed "a lamentable decay in religious affections."[26] Edwards judged the result of the revival by an increase in charity toward the poor, "though [he wrote] I think with regard to this, we in this town, as in the land in general, come far short of Gospel rules."

Edwards, in the "Treatise on Religious Affections," provided a thoroughly rational analysis of the revival experience and put forward the characteristics by which a pastor might distinguish a true conversion from mere emotionalism. His psychological analysis of religious experience, drawn from the work of John Locke, laid the groundwork for that of William James two centuries later. Edwards challenged the prevailing view that the heart is only emotional and the mind is only rational. Gracious affections, those that accompany a true conversion, are of both mind and heart. "Gracious affections do arise from the mind's being enlightened, rightly and spiritually to understand or apprehend divine things," but also they "soften the heart, and are attended and followed with a Christian tenderness of spirit."[27]

The historian of American religious thought, William Clebsch, has argued that Edwards' most radical religious insight was this:

> Persons who received true religion (= true virtue) would sensibly know and palpably display it. Spirituality would inexorably become outward in practice. By empirically demonstrating this principle, Edwards turned inside out the traditional Protestant emphasis on spirituality as inward, hidden, unknowable, and mysterious.[28]

Edwards' Christianity was an embodied religion, a concrete experience in which true virtue becomes visible in the actions of the believer. Not only the heart and the mind, but the body as well share in the experience of conversion. Clebsch characterizes Edwards' theology as a "dynamic liberalism"[29] in contrast to the rationalist liberalism of the Deist and the later Unitarians. Edwards' embodied spirituality, the beauty of virtue, was translated by later American theologians into a "sense of a welcoming universe."[30] Edwards did not create a consistent Calvinism, though his later New Divinity followers did, nor did he reduce religion to feeling in contrast to thinking as his revivalist heirs tended to do. Instead he held the two together under the categories of beauty and virtue.

At the end of his life Edwards had synthesized his Enlightenment analysis of religious experience and his Pietist awe of the working of God in the human heart into a spirituality that influenced subsequent American thinkers from Ralph Waldo Emerson to Horace Bushnell. His work on "The Nature of True Virtue" (published posthumously in 1765) contains some of the most important of Edwards' work for shaping a liberal style in subsequent Congregational thinking. Edwards linked beauty and virtue, giving spirituality both an aesthetic and an ethical aspect.

> Virtue is the beauty of those qualities and acts of the mind, that are of a *moral* nature, i.e., such as are attended with desert or worthiness of *praise*, or *blame*. Things of this sort, it is generally agreed, so far as I know, are not any thing belonging merely to speculation; but to the *disposition* and *will*, or (to use a general word, I suppose commonly well understood) the *heart*. Therefore, I suppose, I shall not depart from the common opinion, when I say, that virtue is the beauty of the qualities and exercises of the heart, or those actions which proceed from them.[31]

Finally, for Edwards, the actions which proceed from the beautiful qualities of the heart result in a harmonious, that is a just and benevolent, society.

Nineteenth Century Liberalism

Meanwhile, in the German universities in particular, theologians and biblical scholars were entertaining doubts about the assumed historicity of Biblical texts and the validity of philosophical assumptions about God, setting the stage for the development of important characteristics of liberal Christianity. Chief among these thinkers was Emanuel Kant, who taught philosophy at the University of Königsberg in the eighteenth century. Kant's questions about human ability to know God or to speak comprehensibly about issues such as immortality, posed unprecedented challenges to Christian theologians. The work of Kant and his students, for example Johann Herder, raised questions about the relation of truth to human language and culture, and opened the question of the cultural relativism of religious ideas and moral practice. As with Jonathan Edwards discussed above, in the following few pages I can do no more than sketch the main figures of this German tradition shaping the nineteenth-century American Protestant liberal style.

Five important theological developments need attention in order to understand the complex foundations and internal differences in today's liberalism. First, one cannot understand any of the liberal traditions without a word about Friedrich Schleiermacher (1768–1834). His focus on the gathered community, its Christocentricity, and the sensibility of absolute contingency underlying all human religion continue to underlie the liberal style in the United Church of Christ, not only in the Evangelical Synod tradition of which Schleiermacher was a major theologian, but through Philip Schaff and John Nevin in the Reformed tradition, and through Bushnell in the Congregational tradition as well. Second, one must follow the liberal emphasis on unity based on the common Enlightenment and Pietist understanding of the outward Christian life more than insistence on creedal orthodoxy. Both the Christian churches and the Mercersburg movement participate in this liberal style. Third, Horace Bushnell sought, based on an understanding of Edwards' psychology and a continued critique of the revivals, an understanding of Christian nurture that made room for the believer's growth in both understanding and moral practice. Fourth, the liberal Protestant tradition sought to make Biblical criticism and Darwin's work on evolution accessible in a setting where the older Calvinist orthodoxy was collapsing. Bushnell was a critical figure in this development as well. Finally, returning to Schleiermacher's view of sin as corporate rather than individual, we must pay attention to the development of the Social Gospel.

By the end of the nineteenth century, there were varieties of liberal Christianity in the United States. They shared a loose set of characteristics. All of them entertained doubt about traditional orthodox creedal formulations as adequate to make Christian faith understandable in their time. They all entertained various forms of doubt about the literal truth or infallibility of the Bible. They tended to doubt the ability of the law, religious or secular, to form a just and happy society. And they tended to doubt both a religion based on reason alone, that had no room for the affections, and to doubt a religion based only on emotionalism with no room for the working of the mind in understanding truth. The nineteenth century was a particularly unsettled time as doubts multiplied faster than the churches could respond. The extreme attempts by some Christians to either make Christianity a religion of reason, or the effort to distance Christianity from any corruption from human rationality, led many, by the end of the century, to conclude that unbelief was the best course.[32] All the traditions of the United Church of Christ chose to engage their doubts, even to welcome the struggle. There are those who would argue that the United Church of Christ thereby sacrificed a sense of doctrinal certainty and identity that has plagued us since. However, that loss of doctrinal clarity is more likely because we are a united and uniting church. In many ways the identity the UCC traditions shared and transmitted into the United Church of Christ is precisely the willingness to engage the culture, to entertain doubt, to think actively, and to forge in each new generation a more united Christianity that answers the deepest human concerns of their times.[33]

Schleiermacher framed the beginning and the end of nineteenth-century liberal development as I have presented it here. Building upon Kant's philosophy and its critiques of the Enlightenment, his thought marked the beginning of liberal theology, but later his theology or a stereotype of it, became the foil for twentieth-century theological disillusionment. He came from a Pietist milieu in Berlin and Halle. Participating in the formation of the Church of the Union in Prussia, a union of the Lutheran and Reformed churches in that area, he developed an acute sense of Christian community as the source of Christian theological discourse. He also faced squarely the growing disinterest, even hostility toward Christianity in his culture.

In his "Speeches on Religion to its Cultured Despisers (On Religion)" (1799), he countered those who wanted only a "natural" or rational religion by arguing that all religion is characterized by an intuitive human feeling, sensibility, or experience of finitude in the face of the Infinite.[34] His more famous formulation is found in *The Christian Faith*. "The common element in all howsoever diverse expressions of piety, by which these are conjointly distinguished from all other feelings, or, in other words, the self-identical essence of piety, is this: the consciousness of being absolutely dependent, or, which is the same thing, of being in relation with God."[35] This feeling of dependence is not a feeling of helplessness, nor an invitation to a passive Christian existence, rather it is a sense of contingency, that we are not here by our own effort, that our life depends upon the world, the community, and ultimately upon God. Many of Schleiermacher's later critics accused him of reducing Christianity to a good feeling about ourselves and a happy optimism that such good feeling is all that is necessary for transforming the world. However, contrary to this critique, he did not stop with this, but insisted that religion also requires that this feeling should accompany our active life.

Schleiermacher the Pietist insisted that spiritual experience should result in acts of love and justice, and he had an acute sense of the depth of social sin found embedded in the structures of society.

> If sin as an organic whole can be rightly understood only as the corporate action of the human race, its causal action relatively to evil can only be understood from the same point of view. In fact, the most definite expression of this conviction lies, for each of us, in the general statement that throughout the human race as a whole, increase of sin is necessarily attended by a corresponding increase of evil (though as the effects of sin naturally ensue only by degrees, it is often the children and grandchildren who first suffer for the sins of the fathers), (Ex. 20:5) and that, in like manner as sin diminishes, so will evil diminish.[36]

In *The Christian Faith,* Schleiermacher made this outward expression of religion more explicit. For Schleiermacher, human reality is a tension between sin and grace, between that which allows community and that which destroys it. His analysis of sin stressed its corporate nature. Sin was not the burden of the individual alone, but of the entire social structure in which the individual lives. "It can be called guilt with perfect accuracy only when it is regarded simply as meaning the totality of the whole race."[37] The social context of the individual serves to transmit sin to that individual. In the same way the redeemed community, the Church, serves to transmit redemption.

> Just as creation is not concerned simply with individuals (as if each creation of an individual had been a special act), but it is

> the world that was created, and every individual as such was created only in and with the whole, for the rest not less than for itself, in the same way the activity of the Redeemer too is world-forming, and its object is human nature, in the totality of which the powerful God-consciousness is to be implanted as a new vital principle.[38]

Operating through the Church, the Redeemer brings the love, justice and wisdom of God to bear in human society and in the end thus will establish the Realm of God. The church has a multiplicity of visible forms, but a unity in the mind of Christ.

The ideal of the unity of the church is a critical aspect of Protestant liberalism, while the political ideals of individual liberty rooted in the Enlightenment and the Protestant principle of the liberty of the individual conscience to approach God tend to produce a pronounced individualism in nineteenth-century liberal Christianity. Individualism is always in tension with unity and the tension is rooted in a sense of corporate sin and redemption. Schleiermacher shared this tension if it did not originate with him. In 1818, Schleiermacher wrote in support of the union of the Lutheran and Reformed Churches in Prussia.

> The work of the Reformation was not, therefore, to found a Lutheran Church–against which, indeed, no one protested more warmly than Luther himself–nor was it to found a Reformed Church, but to bring forth in renewed glory the Evangelical Church, which is guided and governed by its founder, Jesus Christ, the eternal Son of God.
>
> He is the quickening centre of the Church, from Him comes all, to Him all returns: He is the beginning and the End: in Him we believe, and through Him alone we are blessed . . . . We ought not, therefore, to call ourselves Lutheran nor Reformed, but we ought to call ourselves Evangelical Christians, after His name and His holy evangel; for in our name our faith and our confession ought to be made known.[39]

The heirs of this union in the United Church of Christ formed the Evangelical Synod of North America, an American counterpart to the

German EKU (Evangelische Kirche der Union) now the UEK (Die Union Evangelischer Kirchen), and the UCC remains in full communion with this church.[40] However, in the traditions of the United Church of Christ this unitive ideal was most powerfully articulated by the Christians.

The ecumenical spirit that the Christian Connection contributed to the liberal style of the UCC rested in profound doubt about the wisdom or theological ground for separate denominations in Christianity. "Gospel liberty" became their central value. This liberty allowed them to cross doctrinal lines with ease. In Christian ranks, Republican Methodists, Calvinistic Baptists, and Unitarians could meet in a common enterprise. They flourished under the newly articulated political freedom of religion from the state and the new American democracy. Like other liberals, Christians tended to share aspects of both Enlightenment and Pietism. They trusted people's experience of God over traditional doctrines, though they honored those doctrines in so far as they judged them to be congruent with experience.[41]

Through the freedom of their ecclesiastical structures, women gained their first significant entrance into American Protestant pulpits. African American Christians formed churches expressing their own culture as well as their own Convention, with its own publications independent from white control. In the first case, Christian liberalism lay in their mode of construing the biblical texts regarding women's role in the churches as well as in their adoption of particular forms of church life that stressed the role of the laity in the governance of the church. They were willing to entertain doubt about the common application of Paul's prohibitions on women speaking in church and the related doubt of women's intellectual ability. "If God has declared, in the most positive terms, that, under *the new dispensation,* his daughters shall prophecy, who dares to say they shall not? Let such reflect that it is a fearful thing to be found fighting against God."[42] So wrote Rebecca Miller, a Christian preacher, in 1841. "Under the new dispensation" all the old traditional forms came under question. The Christians claimed, based upon their experience of God's call in their own generation, the Gospel liberty to do what had not yet been done, or to recover an ancient practice.

African Americans had to engage an even more difficult set of assumptions. The women had grounds for their doubt of the customary prohibitions of their participation based on a complementary and clear set of biblical affirmations. The African Americans had to entertain their doubts of the social order without Scripture that clearly named them as participants, in the same way that it named the daughters who would prophesy. And one of first tasks of the African American Christians was to secure the education that Enlightenment and Pietist liberals alike claimed to be the necessary underpinning of responsible freedom and which the Christians had already offered to women.

> The Christian denomination in North Carolina and Virginia are behind all other denominations in education. Why are they behind? Because they have had no help since they were freed from bondage. The white people in the South are very agreeable and admire the prospect of industry, but do not desire the improvement of elevation and education among the colored people, and therefore they will not teach a colored school. I say that we are behind all others in schooling our ministers, and in educating our children.
>
> The Baptist people, . . . have built up schools for the colored Baptists. The Methodist white people have come from the north and built up schools for the Methodists. . . . Our inducements are by other denominations saying, come and join us and deny your name and take ours and we will educate you.[43]

So wrote George W. Dunn in 1879 to the Christian churches in the North, asking for aid for education so that the Christians of the South would not have to give up their Christian ideals to gain an education. In his letter, Dunn recites the main principles of the Christian tradition, among them "Christian character or vital piety is the one scriptural test of fellowship and church membership." This principle allowed the Christians to develop an inclusive style that, despite their small numbers in the original union, remains a legacy to the United Church of Christ.

We can also find the active ecumenical spirit of United Church of Christ liberalism in the Mercersburg tradition of the German Reformed Church. Philip Schaff (1819-1893), in *What is Church History?* (1846), echoed both Schleiermacher and the Christians in their understanding of Christian unity that transcended denominationalism. Speaking about the historian August Neander, Schaff wrote,

> His liberality proceeds partly from his mild, John-like nature, and partly from his genuine Protestant toleration and high regard for individual personality; or from such a *subjectivity* as formed a barrier against ultra-Protestant and sectarian bigotry no less than against Romanism, where individual freedom is lost in the authority of the general. In this he is a faithful follower of Schleiermacher, who, though he based his philosophy on the pantheistic system of Spinoza,[44] had nevertheless an uncommonly keen eye and a tender regard for the personal and individual. . . . He (Neander) was fully convinced that the free spirit of the gospel could never be concentrated in any one given form, but could be completely manifested only in a great variety of forms and views.[45]

Schaff's view represented a different solution to the problem of denominationalism. While the Christians proposed that each denomination give up its name and distinctive claims and simply become Christian, Schaff proposed, as Schleiermacher had, that the variety of forms was actually necessary to fully represent the free working of the Gospel. In either case, the liberal view emphasized Gospel liberty, not to satisfy the individual believer, but to make the Gospel more compelling to its, by now many, "cultured despisers." To do this both Christian unity and the believer's own Christian faith needed to be outwardly visible.

The issue of education continued to generate new questions for liberal Christians in the nineteenth century. Nearly all American Protestants agreed that education was necessary for both political participation in democracy and for church life. The role education played in Christian experience, particularly in conversion, was a matter of debate at the time. For a theologian such as Jonathan Edwards, education prepared the mind for conversion, but that was all. However necessary education was for secular life, it played no necessary role in the most important aspects of Christian experience. God converted the heart. Many, but not all, of the revivalists believed that a person could choose to respond to the grace of God, to convert,[46] but debated whether education fostered or got in the way of a person's willingness to make the choice. Those revivalists tending toward a liberal style in their expression of nineteenth-century American evangelicalism, Charles Finney for example,[47] tended both to affirm individual choice in the religious life, as well as to value education. Finney, like Edwards undertook a rational analysis of the revival experience and concluded, unlike Edwards who believed revivals of religion depended on God alone, and not on human effort, that such phenomena were not miraculous, but reproducible by using particular methods. The methods originated with God, but pastors needed to know and use them.[48]

The Sunday School movement, a contemporary movement with revivalism, rested on the principle that education could, in fact, foster in the student a desire to choose conversion and the knowledge of how to accomplish such a move. Others with a liberal style were entertaining doubts about the process and necessity of conversion itself. They had seen too many examples of conversion that seemed socially coerced or falsely claimed. In addition, they could point to people of Christian character and even "vital piety" who had not undergone any conversion experience they could identify nor could they point to the day when they had decided to be Christian.

Chief among these pastors and theologians was Horace Bushnell (1802–1876). Like Schleiermacher in Germany a generation before, Bushnell began a liberal theological movement in the United States. Like Schleiermacher, his thought had weaknesses that made easy marks for opponents of liberalism. However, his thought also repays deeper study and has much to contribute to us both in historical understanding and in ideas that have not yet been mined to their depths. Bushnell is most famous for his work *Christian Nurture*. Here he addressed the problem of how a person becomes a Christian, asking whether it was by conversion or by some other means. He is particularly concerned by what he regards as "ostrich nurture," the practice of allowing a child to grow up completely free from parental prescriptions about life. As a result the children can do nothing except follow their instincts without the benefit of accumulated human wisdom, established institutions to support their human development, and without history to give meaning to the present.[49] It is even worse for children in the church.

> There is no church nurture for them proper to their tender years; they can not be in the church till they are sufficiently grown to believe. And so it is settled that there is no church mercy for them. The church turns her back and leaves them, separated even from their parents, to try their fortunes, like the wild ostriches, in the desert sands without.[50]

Bushnell's principle was "*that the child is to grow up a Christian, and never know himself as being otherwise.*"[51] Bushnell assumed, as all orthodox Congregationalists of his day, the corruption of human nature. He argued though, that the pliancy of the young allows parents to teach by example where in later years force would be necessary. A child brought up by Christian parents, nurtured in body, mind, and spirit according to principles of Christian love, will grow up to embody Christianity and have no need for conversion. "The whole scheme of organic unity in the family and of family grace in the church, is just what it should be, if the design were to propagate religion, not by conversions only, but . . . by the populating force embodied in it."[52]

In all of this teaching, Bushnell relied on a particular understanding of language and the way in which language shapes human individuality and society, and this, more than his idea of Christian nurture, made him liberal in his theological style. We find his most explicit views of language in his work *God in Christ.*

> Words of thought or spirit are not only inexact in their significance, never measuring the truth or giving its precise equivalent, but they always affirm something which is false, or contrary to the truth intended. They impute *form* to that which really is out of form. They are related to the truth, only as form to spirit–earthen vessels in which the truth is borne, yet always offering their mere pottery as being the truth itself.[53]

Bushnell here represents a stream of thought already apparent in the Reformation and growing stronger with each passing decade of the nineteenth and twentieth centuries. Increasingly entertaining profound doubts about the ability of human language to convey the truth in any simple way. Yet, since language is all we have, Bushnell strove to understand how we can know anything. In *God in Christ,* Bushnell outlines his distrust of both rational logic and Christian dogma. In essence, he thought both stifled the Spirit.

> Religion has a natural and profound alliance with poetry. Hence, a very large share of the bible is composed of poetic contributions. Another share, equally large, is that which comes to us in a form of history and fact; that is, of actual life, which is equally remote from all abstractions, and, in one view,

> equally poetic; for history is nothing but an evolution or expression of God and [humanity] in their own nature and character. The teachings of Christ are mere utterances of truth, not augmentations over it. He gives it forth in living symbols, without definition, without *proving* it, ever, as the logicians speak, well understanding that truth is that which shines in its own evidence, that which *finds* us, to use an admirable expression of Coleridge, and thus enters into us.[54]

Such a principle may remind us of John Robinson's statement, now part of Congregational lore, that "there is yet more light and truth to break forth from God's word." Bushnell placed a high value on the role of the Spirit in discerning the meaning of the Word of God. He shared a characteristic liberal openness to the poetic and to the idea that truth is not given for all time, but is progressive or evolutionary in nature. These characteristics proved especially useful when the Congregationalists engaged Darwin a decade later. But they proved also to have raised the troubling question of the exact nature of the difference between historical fact and symbol.

Until 1859, and the publishing of Charles Darwin's *The Origin of Species,* theologians influenced by the questions of the rationalist Enlightenment were content to argue the obvious design of the universe, and thus the existence of a Creator, without the need to appeal to a literal understanding of Genesis. But, though Darwin claimed belief in God, or at least admitted its possibility, in the work itself, his idea allowed for a nondivine explanation of the development of life.[55] In his autobiography, Darwin wrote about his belief at the time he was working on *The Origin of the Species:*

> Another source of conviction in the existence of God, connected with the reason and not with the feelings, impresses me as having much more weight. This follows from the extreme difficulty or rather impossibility of conceiving this immense and wonderful universe, including man with his capacity of looking far backwards and far into futurity, as the result of blind chance or necessity. When thus reflecting I feel compelled to look to a First Cause having an intelligent mind in

> some degree analogous to that of man; and I deserve to be called a Theist.[56]

Later he modified his view, or perhaps elaborated the one he had already stated. "The mystery of the beginning of all things is insoluble by us; and I for one must be content to remain an Agnostic."[57]

Bushnell's ideas about language proved inadequate to the problem Darwin posed for Christian theology. For Darwin and others, it was not that the Biblical accounts interpreted as poetry and legend rather than as historical fact that bothered them. It was the capricious nature of the ethics they contained, that in one place they proclaimed a just God and in another seemed to condemn the innocent to hell simply because they had not heard the Gospel. Darwin's most critical challenge to the religion of his contemporaries was that his theory explained the development of living things without reference to their purpose. From the beginning, Christians had assumed that all life existed to serve the needs of humanity, and that humanity was a special creation of central importance in the universe. Darwin posited the theory that life emerged and developed without reference to any end or purpose, and in the *Descent of Man* (1871) he applied that theory to human beings, concluding that we also experienced evolution just as the rest of the living world. While Darwin (who had in his early years studied theology thinking to become an Anglican priest) did not venture to explain what mechanism set the evolutionary process in motion in the first place, those who read his work either argued or feared it could be argued that God as Creator became unnecessary for explaining the existence of the world or for teaching a particular religious vision for human life.

The American mainline theologians of the nineteenth century, particularly in the Congregational tradition of the UCC, did not long concern themselves over the question of to what degree Darwin's thought led to irreligious conclusions. Rather they embraced his theory of evolution as of an intellectual piece with the cultural progress they celebrated. The nineteenth century mainline Christian theologians in the United States viewed the nation's extension over the continent as a tangible sign of God's purpose. The progress they believed they witnessed in that territorial expansion, and in the economic rise of their own middle class in the industrial and technological developments of the day persuaded them that God blessed their application of human reason and effort to the problems of the day. They came to hold an evolutionary view of the coming of the Realm or Kingdom of God. Orthodox liberal thinkers and those who had discarded specifically Christian theological beliefs as well as the more theologically conservative anti-Darwinists, agreed that science fostered positive developments for the comfort and well-being of humanity.[58] A group of later English and American thinkers, the social Darwinists, argued that human society was inevitably shaped by the law of the survival of the fittest. They reasoned that the Anglo-Saxon race, because of its success, was destined to prevail and rule the earth.

Parallel to this cultural development was the rise and fall of the Social Gospel, more generally termed social Christianity. The Social Gospelers argued, in contrast to the social Darwinists, that the Christian had an obligation to follow the teachings of Christ and the earlier Hebrew prophets in working for just conditions for the poor, particularly in their economic life.

One of the industrial developments of the post-Civil War period, unrestrained monopolistic industrial capitalism, figured in the displacement of farm workers, a sharp rise in urban poverty, and the economic exploitation of labor. The era was characterized by sharp peaks and dips in economic prosperity. Long working days, unsafe conditions, and low wages necessitating the work of women and children in the factories put pressures on working-class family life. Liberal Protestantism dealt well with individuals, encouraging a temperate and hard-working lifestyle, celebrating the freedom of each individual to live out his or her calling in the world. This theology worked well for those who were middle class, healthy, prosperous, and well-educated. But it did not take account of the need of capitalism for a pool of the unemployed in order for the free market in labor to work. Liberal Protestantism, including most in the traditions of the United Church of Christ, tended to blame the unemployed for their situation; they were lazy, drank too much, or were spendthrifts. In addition, liberalism was, as it turned out, too optimistic about the inclination or ability of wealthy to alleviate the problems of the poor by private charity.

As the economic condition of the working class deteriorated, a few urban pastors, like Schleiermacher before them, began to rethink the nature of sin and grace. They began to recognize increasingly the corporate character of human sin, the way in which it was woven into the very structures of society to produce injustice and suffering in spite of the goodness of individuals. American Christians in general, and those in the United Church of Christ traditions in particular, were alarmed by the antireligious sentiments of the growing labor-rights movements and especially so by Karl Marx who advocated violence in the pursuit of justice. *The Communist Manifesto* (1848) made a religion-less appeal for economic justice, implicating the churches in the oppression of the working class.[59] Though Marx based his arguments in deeply held principles of the Judeo-Christian tradition, it is perhaps little wonder that the churches found it hard to take in the social analysis of Marx apart from his indictment of the church. However, the most radical among the social Christians adopted a socialist interpretation of the Gospel and in the early years supported the Communist movements growing from Marx's economic theory. In this way, the Social Gospel concerned itself both with the teachings of Jesus and the systemic nature of economic evil, particularly as suffered by the working class and the poor.

The Social Gospel developed in the space between Marx's critique of the middle class and mainstream American Christianity's belief that poverty was a problem of individual morality. For the most part, the Social Gospel theologians believed that the necessary remedy to social sin entailed a change of social mind. Washington Gladden, a most well-known Congregational proponent of the Social Gospel, attributed the Church's failure to address the social crisis of the cities as a failure to recognize its own purpose. In *The Church and the Social Crisis* (1907) he wrote:

> It is only necessary that the Church shall know that she is here in the world to seek first the Kingdom of God and his righteousness; to seek it, not by turning her eyes to the skies, but by fixing them upon the world; to seek it and find it here. . . . If the Church can rally such moral forces that injustice will be overcome and fresh red blood will course in a sounder social organism, it will itself rise to higher liberty and life. Doing the will of God, it will have new visions of God.[60]

The most popular Social Gospel work was the novel by Charles M. Sheldon, *In His Steps: What Would Jesus Do?* (1896). As in the case of

Gladden, Sheldon applied the Sermon on the Mount to everyday life in the effort to build the Kingdom of God. He regarded it as a task within human possibility. God had provided the instructions and in terms reminiscent of Pelagius in the fourth century, Sheldon argued that Christians not only could but must work to build the righteous society God intended.

Out of the context of the Great Depression of the 1930s, Elmer Arndt, a professor at Eden Theological Seminary of the Evangelical Synod and later active in the Evangelical and Reformed Church Commission on Social Action, wrote in a similar vein.

> Mere proclamation of ideals is not enough. Ideals to be effective must be brought into relation with concrete events. It is not only necessary to realize the antitheses between the world with its injustice, its inequalities, and its lust for comfort and security even at the price of justice and righteousness and the principles of the gospel with their emphasis on justice and mutuality and repentance. These principles must be brought to bear on the world. . . . The function of the Christian church is neither to protect the position of the middle class nor to veneer its lusts with the phraseology of religion, but to teach [people] to criticize their inherited and accepted class ambitions and generate the moral energy necessary to extend the principles of justice and mutuality beyond the limits of class–even when it is contrary to their own self-interest.[61]

The Social Gospel was in many ways a powerful prophetic movement, and provided religious ideals for the wave of progressive legislation in the early twentieth century including the right of labor to organize, an end to child labor, the beginning of protections for workers in the work place, and protections for the nation's natural resources and environment. The Social Gospel shared common characteristics with other liberal theological movements; optimism that an informed individual would choose the right course; belief that God had endowed humanity with the power to do good; and in the revelation of the Gospel, had shown us how to accomplish what was necessary to bring about the Realm of God; and shown us the willingness to entertain doubts about the economic structures of society.

Twentieth-Century Expressions of a Liberal Style

The entertainment of doubt led Protestant liberal pastors and theologians to question even liberalism itself in the face of the horrific events of the World Wars and the economic devastation of the Great Depression. As the twentieth century progressed, liberalism's most powerful critics were liberals themselves who dared to question their own beliefs in light of the social suffering of their times. Two of the most famous of these critics in the traditions of the United Church of Christ were H. Richard and Reinhold Niebuhr, brothers raised in the Evangelical Synod tradition. H. Richard Niebuhr's critique of liberalism centered on its unreflective allegiance to the middle class. Niebuhr characterized liberal Christianity in his time as placing a high value on the individual, having an optimistic sense that the believer could work cooperatively with God, while holding the idea that salvation meant a fairly easy agreement with a rational approach to Christian truth rather than a radical change in one's lifestyle, and allowing the individual to choose among doctrines those which most fit her or his experience. All these characteristics expressed values important to the American middle class. Though the Social Gospel theologians had questioned the social structures that led to poverty, they continued to assume that American middle class life was the norm toward which to shape society.

H. Richard Niebuhr identified three ways in which the liberal church had become entangled in the world; through its economic dependence on capitalism, shown in its reliance on endowments for its financial support; through its identification with nationalism, shown in its blessing of national imperial expansion as the nation's God-given destiny; and in its "anthropocentrism" or glory and confidence in human (a late twentieth-century feminist might add male) achievement.[62] H. Richard Niebuhr returned to Schleiermacher's starting point.

> The church's declaration of independence can begin only with the self-evident truth that it and all life are dependent upon God, that loyalty to him is the condition of life and that to him belong the kingdom and the power and the glory. Otherwise the emancipation of the church from the world is impossible; there is no motive for it or any meaning in it. . . . Such words must seem to many to be pious and meaningless platitudes . . . That this is so is but another illustration of the extent to which

> the faith of the church has been confounded with the belief in the ideas, wishes and sentiments of men, and to which the word God has been made the symbol, not of the last reality with which man contends, but of his own aspirations. It remains true that loyalty to the "I am that I am" is the only reason for the church's existence and the recovery of this loyalty is the beginning of true emancipation.[63]

Reinhold Niebuhr, on the other hand, focused his critique less on the church as a social system and more on the dilemma of the individual who is able to be somewhat moral as an individual, but, as part of a social group finds morality impossible to achieve. The human being is caught between overweening prideful optimism that needs no God and a paralyzing despair in the face of human finitude and simply gives up. For Reinhold Niebuhr, the response of faith requires a person to struggle forever between pride and despair, to never be able to rest in one or the other. Thus Reinhold Niebuhr characterized liberalism's optimism as human pride, and the reluctance of the liberal churches to act in the face injustice as despair.[64]

If one characteristic of liberalism is to engage modernism, in contrast to fundamentalism which rejects it utterly, and equally in contrast to secularism which embraces modernism. Then in the mid twentieth century liberals struggled with the larger society's high regard for modernist values. Liberal Protestantism found it tempting to embrace modernity including the objectivity that encouraged neat categorization for the sake of efficiency, emphasized quantity over quality, and encouraged homogeneity and unity rather than diversity. But modernism was not the explicit goal of liberal theologians. Liberalism entertained modernist values and methods but, in the end, centered and recentered itself in a basic search for truth, embracing modernity and its methods because they seem suited to that end.[65]

After the second World War, the doubts facing liberal Christian theologians increased. First the economic class issues of poverty and injustice remained. The Civil Rights movement was in full swing and the problem of racism challenged otherwise righteous Christians to see the color lines in society and acknowledge the prejudice behind them. Increasingly small and unclear wars eroded liberal American Protestant support for the country's expansion while the realities of potential nuclear warfare were sinking into the American conscience. Then in the sixties, a renewed women's movement challenged the very language of Christian theology, and joined by those bringing forward increasingly complex and fluid expressions of sexual orientation, began to confront inequities of society and the church based upon traditional constructions of gender and family. At the same time, these issues remained contested within all American denominations in one way or another. These issues illuminated deep differences among Christians, even within the UCC, about the role of Scripture in the life of the Church, the degree to which the Church could accommodate itself to human culture, and the degree to which traditional orthodoxy could be translated from the fourth-century Greek philosophical categories in which it had been expressed into a very different philosophical and cultural language.

To their credit, liberal theologians in what is by now the United Church of Christ have tried to entertain all of these doubts faithfully. The price has often been a deliberate unclarity about theological categories. It is safer to say little, with the risk of the United Church of Christ almost losing its theological voice, rather than engaging in active theological thinking and discourse. The denomination for the most part became theologically paralyzed in unappeasable doubt. As society raised issue after issue, the church responded well with pragmatic action, but increasingly avoided theological reflection.[66] Many in the United Church of Christ take a more classically evangelical stance, reaffirming the basic Nicene creedal position of the Reformation churches, embracing the doctrinal orthodoxy rooted in the seventeenth-century Calvinist tradition of both the Puritan and Reformed churches. A few more conservative members declare the infallibility of the Bible. Primarily represented by the Biblical Witness Fellowship, they urge the church to deal with the rising doubts by defending the faith and traditional morality, particularly with regard to gender roles and human sexual identities.[67]

In 1983 and 1984, a number of more liberal groups in the United Church of Christ grappled with this loss of theological voice. On Reformation Day 1983, thirty-nine professors in theological schools addressed the church in a document entitled "A Most Difficult and Urgent Time." The document noted "a void in sustained, disciplined reflection that can claim the assent of the church. . . . We yearn for an articulation of faith in the life and witness of the church that may claim the assent of the church precisely because it faithfully witnesses to the bedrock truth of Jesus Christ in our common life."[68] The Craigville Colloquy, a group of lay and clergy members of the United Church of Christ issued yet another letter to the church in 1984 on the Fiftieth Anniversary of the Barman Declaration, the declaration of the churches in Germany against the church's participation in support of the Nazi government. They urged the clergy to take time for theological reflection and spiritual practice and above all to reaffirm loyalty to the founders faith in Jesus Christ. The Colloquy was concerned by the divisions within the United Church of Christ over the church's responses to social issues, and urged common prayer, study and mutual care, seeking the unity of the mind of Christ.[69]

In all three of these recent documents, is a pervasive uneasiness and call to find some new or old certainty. In the 1980s, the United Church of Christ seemingly longed to rest in belief rather than engage doubts, and understandably so in a complex world. However, from the margins of the church, theological voices urged the UCC to receive and continue to use the characteristic liberal entertainment of doubt. They called the church to doubt even that uncertainty has the last word. James Smucker of the Christians for Justice Action wrote, "Instead of worrying about a return to ancient truths or reestablishing a theological center or base, we are called to plunge into the world with its division and despair as well as its joy–and there to discover what the Spirit is saying in our time."[70] Susan Brooks Thistlethwaite observed in these documents an attempt to dismiss our Enlightenment, liberal heritage, a dismissal that she both understands but also finds impossible.

> The key thing, as I see it, is how we assume our heritage, Enlightenment included, in view of the demands on us today. The Enlightenment performed a great and necessary service to Christian thought in turning attention toward humanity. But there was also error in this turn. Enlightenment theologians limited their definition of what it means to be human to the experience of Anglo-Saxon, middle-class males. Further, their attention to human concerns often resulted in the limitation of the theological task by the values of a particular culture. This means that theologians could gain no critical distance

> from their individual culture. Theology came to be identical with North Atlantic bourgeois culture.[71]

The theology professors, in their 1983 letter, were going to ask for the establishment of a theology commission, a national body charged with clarifying theological matters for the United Church of Christ. However, Thistlethwaite noted that another woman objected to this plan. Barbara Brown Zikmund wrote:

> For centuries the church has shaped its theological stance in councils and commissions. Given the limitations of literacy and communication in past eras, this was understandable. . . . But I also know as a woman . . . that I cannot support "top down" theological formulations in these times.[72]

In their contribution to the theological ferment of the 1980s, a working group from Christians for Justice Action made their contribution to the discourse. They also cautioned against a move in the direction of intellectual reflection alone, and a simple return to a well-defined faith. They pointed out that "the biblical vision assumes life in community."

> We who are members of CJA affirm the centrality of Jesus the Christ as our witness. At the same time, we affirm that God's Spirit has been and is revealed through many faiths and tongues in every age. Therefore, we work with all the worlds God has called into being. As we understand scripture, we must fight the urge to make God too small. Our faith is inclusive and not exclusive. And thus we return to the cost and joy of discipleship which is the basis of our identity and our mission as the United Church of Christ. God is not finished, and thus we remain open to the call of the Spirit to cry aloud and spare not, to lift up our voices like trumpets and declare to our people, and to ourselves, our transgressions and our hope.[73]

Our UCC theological identity has never been found in a concise set of shared beliefs, nor in a common way of worship. It is certainly not found in our polity (though ours is uniquely complex). It is found precisely in our doubt. Our identity as the United Church of Christ lies in our doubt of the adequacy of any human containers of the Word of God. We doubt that the depths of God's Revelation in Jesus Christ have been fully explored.[74] Our identity does not lie in a set teaching or structure, but in a process. Our task today, as it was in our past traditions, is to think more clearly and openly about God, about Christ, about the Church so that we may recover our church's theological voice, so that the Gospel sings again from our minds, our hearts, and our actions.

Culture and style are not the same thing as an ecclesiology. In this chapter, I have tried to illustrate the intellectual traditions that have shaped the United Church of Christ as a complex theological culture. It is extraordinarily diverse, as I illustrated in the first chapter of this volume, but it is rooted solidly in the Protestant Reformation tradition, indeed attempting to hold much of that fractured tradition together, and it is shaped by the American Protestant theological engagements with modernity, particularly science. Liberalism in the United Church of Christ has never been a uniform position, and certainly never has been an official doctrine, but, it has been a prevailing style of theological thinking that continually places the traditions of the Christian faith in dialogue with the questions of the present. Andrew Walls, a missiologist at the University of Edinburgh puts forward the thesis that Christianity survives and grows by constantly translating itself into new cultural forms, and that when that translation stops the Church in that area begins to decline. He argues that in Europe and North America, the churches have failed to translate the Christian faith into the new cultural language of the late twentieth, early twenty-first centuries. The result is a steeper or more gradual decline, depending on the place, and a growing disinterest in Christianity, even where there is a lively religious conversation in society. For the future of United Church of Christ, it is important that we situate ourselves not in a theological project that tries to recreate the doctrinal positions of the Reformation and the Christendom that accompanied them, but rather that we engage in a much larger theological dialogue. Walls writes,

> Perhaps the most striking single feature of Christianity today is the fact that the church now looks more like that great multitude whom none can number, drawn from all tribes and kin-

> dreds, people and tongues, than ever before in its history. Its diversity and history leads to a great variety of starting points for its theology and reflects varied bodies of experience. The study of Christian history and theology will increasingly need to operate from the position where most Christians are, and that will increasingly be the lands and islands of Africa, Asia, Latin America, and the Pacific. Shared reading of the Scriptures and shared theological reflection will be to the benefit of all, but the oxygen-starved Christianity of the West will have most to gain.[75]

To fully engage in that conversation and process of translating Christianity once again into new cultural forms, we will need our liberal style, but not a set of doctrines we developed in the past using that style. Certainly we will run the risk of getting it wrong from time to time, but our alternative is to defend what we think now until no one cares any longer. Generosity of spirit, willingness to doubt the sufficiency of our theological formulations however orthodox, and our ability to sit with and learn the language of people we find strange and perhaps even uncomfortable, these hallmarks of the liberal style will be necessary if we are to move beyond our current Christian beliefs and commitments to deeper ones.

In these two chapters dealing with theological traditions and style, I have said little about the nature and purpose of the Church. These discussions serve to set the stage for the next chapter in which I will discuss the development of ecclesiological themes in the life of the United Church of Christ. Particularly important are the ways that our concepts of the beloved community, covenant communion, and the mission of God, call into question our central ecclesiological principle of congregationalism. Our openness to multiracial and multicultural expressions of the faith, the theological diversity of our Reformation heritage and our legacy of a liberal style all prepare us to live into an ecclesiology well suited to translating the Gospel authentically and with integrity to a new generation.

Five

Covenant Community

Congregationalism and Its Discontents

One could argue that this book should begin with this chapter on the question of the relationship of covenant and congregationalism in the life of the United Church of Christ. But to do that one would have to argue that this is the central issue among us, and I think it is not. Listening recently to the business of the Twenty-Fourth General Synod in Minneapolis, I reflected that the questions of diversity, cultural and theological, are much more at issue among UCC people. But as we struggle with these divisive issues, the ecclesiological question shows up in sharp relief. Where are these questions to be settled and with what authority for the rest of the Church? In the first chapter I explored the issues raised by our common origin story and its ecumenical idealism for a world that proved much more complex than its founders realized. In the next chapter, I opened up the question of that complexity as it emerges in the racial and cultural diversity of both our Church and in its larger cultural context. In the next two chapters, I traced the theological resources available in the United Church of Christ for discussing matters of diversity, both the theological diversity manifested in the Protestant Reformation, particularly the way in which the United Church of Christ attempts to hold those diverse streams together, and in the openness of the liberal style in theological thinking to entertain unusual questions and new ideas in the light of the Christian Gospel. However, I wish to illustrate the evolution of a culture, both intellectual and practical, in the United Church, not simply trace a theological trajectory. This project requires that we turn next to how these particular theological developments and the diverse cultural context of present-day American society come together.

The engagement with cultural diversity is far more obvious in the national setting of the UCC, or in the Conferences, than it is in the local congregations, partly because the conversation is more concentrated and its ongoing expressions are more readily available. However each of these settings of the Church holds authority and uses it to shape the whole Church. For this reason, the dilemmas posed by a covenant ecclesiology expressed in a congregational form affect both the way we as a church define ourselves and how we live. For many, the key concept in our ecclesiology is contained in the Constitution and Bylaws of the United Church of Christ, and some might argue that this statement is the closest thing we have in the UCC to a dogma.

> The autonomy of the Local Church is inherent and modifiable only by its own action. Nothing in the Constitution and Bylaws of the United Church of Christ shall destroy or limit the right of each Local Church to continue to operate in the way customary to it; nor shall be construed as giving to the General Synod, or to any Conference or Association now, or at any future time, the power to abridge or impair the autonomy of any Local Church in the management of its own affairs, which affairs include, but are not limited to, the right to retain or adopt its own methods of organization, worship and education; to retain or secure its own charter and name; to adopt its own constitution and bylaws; to formulate its own covenants and confessions of faith; to admit members in its own way and to provide for their discipline or dismissal; to call or dismiss its pastor or pastors by such procedure as it shall determine; to acquire, own, manage and dispose of property and funds; to control its own benevolences; and to withdraw by its own decision from the United Church of Christ at any time without forfeiture of ownership or control of any real or personal property owned by it.[1]

The critical importance of this paragraph in the formation of the United Church of Christ has been discussed in other places, so I will not work through that matter again here, but only note that the United Church of Christ is fundamentally defined here as a collection of congregations. However, the paragraph preceding this paragraph, often overlooked in discussions of the role of the local congregation in the life of the UCC, changes the complexion of this congregationalism with the introduction of the context of fellowship within which we are to place all considerations of the local congregation.

> The Local Churches of the United Church of Christ have, in fellowship, a God-given responsibility for that Church, its labors and its extension, even as the United Church of Christ has, in fellowship, a God-given responsibility for the well-being and needs and aspirations of its Local Churches. In mutual Christian concern and in dedication to Jesus Christ, the Head of the Church, the one and the many share in common Christian experience and responsibility.[2]

While the independence of the local congregation is inalienable that independence never exists theologically outside of the covenant binding the whole Church together. Therefore, one of the key words today in the ecclesiology of the United Church of Christ is covenant, and it is prominent in the 2001 revisions of the Constitution and Bylaws. However, this has not always been the case.

While we think its use goes back to the Puritan era and has continually been part of our ecclesiological vocabulary, the word 'covenant' appears in United Church of Christ usage for the first time in the Statement of Faith (1959), "The Holy Spirit binds in covenant faithful people of all nations tongues and races."[3] But the vocabulary of the Statement of Faith did not immediately appear in governance documents. Aside from the continued tradition of local church covenants in the Congregational Christian churches, the idea of covenant as a particularly important idea in the UCC is relatively new. The term covenant first appears in the Constitution of 1984 and in the 1986 Manual on Ministry as a theological idea underlying the commitments between authorized ministers, local churches, or other calling bodies and Associations.[4] The 1984 Constitution and Bylaws, Article V Paragraph 22 reads "The Call of an Ordained Minister to a Local Church establishes a covenantal relationship . . ." The 1986 Manual on the Ministry indicated (page 3) the import of the addition to the constitution as providing for "new covenantal understandings and commitments between persons authorized for ministry, local churches, calling bodies, and the

United Church of Christ." Most recently covenant served as the central theological concept in the restructuring of the national setting of the church. In the 2000 edition of the Constitution and Bylaws, the new Article III defines a covenantal understanding for the whole church.

> Within the United Church of Christ, the various expressions of the church relate to each other in a covenantal manner. Each expression of the church has responsibilities and rights in relation to the others, to the end that the whole church will seek God's will and be faithful to God's mission. Decisions are made in consultation and collaboration among the various parts of the structure. As members of the Body of Christ, each expression of the church is called to honor and respect the work and ministry of each other part. Each expression of the church listens, hears, and carefully considers the advice, counsel, and requests of others. In this covenant, the various expressions of the United Church of Christ seek to walk together in all God's ways.[5]

This represents a recovery into the late twentieth century context of an idea from the Puritan tradition.

United Church of Christ definitions of the Church and the ecclesiastical practices the denomination nurtures derive theologically from thinking about the nature of the Church as primarily covenantal, even when it has not been explicitly stated. In tension with this theological base is Congregational ecclesiology from two of the historical traditions within the church. While the Congregationalists developed the covenant theology out of the Reformed traditions of the Reformation, the addition of different understandings of the way covenant bestows authority has complicated any attempt to describe United Church of Christ ecclesiology simply as covenantal to the satisfaction either of those within the communion or those without.

The dilemmas of covenant in conflict with congregationalism are almost notorious within the United Church of Christ. In order to understand, and eventually resolve, these dilemmas it is necessary to look carefully at the nature of covenant, as it is found in the Bible to which they all refer, and how it was understood in the traditions, as well as the ways the United Church of Christ people currently understand it.

The Congregational, Reformed, Christian, and Evangelical traditions all had within their understandings of the nature and purpose of the Church some idea of a covenantal relationship both of the Church with God and the Church and its people with one another. Definitions and emphases differed in each communion. While each tradition drew its theology of covenant from the Bible, it is helpful to look historically at the traditions themselves and then look at the ways in which they used the Biblical texts. Finally we will look at the way in which the idea of covenant took shape in the formation and life of the United Church of Christ. All four traditions have also placed responsibility in the local congregation for being the church in its time and place, and given local congregations the freedom to develop their own ways of doing things and their own theological emphases in order to carry out that responsibility.

After considering this historical background, I wish to look at three cases which have tested aspects of covenant theology in relationship to congregationalism; the ordination of women, the issue of racism in the church, and the questions of sexual orientation. These issues have not only been points at which covenant and congregational ecclesiologies have been at odds, they are also points which test the covenant relationships of the United Church of Christ with the whole church in its ecumenical relationships. All of these examples challenge the idea that congregationalism alone defines UCC ecclesiology any more than covenant alone does. In all of them theological themes of the beloved community, covenant communion, and the mission of God emerge as the Church and the churches wrestle with their challenges.

The Biblical Ideas of Covenant and Local Congregation

In order to make some sense of these ideas of covenant within a Protestant American Christian understanding of the Church, let us look more closely now at how the idea is used in the Bible. The word occurs in Genesis early in the saga of the Hebrew people, first with Noah after the great flood, then with Abraham and Sarah, and finally with Moses and the people at Sinai. The word in Hebrew is *berith*, based in the verb meaning "to cut down the middle." And to mark a covenant a sacrificial animal was cut down the middle and burnt as an offering to God. *Berith* means to make an alliance of friendship, an agreement or pledge, a treaty, or a constitution between monarch and people. In the Hebrew language, it is an alliance between unequals.

One party is condescending to another. It is not the people who make a covenant with God, but God who makes a covenant with them. The terms of the covenant are not the same on both sides, the people promised faithful obedience, God promised faithful care and protection. In the case of the Church, in its covenant of grace with God, God has condescended to offer grace to humanity.

Translated into Greek, the Hebrew term loses its unequal connotation. *Diatheke* means a declaration of one's will or testament. But here the idea is one sided, the first party, the one making the will or covenant, is always understood but the second party, the one addressed, is implied and does not necessarily have any reciprocal will or testament to make. Later, when the Hebrew Bible was translated into Latin, three different Latin words represented *berith* in different contexts. The first was *conventio*, literally "come together," signifying an agreement or pact. The second term was *constitutio*, to ordain, or to make it so. The third was a literal translation of *diatheke, testamentum,* to declare one's will. Those who translated the Bible into English, whether from Hebrew, Greek, or Latin found the Latin based *convene*, "to come together" most satisfying translation for the Greek and Hebrew terms and, along with the noun derived from it, *covenant*, this became the preferred English term for translating the Biblical words.

The question a present-day interpreter must ask, especially when a term is recovered for significant theological use in forming a community, is does the inequality inherent in the Hebrew *berith* carry over into the English *covenant* when used by the United Church of Christ to describe its ecclesiology? This is particularly relevant when we seek to base our theological language on Scripture. Certainly, the Church's covenant with God remains an unequal covenant although certain theological streams in the United Church of Christ allow us to think of a God who "empties himself[/herself] and takes the form of a servant"[6] thus an equal. The question nags where the term refers to our relationships with one another. At least for now, I believe we have taken the word only in its Latin connotation of an agreement among equals and that we use the word in its Biblical sense to recognize the gravity and spiritual power of our completely equal agreements to live together as God's people.

The idea of 'congregation' also occurs in both the Hebrew and Greek scriptures. In the Hebrew the word is *kahal* and can mean simply assembly of people, but theologically it refers to the assembly of the people of Israel to hear from God, as when Moses spoke to the people or when King Josiah called for an assembly of the people to hear the scroll of Deuteronomy read.[7] In the stories of the return of the people from exile in Babylon, the *kahal* referred to the assembly of the redeemed in Jerusalem.

In the New Testament and the Greek translation of the Hebrew scriptures, the Septuagint, the word for the congregation is *ekklesia*, meaning "called out from," also the term for a political or religious assembly. In the New Testament, the word for *ekklesia* always refers to the congregation, the assembly of the people, rather than, as we think of it in the English term "church" or the German "*kirche*" as ambiguously referring also to the building in which the congregation meets.[8] Those who translated Christianity and its writings into Latin simply adopted the Greek term Latinizing it as "ecclesia." The Romans already used the term with respect to the political governing assemblies in the Greek cities. To them, the Church was simply another kind of Greek assembly. This minor fact suggests a deeper cultural current in the formation of Christianity. The Church took shape as an institution in a Greek cultural context, in which the governing authority rested, not with a single individual, or with a representative body but with the whole assembly of the citizens. It has of course been translated into many other cultural forms in the course of centuries, but the sense of congregation as a basic location of the wholeness of the Church has very deep roots. From this biblical vocabulary, later theologians shaped the theologies of the Church.

Calvin's Understanding of Covenant and Congregation

Calvin's interpretation of the biblical use of covenant has been most influential in the traditions of the United Church of Christ. He carefully preserved the inequality between God and humanity, but the equality of human beings with each other within the covenant Calvin regarded both Testaments to be witnesses to the same covenant. "The Old Testament was established upon the free mercy of God, and was confirmed by Christ's intercession."[9] From our perspective it is sometimes difficult to remember that Calvin's great objective theologically was to defend the freedom of God, not the freedom of the congregation. The *testamentum* or covenant of Scripture was the declaration of God's will. In Calvin's theology, the first covenant, the covenant God made with

Adam and Eve in the garden, reaffirmed in the covenant with Noah and his family, with Abraham and Sarah, with the Israelites in their "baptism" in crossing the Red Sea, and finally with the whole people of Israel at Mt. Sinai (or Horeb) is a covenant based on what human beings must *do* to be blessed. It was a covenant of *works* and human beings violated it from the beginning. However, Calvin regarded it as a covenant of *grace* for precisely this reason. Since no human being could keep all of its terms except by God's grace, the covenant of grace did not begin with Christ, as Christians often thought, but existed from the beginning. This was a covenant of unequals, and only by God's grace was humanity ever able to stay in the covenant at all.

In Calvin's thought, the covenant of grace is, for Christians, sealed in their participation in the sacraments. As circumcision was for the Jews, Baptism is the initial recognition of our incorporation into the covenant. "All believers have one common vow which, made in baptism, we confirm and, so to speak, sanction by catechism and receiving the Lord's Supper. For the sacraments are like contracts by which the Lord gives us his mercy; and we in turn promise him obedience."[10] Calvin was in favor of infant baptism because he viewed incorporation into the covenant of grace as God's gift to us, not something we can ever understand or do for ourselves.[11] From the moment the elect are conceived they are in the covenant of grace and baptism is simply the outward sign of that incorporation. This is why for Calvin, it was important that each person know of her or his own baptism, not necessarily the literal story, but that each knows what baptism is, because we rely on this memory when we fall away from grace, as we all inevitably do, to find our way back. It becomes a light, a rope to hang onto, a map, a compass (to use a metaphor Calvin might not have known).

Communion for Calvin is also a sign, a seal of the covenant of grace, it is a sign of the "new" covenant, or the covenant written on the heart, not that written in the law.[12] Communion signifies the redemption of the person suffering under original sin. Original sin[13] then is the inevitability of our falling away from the covenant. Inevitably we will break the covenant of grace and will not be able to find our way back unaided. Calvin's account of the atonement is based upon Augustine's reading of Paul, that humanity required a mediator to bridge the infinite gap between human and divine, a gap that for Calvin would have existed whether humanity sinned or not. Christ the

Redeemer as both human and divine is able to serve as this bridge.[14] At the table in the Lord's Supper, a mystery fundamentally impervious to human curiosity, we receive this seal of redemption. Calvin said surprisingly little about communion, perhaps because of his interest in healing the breach between Luther and Zwingli on this matter. For our purposes it is important to note the role of the symbols of sacrifice and blood in Calvin's theology of the sacraments. For him the covenant is "cut" between God and human beings through a sacrifice that entails spilling blood (read life) by God the powerful one on behalf of the powerless. This covenant is a mystery, but also contains a visible aspect in the revelation of the Law as a guide for keeping within the covenant of grace. Communion signifies participation in the covenant. While Calvin never asserted that the congregation could know whether an individual was among the elect or not, the congregation, he thought, ought to take care that those whose lives were not lived according to the covenant did not receive communion because this possible violation of the covenant would endanger their souls even more.

The Covenant and Congregation in the Ecclesiology of the Traditions of the UCC

Covenant theology in the traditions of the United Church of Christ is rooted in the role the idea of covenant played in the Reformed traditions of the Reformation. We noted that it is necessary to understand the Reformed tradition as plural, and to note the differences between Zwingli and Calvin in the Reformed tradition of the Swiss cities, the German Reformed tradition that developed in proximity with the Lutherans, the Presbyterian expressions found in Scotland and England, and the more radical understandings of the Zwinglian Anabaptists and many of the English Puritans. In the United Church of Christ context it is sometimes helpful to note the connection of the Reformed and Lutheran traditions in the Evangelical Synod, and the Reformed roots of the Baptist and Presbyterian parts of the Christian tradition. By 1957 none of the four traditions of the United Church of Christ could be simply identified as Reformed as if that were a singular form of Protestantism. Each of them had developed a slightly different understanding of covenant.

In the United Church of Christ, we often regard Congregationalism as the tradition who introduced covenant into our discussions of ecclesiology. There is no doubt that the classic tradition contributing to the United Church of Christ understanding of covenant is Congregationalist. However, it is not the only tradition to use ideas of covenant when discussing the nature and purpose of the church, and even in this tradition, the use of the idea of covenant occurs somewhat late, in the American context. The Puritan traditions placed emphasis in Augustinian forms of theology as interpreted by the reformers, particularly Zwingli and Calvin. In none of these traditions does the concept of covenant receive extended attention, except when theologians investigate the understanding of covenant in the Bible, or the nature of the new covenant in Jesus Christ, neither did William Ames, the primary Puritan theologian of the time. Ames' textbook, *The Marrow of Theology* (1629), originally written for children, but soon becoming required reading at Harvard and Yale, was for nearly a hundred years the standard in the field.[15] Ames never used the concept of covenant to explain the nature of the church.

✦

The Puritan concern with covenant[16] began with the Reformed idea of the covenant of grace, particularly as Calvin had articulated it. For Robert Browne, the use of the term covenant with regard to the Church made it mutual among the members of the congregation with Christ understood as the monarch[17] under whom the Church lives. The sacraments are the outward signs of that covenant. In particular, Browne argued that the covenant is voluntary on both sides, and therefore, a state church is an idea completely contradictory to the Gospel.

> "In the meane time let them knowe that the Lords people is of the willing sorte. They shall come unto Zion and inquire the way to Jerusalem [Jer. 50:5], not by force nor compulsion, but with their faces thitherward: yea as the hee goates shall they be before the flocke, for the haste they have unto Zion, and they them selves shall call for the covenaunt, saying, Come let us cleve faste unto the Lorde in a perpetuall covenaunt that shall never be forgotten.[18]

Later, most clearly in the American context, the Congregationalists in the Cambridge Platform developed the concept of the covenant as defining the establishment of a church. To fully understand the ecclesiology of the Cambridge Platform 1648, it is necessary to look at two related contemporary statements of the nature of the church, the Westminster Confession of 1647 and the Savoy Declaration of 1658. The Westminster Confession was crafted by a council of English Puritan church leaders, both Presbyterian and Congregational or Independent, meeting to advise the primarily Puritan English Parliament of that time on theological and ecclesiastical matters.[19] Though they were all Reformed (Calvinist) in theology, Presbyterians held the majority at the Assembly, and therefore, their Confession has a Presbyterian flavor. For the Westminster Assembly ecclesiology rested on the theology of God's covenant of Grace.

> The distance between God and the creature is so great that although reasonable creatures do owe obedience unto him as their Creator, yet they could never have any fruition of him as their blessedness and reward but by some voluntary condescension on God's part, which he hath been pleased to express by way of covenant.[20]

The Cambridge Platform stated the definition of a congregational (the Platform specifically rejected the term "independent") church in this way.

> A congregational church is by the institution of Christ a part of the militant visible church, consisting of a company of saints by calling, united into one body by a holy covenant, for the public worship of God and the mutual edification one of another in the fellowship of the Lord Jesus.[21]

This idea of covenant, also under the monarchy of Christ, defined as well the relationship of a group of congregations to each other. This covenant was between Christ and a group, an Association, of equal congregations. Their covenant with each other existed to further work of Christ in the world. The Cambridge Platform also delineated the reasons for this covenant.

> When a company of believers purpose to gather into church fellowship, it is requisite for their safer proceeding and the maintaining of the communion of churches that they signify

> their intent unto the neighbor churches, walking according unto the order of the gospel, and desire their presence, and help, and right hand of fellowship, which they ought readily to give unto them when there is no just cause of excepting against their proceedings.[22]

The Cambridge Platform delineated the other matters besides assisting in the formation of new churches, which belong to Synods and Councils of churches. They were charged with debating and determining "controversies of faith and cases of conscience." The results of such deliberations by synods and councils of churches were "so far as consonant to the Word of God, . . . to be received with reverence and submission, not only for their agreement therewith (which is the principal ground thereof and without which they bind not at all) but also secondarily, for the power whereby they are made, as being an ordinance of God appointed thereunto in his Word."[23] This is much stronger language regarding the strength of the relation of the individual congregations to each other than is usually given in characterizations of congregationalism. The Congregationalists left open the question of whether the Church meant always each congregation taken alone, or whether Church referred to the whole Church of which each congregation was an expression. The degree to which the covenant among them constituted a Church was never a settled matter in the Congregational communion. This relationship among neighboring churches was most strongly represented among the Connecticut congregations as outlined in the Saybrook Platform that defined the Consociation the final arbiter of disagreements among the churches.[24]

The German Reformed tradition kept a more presbyterian understanding of covenant, and the covenant was expressed in its ecclesiastical structure. The Reformed churches shared with the Puritan Congregationalists Calvin's theology of covenant of grace, that Baptism was the sacrament and sign of incorporation into the covenant.[25] The sacrament of the Lord's Supper they also considered to be a seal of the covenant of grace as Calvin did. In the early eighteenth century, the scattered German Reformed congregations in Pennsylvania faced wide ranging attacks on their unity. Since they were so far from their German church organizations, had no settled pastor among them[26] and were placed in a setting of unprecedented religious diversity, they called upon the Classis of Amsterdam to assist them by providing them with pastoral leadership and a sense of unity.[27] The Classis of Amsterdam already had churches in the area, though Dutch speaking. The consistories of these congregations took this step because they desired to be in covenant with others to preserve their sense of identity. "We were very desirous of enjoying the Seals of the Holy Covenant, which we had not been able to secure in this far-off region according to the custom of the Reformed Church, and for want of which some had resorted to Dissenters."[28]

As the church grew, the German Reformed congregations continued to seek to be in strong fellowship with each other, forming a Synod of their own in 1793.[29] The synod consisted of the ministers and church elders appointed by the congregations. Their purpose was, according to the Preamble to the "Synodal-Ordnung," "to establish a wholesome Christian Discipline and to observe the same, not with a view to invade the rights of the civil authority, but that, governing themselves, they may not be exposed to the censure of others."[30] Very much in the style of the Congregational church covenants, the stated purpose centers in the desire to support the Christian life rather than maintaining a particular doctrine. The "Synodal-Ordnung" did not stipulate a doctrinal standard beyond requiring candidates for ministry to have "a true conception of the doctrines of our Church."

In the mid nineteenth century, the German Reformed Church faced a crisis similar to that in the Congregational communion a century before resulting in the "Half-Way Covenant."[31] Since the German Reformed Church practiced infant baptism, they began to question what it meant in an increasingly secularized society on the one hand and in the environment of the revivals and their understanding of conversion on the other. In addressing this issue, the Reformed understanding of covenant came into play.

> It is presumed no one will question that it is necessary, at least highly important to the temporal and spiritual well-being of families who are in covenant with God, that they should rightly understand the intimate and deeply interesting relations they sustain to the Church of Christ and the duties which belong to such relations. The minute of Synod, in regard to Church membership, declares that *all baptized per-*

> *sons* are members of the visible Church. This doubtless, is true; but it is also true, we think, that *all those who are included in God's gracious covenant with men [and women], are members of his outward Church,* though they may not have received the appointed token of such membership.[32]

Since in the Hebrew tradition, those who were members of the covenant by virtue, for instance, of circumcision, but violated the covenant later in life were held to have cut themselves off from the covenant, so too a person baptized as an infant still had the responsibility of confirming that faith when they were old enough. Nonetheless, it was not the rite of baptism or confirmation itself that conferred participation in the covenant. This definition indicated a broad understanding of who was included in the covenant, and affirmed that it is God who includes people in the covenant, not the church. The letter sent by the Synod attempted to hold together the concern of those in the evangelical or revival camp of the importance of baptism for affirming a person's experience of renewal and forgiveness and those who held that the sacrament conveyed the church's acknowledgment of something God has done and was not itself an act that produced or confirmed salvation.

The Evangelical Synod was the only main tradition to use the concept of covenant, apart from the discussion of baptism. It does not seem to have been an important concept in Christian ecclesiology. The Evangelical Synod shared the general Reformed understanding of the baptismal covenant. In the United States, the German Evangelical churches were far more congregational in their approach to church order than their German compatriots. But the isolated congregations faced several difficulties which drove them to associate with one another just as the German Reformed and the Congregational churches had before them. In his initial call to the Evangelical church ministers to meet together in 1840, Louis Nollau wrote,

> In order to establish and foster such fellowship, we propose, if God wills, to hold a fraternal gathering on Wednesday, October 14, 1840 in Gravois Settlement. It is not intended at this time that this meeting shall be a gathering of a "synod," but for the time being it shall simply afford an opportunity to become mutually acquainted. Some important matters will be

> deliberated upon, and a covenant of fraternal fellowship will be made.[33]

We can see familiar outlines of the need for mutual support among the congregations which led them to associate together in a covenant arrangement that made them more than simply advisory to one another, but nonetheless preserved a high respect for the local congregation and its determinations.

These forms of church life in covenant were not developed apart from broader political currents of the eighteenth and nineteenth centuries. Particularly important was the philosophical tradition that led also to the Declaration of Independence and the formation of the Constitution of the United States. In their constitutional forms, Reformed church structures, like the Congregational forms, incorporated John Locke's thought on the covenantal (in the Latin sense) nature of society.

> And thus every man, by consenting with others to make one body politic under one government, puts himself under an obligation to every one of that society, to submit to the determination of the majority, and to be concluded by it; or else this original compact, whereby he with others incorporate into one society, would signify nothing, and be no compact, if he be left free, and under no other ties than he was in before the state of nature.[34]

However, in the Reformed tradition, freedom signified freedom to obey Christ, not freedom to do simply as one wishes. That would be "antinomy" against order, government or law.

The Idea of the Local Congregation in the Ecclesiologies of the Main Traditions

While covenant is the ecclesiological idea most often associated with congregationalism, what first makes a congregation of people a church is the hope of a beloved community, a place where a person loves and is loved, and thus experiences tangibly the presence of God. This idea of the beloved community was pushed aside in the formation of a state church and existed mainly in the monastic orders if it survived at all. In the early periods of the modern age, as the state church began to weaken, the idea resurfaced among the Protestant ideas about the church. While such Protestant churches as the Lutherans, the Anglicans, and most of the Reformed became national state churches, some followed an alternate path, the Puritan Separatists were among them. These Protestants returned to a New Testament idea of the church as the community of believers in or followers of Christ, who joined each other in such communities for mutual encouragement and eventually for the purpose of carrying out the mission they believed God had entrusted to them. The troubles the Reformed and the Congregationalists had with their venture in the English American colonies to form congregations based not on the model of the state church but on the model of the gathered community of believers, resulted from their inability in the early years to completely discard the idea of the state church of which everyone was a part. They did not know what to do when the believers who met their criteria for determining those whom God had called were so few, compared to the number who gathered for worship and confessed to belief in the doctrines of the church, but who lacked the experience of assurance of being among the elect. In both instances the more idealistic early Puritans had defined the church in terms of a covenant, but which only those who met the proper criteria could own. But what of the beloved community, what of the nature of the community as encouraging one another? I want to turn to the development of the idea of the local church and its independence or autonomy in the traditions of the UCC for some insights into the ways those who ultimately formed the UCC thought about the beloved community and its mission.

The local church in the traditions and especially the idea of its autonomy played a prominent role in the union discussions and remains a central aspect of any ecclesiological conversation in the UCC.[35] The question of the place of the local congregation in the ecclesiology of any church depends on many historical and theological factors. Within the traditions of the United Church of Christ, the Reformation context is important for understanding the concept of the local church or congregation in their ecclesiologies. The Reformed tradition in particular arose in the context of the Swiss cities where the local city population regarded itself as a single congregation, and reform was carried out by the city council with or without the cooperation of the bishop. In this way, the history of the Reformed tradition was different from that of the Lutheran (or Evangelical) tradition where the Reformation began with an individual theologian, but was organized over an entire territory by the decision of the prince. Similarly in the English Reformation, the process began with the decision of the king and affected the whole nation. The Anabaptists or radicals withdrew altogether from the idea of a national or state church of any kind, and were the first to formulate both the separatist idea of a gathered church of the saints, as opposed to the more general idea of the visible church of all the people of the community. The radical reformers may have developed this idea out of necessity since they were excluded from the state churches. They might have followed the state church tradition had they been in the majority anywhere. The traditions of the United Church of Christ developed their ideas of the role of the local congregation out of these possibilities. The Congregational tradition remains the most important for understanding this matter and it is important now to take note of similar or alternative developments in the other traditions.

In the English Reformation, certain of the Puritans, developed the theological concept of the autonomy of the local congregation. The Puritans were the more radical of the English reformers, desiring the Church of England to more fully incorporate the Protestant principles, especially those of Calvin, into its theology and practice. The designers of the English Reformation instead created an ecclesiology and theology that would allow for unity across Protestant and Catholic lines. The central difficulty of this system for the Puritans lay in the continued connection of the church hierarchy with the state. The bishops were in essence state employees. In addition, the crown made episcopal appointments for secular political ends as well as for ecclesiastical purposes and did not take the local church's will into account. The Puritans were concerned when their churches were served by clergy whose theology and practice failed to meet their standards of piety, teaching, and practice. The majority of Puritans, Calvinist in their theology and tending toward a presbyterian understanding of church structure, remained in communion with the Church of England. Puritan pastors and bishops simply sought the affirmation of the congregation for their appointments and actions. The more radical Puritans, more Anabaptist in theology, formed separate congregations in an effort to keep their churches from corruption with state power, or from what they regarded as extra-biblical practices from the Roman Catholic tradition. The Puritans, therefore, developed two streams of thought about the autonomy of the local congregation, one out of a separatist stance and the other from a desire to conform in some things for the sake of the unity of church and society.

Both of the Puritan concepts of the local congregation were rooted in the principle that Christ, not the Queen, or the local magistrate, or any human body, is the head of the Church. The separatist Robert Browne argued that "Yea the church hath more authoritie concerning Church government then Magistrates, as it is written, They shall followe thee, and shal goe in Chaines: they shall fall downe before thee, and make supplication unto thee.[Isa. 45:14]. . . . For all powers shall serve and obeye Christ, saieth the Prophete."[36] Browne's theology of covenant centered on the divine government of the Church and the covenant of the people of God with God formed the foundation of his understanding that the Church should govern itself. In his 1582 "Treatise of Reformation without Tarying for Anie," Browne argued that the civil government or magistrates were not the appropriate rulers of the church, but should rather be ruled by it.

> Be ashamed therefore ye foolish sheepheardes, and laye not a burthen on the Magistrates, as though they should do that in building the Lordes kingdome, which the Apostles and Prophetes coulde not doo. They could not force Religion, as ye woulde have the Magistrate to do, and it was forbidden the Apostles to preache to the unworthie [Matt. 10:13-14], or to force a planting or governement of the Church. The Lordes kingdome is not by force, neither by an armie or strength [Zech. 4:6], as be the kingdomes of this worlde. Neither durst Moses, nor anie of the good Kings of Iuda force the people by lawe or by power to receive the church government, but after they received it, if then they fell awaye, and sought not the Lorde, they might put them to death. For the covenaunte was firste made, as it is written, they made a covenant to seeke the Lord God of their fathers, with all their harte, and with all their soule. . . .But the Lorde shall bring them downe to the dust, and to the pitt, as abhominable carkasses, which would be above the cloudes, yea which dare presume into the throne of Christe Iesus, and usurpe that authoritie and calling in his Church, which is opposed and contrarie to his kingdom and

> government. . . .In the meane time let them knowe that the Lords people is of the willing sorte.. . . and they them selves shall call for the covenaunt, saying, Come and let us cleave faste unto the Lorde in a perpetuall covenaunt that shall never be forgotten.[37]

The Church governed under the covenant that goes back to the time of Moses, in time will exist in the hearts of the people themselves, having no more need of external government. Thus Browne argued for separation from the false state church. Some of his followers eventually came to New England on the Mayflower in 1620 and worked there to establish this ecclesiastical order.

The nonseparating Puritans held a very similar idea, also derived from Calvin's reading of the New Testament on the organization of the Church. Henry Jacob, one of the earliest theologians of this group, believed that the Congregational ecclesiology could be worked out practically within the existing structures of the Church of England. His description of it, contained in his catechism, "Principles and Foundations of the Christian Religion,"[38] is more fully developed than Browne's of fifteen years before. Jacob places membership in the visible Church under the category of the "ordinary Generall means" of salvation.

> The ordinary Generall meanes is, to be joyned a Member in som true Visible or Ministeriall Church of Christ. . . .[A Visible Church is constituted and gathered] By a free mutuall consent of Believers joyning & covenanting to live as Members of a holy Society togeather in all religious & vertuous duties as Christ & his Apostles did institute & practice in the Gospell. By such a free mutuall consent also all Civill perfect Corporations did first beginne.[39]

Jacobs' reading of the early history of Christianity is that the church has always been found in plural form, in multiple congregations. And each of these congregations represents the whole church within itself. "A true Visible or Ministeriall Church of Christ is a particular Congregation being a spirituall perfect Corporation of Believers, & having power in it selfe immediately from Christ to administer all Religious meanes of faith to the members thereof."[40]

John Robinson's "Just and Necessary Apology" offered another development in the concept of the particular congregation. Robinson, a separatist Puritan, developed Jacobs' argument about the New Treatment church, noting that in the New Testament it appears that each congregation consisted of all the believers in a particular place who met together, gathered, or convened, and "with one accord pour out their prayers unto God, when they all partake of one, and the same holy bread, 1 Cor. 10:17; and lastly, when they all together consent unanimously, either in the choice of the same officer, or censuring of the same offender."[41] Robinson wrote his "Apology" to defend his congregation, then residing exile in Holland, against its critics in England. He had difficulty maintaining theologically a way to remain in communion with the Church of England whose bishops he regarded as having corrupted the faith. He believed the godly could no longer fully exercise the Christian religion within the state church. He favored the Pauline idea of individual churches, each of which represents within itself, in its Eucharistic celebration, the body of Christ. However, Robinson did regard the unity of the whole Church as a concern.

> If any object, that there is one visible, and catholic church, comprehending as the parts thereof, all the particular churches, and several congregations of diverse places; as there is one ocean, or sea, diversely called, according to the divers regions by whose shores it passeth; and that therefore this matter is not worth labour spending about it, I answer, first, that the catholic church neither is, nor can be called visible: since only things singular are visible, and discerned by sense: whereas universals, or things catholic, are either only in the understanding, as some are of mind; or as others think better, are made such, to wit, universals, by the understanding abstracting from them all circumstantial accidents, considering that the kinds intelligible have their existence in nature, and is in the individuals.[42]

For Robinson, the unity of the Church could be maintained visibly only in the local congregation. The local congregations can have unity only in a common bond of charity.[43] The beloved community, in his view, expressed itself best in the unity of the particular congregation.

We complete our survey of the ecclesiological thinking of the earliest generation of Puritan Congregationalists with William Ames, the nonseparatist, and most influential theologian among them, especially in the American context. Ames differed from Robinson in his definition of the whole church, and unlike Robinson, he articulated the place of covenant within the constitution of a church in this passage from his *Marrow of Theology.*

> 1. The church living upon earth, though it is not wholly visible, is visible in its parts both individually in its single members and collectively in its companies or congregations.
>
> 2. The first visibility is in the personal profession of men [and women]. This does not make a visible church, except as it exists in these particular members, i.e., it makes the church's members visible; the church itself, in its integral state does not become visible in the same place. Acts 19:1 *Paul . . . came to Ephesus where he found certain disciples.*
>
> 3. That visibility which is in companies or distinct congregations not only makes a visible church, but, so far as outward form is concerned, also makes as many visible churches as there are distinct congregations. Rev. 1:4, *The seven churches'* 2 Cor. 8:1, 19, *The churches of Macedonia. All the churches.*
>
> 4. These congregations are, so to speak, similar parts of the catholic church and partake both of its name and nature.
>
> 5. Therefore a particular church, in respect of the nature it has in common with all particular churches, is a species of the church as a genus; but in respect of the catholic church, which has the nature [*ratio*][44] of a whole, it is a member made up of various individual members gathered together; and in respect of these members it is also a whole.[45]

While Robinson leaned toward the sectarianism of the separatists in that he believed true faith cannot be separated from holiness of life, he located the unity of the churches in profession of a common faith. "They are in God the Father and in the Lord Jesus Christ because of the faith which they profess. 1 Thess. 1:1; 2 Thess. 1:1."[46] However, Ames continued, the church is not simply a collection of believers.

> Believers do not make a particular church, even though by chance many may meet and live together in the same place, unless they are joined together by a special bond among themselves. Otherwise, any one church would often be dissolved into many, and many also merged into one.
>
> This bond is a covenant, expressed or implicit, by which believers bind themselves individually to perform all those duties toward God and toward one another which relate to the purpose [ratio] of the church and its edification. . . .
>
> Therefore, no one is rightly admitted into the church except on confession of faith and promise of obedience.
>
> This joining together by covenant makes a church only as it looks toward the exercise of the communion of saints. For the same believing men [and women] may join themselves in covenant to make a city or some civil society when their immediate concern is for the common civil good. But they cannot make a church except as in its constitution they intend holy communion with God and among themselves.[47]

For William Ames, the intention of the believers to participate in holy communion with God and among themselves, is itself a gift of God's grace. Ames was thoroughly Augustinian and Calvinist in his view of human ability to live in a covenantal community.

> Grace is the basis of that relation in which [humanity] is united with Christ Jesus. . . . The enlightening of the mind is not sufficient to produce this effect because it does not take away the corruption of the will. Nor does it communicate any new supernatural principle by which it may convert itself. . . .This act of faith depends partly upon an inborn principle or attitude toward grace and partly upon the action of God moving before and stirring it up. John 6:44, *None can come to me, unless the Father . . . draws him.*[48]

It was upon these foundations that the New England Puritan Congregationalists elaborated their distinctive form of polity. We turn now to the Cambridge Platform (1648) to note the further developments of this idea.

The two covenants, the covenant of works and the covenant of grace, underlay the Puritan understanding of the church. The church then is "the whole number of the elect, that have been, are, or shall be gathered into one, under Christ the head thereof; and this is the spouse, the body, the fullness of him that fillith all in all."[49] The Puritans agreed also with most Protestants and Catholics of their day, that "there is no ordinary possibility of salvation" outside the church.[50] The few Congregational or Independent delegates to the Assembly agreed with almost all of the Westminster Confession. They differed only on the points regarding church government. The Westminster Confession was, in this regard, definitely Presbyterian.

> For the better government and further edification of the Church, there ought to be such assemblies as are commonly called synods or councils.[Acts 15, 2,4,6] . . . III. It belongeth to synods and councils, ministerially, to determine controversies of faith, and cases of conscience; to set down rules and directions for the better ordering of public worship of God, and government of his Church; to receive complaints in cases of maladministration, and authoritatively to determine the same: which decrees and determinations, if consonant to the Word of God, are to be received with reverence and submission, not only for their agreement with the Word, but also for the power whereby they are made, as being an ordinance of God, appointed thereunto in his Word.[51]

Likewise, in New England, the synod of the New England Congregationalists meeting in Cambridge from 1646–1648 in order to influence English policy toward Congregationalism and to defend their orthodoxy and polity against their Presbyterian neighbors, agreed with the theological substance of the Westminster Confession, differing only in their understanding of the nature of the Church. The Cambridge Platform was the result of their deliberations. They did not claim that Congregational churches were the only true churches, but that, "a congregational church is by the institution of Christ a part of the militant visible church,[52] consisting of a company of saints by calling, united into one body by a holy covenant, for the public worship of God and the mutual edification of one another in the fellowship of the Lord Jesus."[53] In this ecclesiology, the local church is an expression of the covenant of grace, it is gathered, or rather called by God. Individuals have a choice about joining, and do so upon giving an account of a converting experience. Having been called into the church through this experience, they make a voluntary covenant with others who have been so called, or after the establishment of the church covenant subsequent new members own it, make it their own.

> This form then being by mutual covenant, it followeth, it is not faith in the heart, nor the profession of that faith, nor cohabitation, nor baptism. 1. Not faith in the heart? Because that is invisible. 2. Not a bare profession, because that declareth them no more to be members of one church than of another. 3. Not cohabitation; atheists and infidels may dwell together with believers. 4. Not baptism, because it presupposeth a church-estate, as circumcision in the Old Testament, which gave no being unto the church, the church being before it and in the wilderness without it. Seals presuppose a covenant already in being. One person is a complete subject of baptism, but one person is incapable of being a church.[54]

The Cambridge Platform reiterated the principles of the Westminster Confession regarding the role of Synods and Councils but limited the authority of a synod over a particular local church.

> It belongeth unto synods and councils to debate and determine controversies of faith and cases of conscience, to clear from the Word holy directions for the holy worship of God and good government of the church, to bear witness against maladministration and corruption in doctrine or manners in any particular church, and to give directions for the reformation thereof – not to exercise church censures in way of discipline, nor any other act of church authority or jurisdiction, which that presidential synod [the one in Acts 15] did forbear.[55]

The Cambridge Synod reaffirmed the doctrinal position of the Congregationalists in the Reformed tradition, but set forth a different ecclesiology from that of the Westminster Assembly. This ecclesiology, of the Church as a gathered particular local congregation whose members, called into the Church by God through an immediate experience of conversion, live in covenant with one another and live as a congregation accountable in fellowship to the other neighboring churches, remained the foundation of Congregational understanding of the nature of the church. In the Cambridge Platform and in the Westminster Confession, there is nothing said of the church's mission outside of its own fellowship. The worship of God and edification of the faithful remained the central task of the church. In this ecclesiology, the mission of God is the responsibility of the members of the church in their daily work rather than some organized enterprise of the church as an institution. Just as the visible church is more or less apparent in given times and places, so too the complete expression of this Congregational ecclesiology in the Congregational churches was more or less apparent. In key times in the history of Congregationalism, the separatist principle gained ascendancy and the fellowship of the churches among each other thinned out or failed altogether. Always in congregational ecclesiology, the tension remained between the way the local particular congregation comes to interpret the will of God for it and the way its neighbors respond to that interpretation. Even in Presbyterian or more generally Reformed polity the tension existed though the location of the power to act resided primarily in the larger group rather than in the local congregation.

The Christian churches shared the Congregational view that the local congregation was in itself complete. If anything, the Christians were even more strictly congregational in their theology than the Congregationalists. One of the founding theologians of the Christian movement, Rice Haggard, wrote a pamphlet outlining his ecclesiology. "What is a christian church, but a voluntary society, stipulating to walk by the rules of the gospel?"[56] The gospel, Haggard claimed was crystal clear. It needed no ecclesiastical body to interpret it for the individual believer, nor did it need to be clarified by creeds. Haggard elaborated his idea of the Church from the New Testament.

> Let all christians consider themselves members one of another: because in the estimation of scripture they are so indeed. This is illustrated and proved from Christ himself being the foundation, and his church the house, or superstructure built upon that foundation–he is the vine, they are the branches–he is the head, and they are the members of his body, knit together by joints and bands. And therefore they are members one of another in particular. Hence it follows, [t]hat all christians ought to be members of one church. Because we find but one

> foundation for a church, and that is Christ; "and other foundation can no [one] lay." All therefore that is built upon that foundation, is one superstructure, or one body in Christ. This is his mystical body, and no other. And the name of this body originates from its head, which makes it the christian church, or church of Christ.[57]

The Christian movement was reluctant to elaborate further than the imagery and theology of the Gospels and Epistles of the New Testament. They insisted on the independence of the local congregation. This principle, one of the five or six by which Christians identified their movement, was delineated in several places. In the "Last Will and Testament of the Springfield Presbytery," marking the withdrawal of several ministers from that Presbyterian body to the Christian movement, they set forth their congregational ideals.

> We *will,* that the church of Christ resume her native right of internal government–try her candidates for the ministry, as to their soundness in the faith, acquaintance with experimental religion, gravity and aptness to teach; and admit no proof of their authority but Christ speaking in them. We will, that the church of Christ look up to the Lord of the harvest to send forth laborers into his harvest, and that she resume her primitive right of trying those *who say they are apostles and are not.*
>
> We *will,* that each particular church, as a body, actuated by the same spirit choose her own preacher, and support him by a free will offering, without a written *call* or *subscription*—admit members—remove offences; and never henceforth delegate her right of government to any . . . .[58]

On the other hand, the Christians envisioned all churches united on these principles, so that Haggard could hope all Christians to be members of one church. For the Christians the Church also signified the universal Church, whether it could now be said to be visible in its unity or not. From individual membership in a local congregation, to that congregation's membership in a convention, any visible unity was entirely voluntary or uncoerced. In its "Manifesto," the General Convention of the Christian Church declared, "It is the steadfast belief of this body that Christ established but *one* Church, designing that all his followers, as members of that one body, should harmoniously work together for the salvation of the world."[59] While rejecting the division of the Church into "sects," its division into local congregations was its natural form. The differences among them should not be the occasion for division of the whole Church. "It is our belief that entire unanimity of opinion upon matters of theological doctrine and ecclesiastical polity, is unattainable, so long as "we see through a mirror darkly;" but that a unity of love, forbearance and cooperation is fully within the reach of all true christians."[60]

Certainly, the unity of the whole Church, or that of the local congregation did not depend for Christians on a particular statement of Christian doctrine. In his 1838 article in the *Christian Palladium,* Simon Clough, an itinerant minister in Maine, wrote giving an extensive argument against the use of creeds "as terms of Christian communion." The only standard of Christian faith and practice was "the pure word of life, and light, and truth,–the Oracles of the Living God."[61] The Christians began, as an alternative to doctrine and a strict interpretation of an experience of grace, to give a more liberal set of criteria by which a person could become a member of the Church.

> "Church membership is predicable on the same ground with Christian fellowship. [Those] who is [are] Christian [are] fit subject[s] for membership in any gospel church. To be a Christian is to have the love of God and fellowship of Christ, and should be loved and received by all Christians as a brother [or sister], and admitted to all the privileges of the church of God."[62]

Any position, theological or political that clashes with the fruits of the Spirit has no part in the Body of Christ. This theology essentially expressed the idea of the beloved community as the foundation for the life of the local church.

Nicholas Summerbell made the local church the central piece in his instructions about how to organize a church outlined in the *Christian Pulpit* which he founded in 1869. He suggested that all founding members answer affirmatively four questions, "Do you believe on the Son of God?," "Are you living a prayerful life?" "Are you willing to receive the Bible as your only rule of faith and life?" and "Are you willing to fellowship all God's people?" Leaving aside the inevitability of differences of interpretation on these matters, the local church may be organized.

> The church thus organized is independent in faith and fellowship. It controls its own property, chooses its own minister, declares its own faith and fellowship. It may represent itself in conference or convention or not, owing allegiance alone to the Lord, and to the Bible. If it united in conference with other churches, it is yet only bound to them in a larger body, each remaining still free in local matters."[63]

African American Christians did not emphasize the independence of the local congregation, though they were organized congregationally. In the "Revised Ritual of the Christian Church," 1901, the Afro-Christian Convention clarified the relationship of the individual member to the whole church, and the procedures local churches should use for governance and worship, but never mentioned the place of the local church in the larger Christian denomination.[64] Without a strongly developed idea of the relationship of the congregations to one another, only the general theological idea that there is a single Church, the Christians were in practice even more congregational than the Congregationalists.

The Evangelical Synod's ecclesiology, like that of the Christians, predicated all discussion of the church as a local congregation on the premise of the entire body of Christians, the One Holy Universal Christian Church.[65] Schleiermacher's characterization of the purpose of the church written in response to the union of the Reformed and Lutheran churches in Prussia, sounds very similar to American Christian talk about the church.

> The work of the Reformation was not, therefore, to found a Lutheran Church . . . nor was it to found a Reformed Church, but to bring forth in renewed glory the Evangelical Church, which is guided and governed by its founder, Jesus Christ, the eternal Son of God. He is the quickening centre of the Church, from Him comes all, to Him all returns: He is the Beginning and End: in Him we believe, and through Him alone we are blessed . . . We ought not, therefore, to call ourselves Lutheran nor Reformed, but we ought to call ourselves

> *Evangelical* Christians, after His name and His holy evangel; for in our name our faith and our confession ought to be made known.[66]

Like the Christians, the Evangelical Synod placed a high value on Christian unity in the context of a highly congregational practice. The German Evangelical tradition was shaped strongly by the pietism of Philip Jakob Spener. In his *Pia Desideria* he listed six principles by which a Christian should live. They should be well acquainted with Scripture, they should avoid controversy in order to further Christian unity, and they should live a holy life. The clergy should stress the importance of Christian life over knowledge of the faith, though theological training is also important for developing a faithful ministry. Finally, sermons should evoke faith and not merely teach doctrine.[67]

This Pietist style carried over into the American German Evangelical churches. They cultivated a disinterest in theological controversy. In addition, they were reluctant to make doctrine a central concern of the church.[68] They organized themselves congregationally. The *Kirchenverein*, or church society, was an organization of the pastors. Not all of the churches joined the society, but it remained influential. Each congregation was independent and had its own constitution.[69] The congregations elected their own pastors from several candidates by majority vote, sometimes for very short terms, and could dismiss the pastor similarly. Congregations were typically governed by a body of elders or *Aelteste*. Another factor influencing the development of these churches was the presence of a group of "rationalists" who, much like the Unitarians in Congregational circles, desired a more Enlightenment approach to religious life than the pietist approach of the majority of German Evangelicals. These rationalists objected most strongly to any creation of a hierarchical church order because of the danger of ultimately reestablishing a state church. Even the creation of a *verein*, more of a club than an ecclesiastical structure, made them suspicious. Along with the Christians and the Congregationalists, the German Evangelical churches were essentially congregational in their church organization.

Underlying Evangelical congregationalism was a biblical idea of the church similar to that of the Christians. The *Evangelical Catechism* treated the Church under the section on the Holy Spirit, paragraphs 87–100.

> By the one holy universal Christian Church we mean the entire body of true Christians. . . . . The Christian Church is called the "one" Church because it has one Lord, one faith, one baptism, one God and Father of all, as it is written. . . . The church is called holy because the Holy Spirit works mightily in it by Word and Sacrament to the end that all its members shall be made holy. . . .The Church is called universal because God has meant it for all, . . . and because everyone finds in it what he [or she] needs. . . . The Church is called Christian because Christ alone [is] its foundation, its head and its ideal. . . . The mission of the Church is to extend the Kingdom of God, that is, to lead [human beings] to Christ and to establish Christian principles in every relation of life. . . . The Church has indeed existed in all times as the true Church, but has frequently erred and been corrupted; its future perfection, however, is certain, according to God's promise. . . . By the communion of saints we understand that all Christians, as members of one body, should love and help one another in all things. . . .The Holy Spirit calls, gathers, enlightens, and preserves the whole Christian Church on earth and keeps it with Jesus Christ in the one true faith. . . In the Christian Church the Holy Spirit daily and abundantly forgives me and all believers all sins.[70]

This is a highly active understanding of the Church, not focused on the ontology or "being" of the Church but rather on Christian participation in the "Misseo Dei" the Mission of God. In addition, as an expression of the activity of the Holy Spirit, the Church participates in the activity of God in the world. For the Evangelical Synod, the theological idea of covenant did not play a role in its understanding of the local church, nor did it play the kind of role it did in the Reformed Church and the Congregational churches' theological emphasis on the covenant of Grace. But the idea of the unity of all the churches was of central importance.

This brings us to the Reformed Church of the United States and its understanding of the local church. The doctrinal positions of the Reformed Church were perhaps the strongest and most clearly stated of all the traditions making up the United Church of Christ. The primary sources of Reformed doctrine lay in the tradition of Calvin formalized in the Canons of Dort and the Heidelberg Catechism. Both of these contain only brief definitions of the local Church and both regard the Church as gathered by God and preserved, at least as a remnant, until the end of the world. The Heidelberg Catechism, first published in 1563 stated it this way in Question 54:

> What do you believe concerning "the Holy Catholic Church"? I believe that, from the beginning to the end of the world, and from among the whole human race (Gen. 26: 3 b-4; Rev. 5:9), the Son of God (Col. 1:18), by his Spirit and his Word (Isa. 59:21), gathers, protects, and preserves for himself, in the unity of the true faith (Acts 13:47-48; Eph. 4:3-6; 5:25-27), a congregation chosen for eternal life. Moreover, I believe that I am and forever will remain a living member of it eternally (John 10:28).[71]

The answer to this question indicates that the believer's incorporation into the Body of Christ exists both at the level of the Universal Church and that of the local gathered community. The answer to Question 54 is deliberately ambiguous. The Reformed tradition was the least congregational among the traditions of the UCC, though in the American colonial context, the Reformed congregations from necessity exercised considerable autonomy.[72] The earliest German Reformed churches established in Pennsylvania and other areas of the American colonies behaved congregationally. With few ministers, the local congregations relied on lay leadership and initiative. However, unlike the Congregationalists who embraced this local independence, the Reformed people looked to the traditional Reformed presbyterial structures to insure the health of their churches.

> A relatively close-knit denominational life emerged from the frontier soil. . . Foremost for the welfare of the churches was the need to regularize the ministry. Church people had been accustomed to a ministry established according to theologically well-grounded principles. They respected and honored the profession as necessary in the scheme of salvation and indispensable for the religious and intellectual leadership of the Christian community. The radical sects, with their easy

> recognition of self-appointed preachers, scandalized many who saw in the practice the road to religious anarchy.[73]

The ambiguity of the formulation about the church remained as the Reformed Churches formed first the Coetus under the Classis of Amsterdam, and finally an American Synod. Their doctrine theologically defined both the local congregation and the whole Church, and undergirded a church order, a principle that fostered both theological seriousness and competency in the ministry.

In the middle of the nineteenth century, the Reformed ecclesiology received new attention. The Mercersburg theological movement put before the German Reformed Church what its theologians Philip Schaff and John Nevin regarded as an ecumenical ecclesiology more faithful to the New Testament and the early church, and containing the possibility of the reunion of Christianity. The Mercersburg theology created lively debate, and although it was not adopted officially within the church it did remain an open possibility and served in the twentieth century to stimulate thinking in the United Church of Christ, particularly about liturgy and ecumenical life. Nevin, in an article summing up the main points of the Mercersburg theology wrote:

> The question of the Church, in its true form, is at bottom always a question of Christ. It reaches back to the constitution of the Redeemer's person. It has to do at once, where it begins, with the mystery of the incarnation. It lies, in such views, at the foundation of all Christian theology; not because it seeks to place the Church before Christ, as shallow thinkers pretend; but because it seeks to determine the full historical significance of Christ, as "Head over all things to the Church, which is his body, the fullness of him that filleth all in all."[74]

In the traditions of the United Church of Christ, we have two intertwining ecclesiological principles underlying the existence of the local congregations and shaping their understanding of their relationships to each other. They are related in turn to more fully developed theological streams of thought. Three of the traditions, the Congregational, the Christian, and the German Evangelicals locate the fullness of the church as Body of Christ in the local congregation, and its relationship with other congregations is an expression of their mission together, or their shared fellowship in Christ. Three of the traditions, a different three, the Christians, the German Evangelicals, and the German Reformed, ground their understanding of ecclesiology in the idea of the Universal or Catholic Church. Therefore, we find at the two ends of this spectrum the Reformed people who simply did not imagine a single congregation apart from its life together with the rest of the churches, and at the other the Congregationalists for whom the local church was so central, that they said little about the Universal or Catholic Church. As we look further at these ecclesiastical principles, from the vantage point of the early twenty-first century, it is important to note the alternative views, and that some of these positions that we find in the nineteenth century literature were shaped by certain schools of German historiography, namely those of Hegel and Harnack, as well as the Protestant tradition of suspicion of Catholic forms, and the Puritan experience of the political power of bishops.

The Problem of Unity in a Congregational Polity

From the above ruminations on our traditions and their thinking over three hundred years about covenant and congregation, it comes as no surprise to us that ecclesiological questions in the UCC tend to be framed as polity questions, and that they overwhelmingly have to do with authority. The question of who is authorized to serve in what capacity, particularly to represent the church, congregation or denomination, in a wider context, is particularly persistent. Our theology of ministry, in addition, is a matter of interest in late twentieth century as our participation in ecumenical conversations deepens, particularly in the Consultation on Church Union/Churches Uniting in Christ, in our partnership with the Christian Church (Disciples of Christ), and in our participation in the World Council of Churches Faith and Order conversations. Finally, we live in a society increasingly apt to bring its controversies to courts of secular justice, where the church's lines of authority, defined theologically rather than legally, may not be clear. In all of these arenas the United Church of Christ has faced a call to clarify its understanding of the Church, its Ministry, and its mechanisms of granting authority.

Four major works on ecclesiology in the United Church of Christ all agree that while congregationalism is a fundamental aspect or form of ecclesial life in the UCC, it does not serve as an adequate definition of the nature and purpose of the Church as represented in our denomination. In addition, they all tend to focus on the organizational structure of the church rather than its theological meaning. Immediately after its founding, Douglas Horton described the UCC, ecclesiologically, as presbyterian in legislative function because it works through representatives, episcopal in its administrative system since it works through superintendents (Conference Ministers) and congregational in its judicial function, "since the congregations and several groupings make their own decisions and have no judge over them but Christ and the decent respect they have for all their brethren [and sisters] in Christ."[75] Horton confined his discussion of ecclesiology to the formal polity or organization of the church. Jon Fogle, minister of Salem United Church of Christ in Cambelltown, Pennsylvania, followed suit, defining ecclesiology as the way authority is distributed in the church. He argued that the congregation expresses its implicit ecclesiology most clearly in its calling of a pastor, that call representing in concrete form, the call by Christ.[76]

Robert Paul, in his *Freedom with Order* rooted his discussion of the order or polity of the UCC much more explicitly in a theology of the Church as a branch of Christology.[77] "The church points to God through Jesus Christ. . . . to a communal expression of what God revealed to us about the divine nature of Jesus Christ."[78] This theology may be implicit in UCC ecclesiological thinking, but most recent discussions focus on the form of covenant polity we have developed with little connection to Robert Paul's Christological suggestion.[79] We find the most recent articulation of ecclesiology in the United Church of Christ is the statement prepared as a guide for the recent restructuring of the national setting of the church.

> Thus the most fundamental documents of the UCC, the Constitution and the Statement of Faith, set forth the denomination's beliefs about the nature of the church, as a covenant community of Christ's people called to faithful mission in the world. By these authorities of Word, Spirit, the faith of the historic church, and the covenant of "common Christian experience and responsibility," (Constitution, Preamble, 2), the church declares that it is one and whole, . . . that it remains in faithful continuity with the apostolic faith of the ancient and

> ecumenical church, and that unity is fundamental to its nature. These traditional "marks of the church" derived from the ancient creeds—one, holy, catholic and apostolic—are understood by the United Church of Christ as expressions of four basic purposes which have increasingly come to characterize its life: to proclaim the gospel to all the world, to gather and support communities of faith in their celebration and mission, to labor for the creation and increase of God's realm of justice and love in the world, and to manifest more fully the unity of the church, all humankind, and the whole creation.[80]

"The nature of the church, as a covenant community of Christ's people called to faithful mission in the world," begins to set forth the way in which the beloved community, covenant communion, and the mission of God interrelate with one another. The ordering of the Church and its ministry, derive from the nature and mission of the Church. I would not want to leave the reader at this point thinking that the UCC has achieved consensus about the nature and purpose of the Church. It has not, and continues to reflect in its various settings on the meaning of its community, its covenants, and its mission in relation to its understanding of Jesus Christ.

Ecclesiology, Congregationalism, and Questions of Authority

In the final sections, I would like to sketch briefly the outlines of the knotty problem of authority and the beginning of a UCC definition of episcopé. To illustrate the issues before us in developing this part of our ecclesiology, I want to use two cases, that of the ordination of women in the nineteenth century, illustrated by Antoinette Brown, and that of the ordination of William Johnson, an openly gay man, in the twentieth century. Both of these cases illustrate the ways in which formal and informal authority plays between the local congregation and the larger representations of the Church Universal in which it stands in covenant.

The ecumenical movement in which the traditions of the United Church of Christ participated and out of which the idea of a United Church was formed, developed over the course of the twentieth century an understanding of ministry that many believe can be held as a consensus among most Christian churches.[81] Out of our essentially though not completely congregational polity, we are called in responding to these consensus proposals to describe the location, within the United Church of Christ, of the three kinds of ministry set forth in the New Testament, deacons, presbyters (or elders) and bishops. As I write this, we stand at the beginning of a process of engaging these consensus positions and it may not be long before we have more clarity. So far we have seen that in the United Church of Christ, three themes arise in our thinking about the nature of the Church, that the Church is the beloved community of followers of Christ, gathered by the Holy Spirit into covenant communion with each other and with Christ, for the purpose of carrying out God's mission (such as we may understand it in our finitude). This community of followers of Christ is expressed in the United Church of Christ in the local congregation. Our traditions claim a biblical basis for understanding the Church as a local body of Christians both free and responsible for carrying out the mission of God in their setting, but in communion at least, and perhaps in covenant with other congregations in other places. Above we have seen the variety of histories and practice lying behind the basic congregational form.

The ecumenical consensus on ministry we are called to engage now, asks us to identify how the biblical three-fold order of ministry, deacons, presbyters (elders) and bishops are located in our church polity and how they function. These three forms of ministry are found in some form in most churches, and there is a general ecumenical understanding that deacons serve more locally, particularly in charitable activities, serving the needs of the congregation, and in certain liturgical ways; that presbyters are for the most part those who preside at the table and preach in a local congregation, but represent the whole Church in that congregation; and that bishops are involved in oversight and are concerned with the unity of the Church in its belief and practice. We live in a time in the history of Christianity when we know that the Church has never achieved complete uniformity in faith and practice. Nor do most of us any longer believe that it should. However, the churches who participate in the ecumenical movement are concerned with the unity of the Church's witness underlying all of our diversity. The ecumenical discussions about what we can say in common about our forms of ministry proceed hand in hand with discussions about a common confession of the Christian faith. Both conversations remain open and lively.

In the United Church of Christ, deacons are present in many congregations as lay people who serve the church in particular capacities, and are elected or chosen by the congregation and so authorized to do their work. They may have roles in serving communion, helping the pastor with visitation or other pastoral care duties, or may do other things in service to the congregation. But even if the congregation does not have people called deacons, chances are it has some people who perform a similar function within the congregation. Similarly, nearly all of our congregations have a leader who can be identified as a presbyter or elder. For the most part this is the pastor of the church, whether ordained or not. This is the person who preaches, baptizes, probably presides at the Communion table, and generally provides the pastoral care of the congregation. There may be more than one person who serves as pastor and teacher in the congregation. Some of our congregations, especially from the Reformed or Christian traditions, may also have lay elders, ordained or not, who carry out many of the presbyter's tasks. The presbyters, unlike the deacons, are ordinarily authorized by that congregation in covenant relationship with the larger Association of churches in the neighborhood, usually by ordination or licensing. So far, the United Church of Christ is in agreement with the general ecumenical consensus, though we have differences with some denominations particularly over the office of bishop, discussed further below, and over the role of gender and sexual orientation in determining who may be called to these offices. We will look more closely at these matters shortly.

The point where the United Church of Christ fits least comfortably with the ecumenical consensus is that of the office of episcopé or bishop. We are congregational in nature because of historical experiences of a corrupt *episcopé* in the European state churches.[82] Our ancestors rejected the office of bishop,[83] even when they did not reject the idea of a state church. But the work of episcopé exists in all the traditions of the UCC as well as in our own polity. As we have participated as a church in these ecumenical conversations, we have been called upon to give an account of our episcopé to the other churches. We do have people, individuals as well as groups, who give attention to the unity of the church and perform the oversight of our churches and our clergy. The outsider to the UCC expects us to begin our account of episcopé with the Conference Minister. This person looks most like other churches' bishops. However, in the UCC, we must begin with the role of the laity in episcopé before the rest of our structure will be clear.[84]

In a congregational understanding of the Church, and where the congregation itself calls and authorizes its own leadership, whether in consultation with other congregations or not, that congregation of lay people is in fact involved in the oversight of itself and its leaders. The members of the congregation, singly and together, have the responsibility to maintain their unity in the context of their love for one another and to represent collectively the presence of Christ in their larger community. This responsibility calls them to evaluate and take a larger view of themselves. The German Evangelical theologian Friedrich Schleiermacher grounded the oversight of the church, and therefore, the office of bishop in the members of the local congregation.

> While so much can be gathered from our creedal passages, they do not make clear the scope or manner in which this whole office resides in the congregation, or how the congregation exercises it. In point of fact, it exercises it not merely indirectly, by ordering and distributing the offices to which legislation and judgement are formally assigned (for how could the holders of these offices come to have such abilities and faculties, unless they have previously had some experience of them?), but each individual as such also exercises a punitive office, in an independent and informal manner, by the judgements he [or she] passes upon what goes on in the congregation, and by praise and blame. Not only so: legislative action is exerted by each through everything he [or she] does that goes to form public opinion; and public opinion must always be the living fount of expressly legislative acts, for these acts are simply a definite way of gaining recognition for public opinion in Church affairs. If in this sphere anything be attempted which is not a pure expression of the way in which, at a particular time and place, human nature in union with the divine Spirit is seeking to give actual form to itself and its concerns, then the attempt fails, and the law, which is thus incapable of securing its own recognition, simply reveals an imperfection in the church. Inevitably the Church is disturbed, and it is only through controversy that agreement (all the more conscious

> for what has occurred) can be regained, and along with it a less ambiguous state of the whole body.[85]

In our ecclesiology, we maintain that no one outside of the congregation has enough experience of its context to prescribe what that congregation ought to do or which leadership it should call. The congregation is left free to discern its mission and call its ministry and is responsible for doing so. Even in the New Testament it is clear that this is a burden for the churches and they began to seek outside advice. The record of early Christianity also indicates that they gave one another advice whether asked or not. Paul wrote to churches other than the one he resided at in that moment and early leaders such as Clement of Rome who wrote apparently unsolicited letters to the Corinthian church followed in that tradition. In every tradition of the UCC, an initial pure congregationalism gave way to a system whereby Association, Coetus, Convention or Synod grew up to support and advise the churches, and to help them remain in communion with what they regarded as mainstream Christianity.

Because of their ordaining authority in the United Church of Christ, Associations are the most logical place to look in our polity for episcopal authority. Indeed, the Associations perform all the functions of episcopé within the UCC. They bring congregations into the UCC, they examine and ordain the clergy,[86] and they may vote not to approve a minister called by a congregation for standing in the Association or to expel a minister or congregation who violates the covenant with the Association. Thus the Associations hold most of the episcopal or oversight authority in the UCC. Seldom, in my experience, does an Association recognize the import of their authority or their decisions. One of the discontents of congregationalism lies in the willingness of congregations, meeting together as the Association, to advise the neighboring congregations or to approve or disapprove their actions, but when meeting separately as congregations, their discomfort with and failure to receive Association recommendations with which they as a congregation disagree. The covenant among the congregations of an Association does not always hold them in peace or in unity.

While Association, Coetus, Synod, and Convention serve well in their oversight of the clergy in the traditions of the UCC and in the present setting, the oversight of the churches themselves is, for the most part, left in the hands of the lay members of those congregations. The covenant of the clergy with the Associations is usually strong, but the covenant of the churches of an Association with each other is not always. Thus, one of the concerns churches in ecumenical dialogue with the United Church of Christ express is their concern that not all congregations will honor the ecumenical agreements the denomination makes.[87] In the UCC, we live into our covenants rather than make them matters of legislation.

This brings us to the consideration of that office that from the outside seems the most likely candidate for bishop in the United Church of Christ polity, the Conference Minister.[88] With the formal and informal authority lodged already in the local congregation and the Association, what role is left for the Conference Minister who can neither appoint and dismiss clergy, nor exercise any discipline over the congregations. The ambiguity of this office in the UCC comes in part from its history. The Conference Minister is not an office that grew naturally from the colonial era churches, nor did it arise to serve the needs of existing congregations. Instead, the Conference Minister was an outgrowth of the home missionary movement, particularly that of the Congregationalists, but also from the efforts of expansion in the other traditions as well. In each case, a superintendent served to guide the establishment of new churches in a given area. That superintendent, by virtue of being the conduit for funds, took on the role of oversight of the new congregations. Only when a number of self-supporting congregations were established in a neighborhood did an Association develop. By that time the Conference Superintendent already held considerable influence and actual power, and could on occasion over-ride the decisions of an Association.[89] To this day, in the West where Congregational home mission activity was extensive, the Associations are relatively weak and the Conferences strong, whereas in New England, the Associations are generally strong and the Conferences are weak.

An office not even mentioned in the first UCC Constitution, the Conference Minister's role and function in the UCC has been discussed lately, particularly with regard to the recent restructuring of the national setting of the church. Two important articles about the role of conferences and conference ministers in the UCC make the service of the covenants which bind the church together the primary responsibility of the conferences. Rollin Russell argues that in a polity in which every setting of the church is autonomous, the conference is the body best able to call forth mutual accountability and responsibility. The conference is situated, by virtue of choosing delegates to the General Synod, as a link between the local congregations and the national settings of the church.[90] That situation in between makes the Conference Minister the one officer who can call both the local churches and the national setting of the church into accountability for their covenants with each other, to ask whether the church at all its levels is being faithful, and to provide oversight of the mission activities of the whole UCC.[91] Writing after the restructuring of the national setting of the UCC, John Lynes concludes the same thing about the nature of the conference ministry.[92] While the nature of the Conference Minister's office remains without clarity, what the new structure does say is that the Conference serves to foster the covenant relationship between the local churches and the wider settings of the UCC. In the title of his article, Lynes provides a biblical or theological image for the role of the Conference Minister, the shepherd of a flock. Here we have a link to the ancient symbol of the bishop with the shepherd's crooked staff. I would argue, and have argued, that the Conference Minister has an episcopal role in our communion, though always shared with the Association and the local congregations.

If I have discerned correctly that the three main aspects of our United Church of Christ ecclesiology are that the church is the beloved community gathered together in covenant communion to further the mission of God, then I would propose that the role of the Conference Minister and in many cases also the Association Minister, is the oversight of all these things.[93] The Conference Minister has no authority simply by virtue of office to tell a congregation what to do, but does have the right of a pastor to serve the beloved community. If the Conference Minister has done his or her pastoral work among the churches, they will have a basis of trust from which to listen. The Conference Minister is also the servant of the covenant communion, the one who stands in the middle of all the covenantal relationships that serve to organize the life and work of the United Church of Christ and works to strengthen and interpret those covenants. And finally, the Conference is the location of the mission work that is too large for the local congregations to undertake alone, but is nearby in its scope. The Conference Minister is also, as Russell and Lynes have outlined, the person who keeps before the churches their covenant relationships with each other. The United Church of Christ as a body of completely free and responsible congregations, but bound together in covenant, communion with each other at all the levels of the denomination's life. We experience both the gifts and the discontents of this kind of covenant congregationalism. In the final section of this chapter, I would like to illustrate how these gifts and discontents work themselves out, particularly in the ordination process.

Practical Illustrations of the Gifts and Ambiguities of Our Episcopé

Issues of power, authority, and Christian community involved in understanding both the gifts and discontents of congregationalism. Two cases which test two aspects of the covenant—one the internal covenant among the congregations and the second the ecumenical covenant with the whole church—are the nineteenth century ordination of Antoinette Brown and the twentieth century ordination of William Johnson.[94] In both of these cases, the freedom of the local congregation or Association proved to be a factor enabling a revolutionary change, but that same local freedom proved to be a discontent both to the larger body of the church and to the group whose part in the leadership of the church had been newly recognized in a single ordination.

In 1853, the Congregational Church of Butler, New York, ordained Antoinette Brown to be its pastor. Brown was not the first woman in a church in the United States to preach by any means.[95] However, she was the earliest for which we have record, to be ordained in any of the traditions of the UCC. Her ordination illustrates the freedom of a congregation to order its own affairs, to call its own pastor, and to ordain her. This allowed the Congregationalists and eventually the United Church of Christ in the twentieth century to celebrate their pioneering role in the opening of the church to women's leadership. Unfortunately, Brown's ordination and ministerial standing was valid only in the Butler congregation because the Association did not ratify the congregation's choice, and did not participate in the ordination. This irregularity in her ordination limited her service and influence in the Congregational churches and after a short term at the Butler church she left to pursue other women's rights work. She eventually became a Unitarian minister.

The freedom of the congregation allows revolutionary things to happen in the Church but, unless in the larger covenant community everyone agrees, that the congregation becomes isolated and the effects of its revolutionary action are muted. It was over thirty years before a Congregational Association ordained a woman. This was Mary Moorland, ordained in 1889 in the Wyanet, Illinois Congregational Church[96] by a council of the Association known today as the Prairie Association.[97] Unlike the women ordained earlier, and perhaps because of her regular ordination, she served as a minister for nineteen years in four different congregations in Illinois.

The ordinations of Brown and Moorland were noted in those circles interested in women's rights, but they did not generate extensive controversy. In the ensuing decades, until the explosion in the number of ordained women in the late 1960s and 70s, a steadily increasing number of women were ordained to ministry by Congregational Associations and Christian churches.[98] While the prevailing and largely unquestioned assumption in the Congregational churches of the time was that Paul prohibited women from preaching, and therefore, from ordination, many men and women noted other biblical passages that seemed on the contrary to allow it. These churches and Associations that did ordain women found the practical need for ministry and the woman's obvious qualifications to override the prohibitions contained in an ambiguous biblical record.[99] In fact, in the records of early deliberations on the ordination of women, there was not substantial appeal to the bible, except occasionally to the passage in Joel that "your sons and daughters will prophesy." The arguments instead centered on the desperate need of the churches for ministers and the availability of a qualified candidate whose only drawback was female gender.[100] Unlike many denominations that struggled more with the issue, the Methodists and Presbyterians for example, congregations of the UCC remain far more willing to ordain a woman they know to serve someone else's church than to call a woman they do not know to be their pastor. Most of the ordained women in the UCC serve in ministries outside the local congregation, or as associate pastors or pastors of very small churches. In summary, while the ordination of women certainly never became a threat to the unity of the United Church of Christ or any of its traditions, its openness does not necessarily mean that women have full opportunity to serve. Congregationalism made women's ordination possible quite early, but that very congregationalism keeps ordained women out of many UCC pulpits.

More recently, the ordination of ministers of a variety of sexual orientations, has on the other hand caused great public controversy among UCC congregations and has threatened the unity of the church. On the surface, this seems like an analogous situation to that of a century ago when women were ordained. The freedom of the local body, in this case an Association, made it possible for an openly gay man to be ordained in the early 1970s. And as in the case of women, while that local freedom made such an ordination possible, it also made rejection of such a position equally possible and also keeps gay, lesbian, transgendered, bisexual ministers out of most UCC pulpits, even in congregations that pride themselves on being Open and Affirming.

The ordination of William Johnson by the Golden Gate Association in 1973 came as the UCC was challenged by the issues of racial justice, inclusive language for women, the end of the Vietnam War, the legalization of abortion, the precipitous decline of liberal Protestantism and the rise of the Religious Right. The anxieties of the era seemed to crystallize around the issues of sexual and gender identity. If I have read both the support and opposition to this ordination correctly, I believe that the depth of the controversy lies precisely in the connection of sexuality and gender identity with our fundamental understanding of beloved community. A major voice for the opposition, Donald Bloesch, focused on three matters of concern within our life in the United Church of Christ, inclusive language, particularly that which uses specifically feminine theological vocabulary and imagery; tolerance of maintaining women's right to chose abortion to end a pregnancy; and the ordination of LGBT persons to ministry. All of these issues, he argues, contribute to the deterioration of both the quality of family life and our ecumenical relationships. In other words, they strike at the heart of the beloved community and its covenant with God as he understands it.[101]

As with the ordination of women in the previous century, there has been surprisingly little theological work done on the issue within the United Church of Christ, one of the chief complaints of those opposed to it and one of the obstacles standing in the way of the Open and Affirming process as well. As early as 1960, Rev. Robert W. Wood, a gay United Church of Christ pastor published *Christ and the Homosexual,* a work declaring that one need not be heterosexual to be Christian. Shortly after Johnson's ordination UCC scholar James Nelson published a work on sexuality in general, *Embodiment* in which he sought to make a place for human sexual experience in theological thinking. These works laid the groundwork for subsequent developments in trying to understand the LGBT experience of sexuality theologically.[102] Particularly in recent years theological discussion of LGBT concerns as well as women's concerns and those of other marginalized groups has called into question the meaning of the Church's claim that the Bible is authority.[103] Rooted in the liberal approach, the UCC entertains doubt about more traditional understandings of biblical authority, and has not to this moment completely finished considering the implications of this doubt. The Bible, we recognize, may have different kinds of authority. Is it a letter that kills and a spirit that gives life, or is it a law that we are bound to live by to the last iota? Though most in the UCC would agree that Jesus provides for us the lens through which to read the rest of Scripture, we do not all agree on how to use that lens. Congregationalism gives each congregation both the freedom and the responsibility to discern the meaning of the Bible for its life. The covenant communion of the congregations with each other gives each the responsibility of engaging in a common conversation. As these examples illustrate, unity in the United Church of Christ comes only slowly, certainly not by majority vote.

The idea of the Congregation, as completely within itself representing the Church, as the Congregationalists would put it, is a difficult idea to reconcile always with the other ideal of the UCC, that of the unity of the church, "that they all may be one." The key problem for the concluding chapter lies in this question of the relation of the many to the one. What is it theologically that allows for the emergence of the idea of the unity of the churches or congregations out of so many separate expressions?

Six

Conclusion

The United Church of Christ as an Ecumenical Project

In the previous chapters, I have addressed a number of aspects of the search for unity and identity in the United Church of Christ by focusing on some emerging ecclesiological themes. Rather than identifying our ecclesiology with our polity, or describing it simply as what we do as a Church, our mission, or our part of the Missio Dei, I have incorporated other aspects of our thinking about the nature and purpose of the Church. Additional expressions of our ecclesiology in the UCC include our understanding of the beloved community (beloved by God and by each other) and living in covenant communion for the purpose of carrying out the mission of God. In the first chapter, I began with the historical resources commonly used in the UCC, and the common interpretations of our life as a Church and traced the development of our understanding of our identity, outlining what still remains to be explored theologically and in our life together. In the second chapter, I opened up the question of the relationship of cultural and racial diversity to our longing for Christian unity. In the next two chapters, I looked back over the development of both theological diversity and our openness to questions from modern and post-modern secular culture. And, in the last chapter, I explored the gifts and discontents of congregationalism in our understanding of the relationships of the churches to one another. After this review, the question remains, upon what ground do we claim unity amid all this diversity?

Is the United Church of Christ still, as it was in its beginning, fundamentally an ecumenical project requiring a certain natural flexibility or fluidity, or has it become so caught up in fostering diversity, culturally and theologically, that it has become lost and truly has lost its theological voice? Can we answer the question, "Who are we?" or can we only say what we do.[1] Our most typical short answer to a question such as this is that we are a multiracial, multicultural, just peace church, open and affirming, and accessible to all. This answer states clearly what we do, but not why we do it. It is a character we work toward, not one we have achieved. There are other churches that have done each of these things better than we have, though perhaps very few have tried to do all of them together. In this concluding chapter, I would like to explore the possible roots for our emerging ecclesiology in our original purpose as a united and uniting church in such a way that we can begin to see how our understanding of what we do as a church is nourished by an unarticulated but quite old and strong underground theological stream. The task for the future will be to translate this living theological heritage and this fuller understanding of the nature and purpose of the church for a coming generation where few know this language.

Recognizing that the divisions among us as Christians go far beyond the issues of faith and order with which our predecessors in the early ecumenical movement struggled, as a United and Uniting Church we have to work as well with issues of economic division, divisions based in gender and sexual identity, and differences of race and culture that are not simply born of misunderstanding and ignorance, but also of histories of deliberate violence and deep-seated denial of each other's very humanity.[2] We are no longer purely a Reformed church, nor are we purely a Congregational church, but the divisions of faith and order are not the only ones we must overcome. In addition to the multiple divisions we have had to address and continue to work to reconcile, our thinking about the nature of our church must include reflection on the purpose for which we united. Did we unite simply to achieve greater efficiency in our mission (this was a big piece of the argument in favor of the union) or did we unite for the purpose of bearing witness to Christ's reconciliation of the world to God? Did we unite simply to enhance our survival among the many denominations competing for the attention of the Christian people of the United States (again and again the size of the new denomination was celebrated), or did we unite in order to begin healing the wounds of human division and to give more effective service to our neighbors?

Can reconciliation, healing, and service be measured in the modernist terms of efficiency and large size?[3]

Inclusivity and Catholicity

In order to more clearly investigate the kind of unity the United Church of Christ seeks, and how that search for unity is expressed in our embrace of racial/cultural as well as theological inclusivity, it will be important to distinguish between *inclusivity* and the more common ecclesiological term *catholicity.* This is particularly important in a postmodern context in which any kind of universalizing, and catholic does mean universal, is open to question. Inclusivity is the broader term, and used theologically in this work it simply means the absence of barriers put up by the church or by God to inclusion at the Table. I base the term upon strands in the Bible quoted over and over again in the United Church of Christ, such as the hospitality Jesus shares with all kinds of "sinners" and his admonition not to judge people as if we were God. Also, the term's meaning rests primarily in the strands that emphasize faith, love and justice over purity and holiness codes of behavior.

Tensions arise related to questions of inclusivity because the biblical tradition, which Protestants hold as central, is ambiguous on these matters. It is difficult to tell to what degree one strand is to be held over another. There is a broad consensus, but not complete agreement, within the UCC that the principle, indeed the commandment, of love of God and neighbor overrides all other commandments—that the lesser commandments were made to serve humanity, but where keeping one would violate the commandment to love, our choice must be to act with love. How far is it from this position to one saying that anything goes and there is no sin if we think it is love, and no behavior we can judge anyway? There will never be a clear line, short of a legal code, to guide us here, and all of us are tempted at one time or another to dispense with thinking the question through when we are not sure we want to know the answer. We remain obligated to engage in conversation with those who hold positions different from our own, since none of us can see everything clearly. Whether we structure our ethical position deontologically, identifying our duty to love and practice justice, or teleologically, identifying our end goal as a loving and just society, people within the UCC traditions tend to begin their conversations over different understandings of inclusivity with the activity of love rather than with a prior ethical or biblical principle.[4]

Catholicity, on the other hand, is a more narrowly theological term. From the first Christian council in Jerusalem, the Church has been concerned with those things that are basic to its unity, a unity bestowed by Christ.[5] I am persuaded (albeit not as a scholarly expert on late antiquity and the rise of Christianity) from the earliest historical record, including biblical, theological and archeological evidence, that the Church has never enjoyed either unity or purity.[6] However, there always seems to have been a set of marks by which Christians recognized their sisters and brothers in the faith. Understanding of these marks varies. For some there are very few required for recognition, any boundary for these Christians is inherently a vehicle for judgement upon both those within and without. They are willing to risk admitting to the beloved community some who may not be Christian either in belief or practice, rather than risk keeping out one of the saints who comes in unfamiliar dress. However, Christianity is not Buddhism, nor is it Islam or Judaism however closely related or even overlapping they may be in history or thought. And there are boundaries to other faiths I believe we are bound to respect, even if we think we recognize Christ in the Buddha or in Mohammad.

Clearly the United Church of Christ has chosen a more permeable boundary than some other churches recognize. If the UCC is to fulfill its ecumenical commitments faithfully, it has a two-fold responsibility. Just as Paul first took responsibility for proclaiming the gospel he received, not from human agency but from Christ, we are called to proclaim the inclusion of those whom we believe God has led us to recognize as Christian. But we are in covenant communion with other churches and remain responsible to give an account of ourselves so that together the witness of the churches to the world remains recognizably Christian.[7] This is the task of catholicity. We may not see a way just now to reconcile our inclusivity with our responsibility for catholicity, and some among us will give priority to one or the other. Nonetheless, our calling as a united and uniting church must be to wrestle with both parts of our calling without always being able to see the way ahead clearly.

The Ecumenical Project of the United Church of Christ in the Context of the High Tech Era

In preparing for the Seventh International Council of United and Uniting Churches, the organizers reminded the presenters that "one important issue is how unity can be understood in a world which is "post-modern" (a phenomenon apparent to some cultures, but not in all!)." This reminder that the world has changed yet again bears on the life of the United Church of Christ especially since in the United States modernity reached its pinnacle and the clash between modernity and post-modernity has multiple facets. In addition, the UCC participated in its history in North American colonialism and now must come to terms with post-colonial relationships with former mission churches both within the denomination itself and in its relationships with the churches of the world.

The religious historian Bruce Lawrence refers to our times as the High Tech Era.[8] In this High Tech Era, the context of religious life has a complex character. While modern ideals and world view still prevail, it is also a time of revolt against these modern values, from those who would go back and from those who would move on. Whatever our views of it, all of us in the High Tech Era have, on some level, to deal with modernity. Churches use cellular telephones, communicate by Web site and e-mail, and quite often have LCD projectors in the sanctuary. Modernity is characterized by rationality, bureaucracy, nation states, technology, and global economic exchange. However, modernity also has created a set of values people adopt as the ideology by which they live their lives. Those values include nationalism (often, but not always understood as best governed by representative democracy), efficiency, change, quantity, and consumer-orientation (most often in a capitalist economic system), and the modernist believes them to be the values best supporting the technological progress that will make life better for everyone.

Another historian Leonard Sweet delineated the ways in which mainline Protestants in the United States coped with modernity by embracing modernism at the beginning of the twentieth century.[9] Concern for quantity before quality, efficiency, including the adoption of business models for pastoral work and the use of movable altar furniture in order to use a single space for many purposes, and consumer orientation, including the use of market analyses, advertising, and entertainment to shape worship and theological meaning became increasingly evident in a large number of American churches. Sweet even points to those churches who located themselves in buildings that deliberately resemble a shopping mall in order to provide a comfortable space for those completely unfamiliar with traditional Christian ritual and symbolism.[10]

However, by the end of the twentieth century, these same modernist Protestants had concluded that modernism proved inadequate to the task of proclaiming the gospel, and after the sixties, their leadership became ever more critical of modernism, though along with ordinary church members, they had trouble divesting their churches from modernist ways. In the High Tech Era, the United Church of Christ, one among the mainline modernist Protestant churches, faces the task of reconstituting its identity without on the one hand continuing to embrace modernism uncritically, or on the other hand turning toward an antimodern dogmatism. Of course, it is a completely modernist characteristic that the alternatives seem so clearly dualistic.[11] One of our alternatives is to continue to be a modernist church. However, it is my opinion that we cannot develop a deeper ecclesiology while still embracing modernism's insistence on efficiency, numbers, and continual change to please consumers. Those things may always serve us in some ways, but to make them our primary goals, implicitly or explicitly, will not allow us to develop the beloved community, covenant communion, nor will they allow us to consider the mission of God in all its complexity. I also do not believe that a simple embrace of tradition will further this ecclesiological character.

Definition of Postmodernity

If the United Church of Christ came into being during the period when the American mainline Protestant churches prided themselves on being "modern," what does it mean that the denomination has lived through three decades or more of cultural trends that have come to be known as "postmodern?" As the church continues to face the question of communicating with the generations following the "Baby Boomers" who themselves for the most part stopped participating in mainline denominations after their confirmation,[12] our unspoken postmodern assumptions based in the cultural transformations of the 1960s and 70s become more clear. Generally speaking, the modern is characterized by its interest in the rational application of technology to human problems, its idea of linear progress and search for a universal understanding binding humankind into one, and its emphasis on efficiency, sorting reality into manageable categories, and working to achieve a standard way of doing things by which progress can be measured. Postmodernism, on the other hand, perceives the weakness in the modern approach. It is characterized by recognition that chance and irrationality play a part in natural and historical processes, that technology does not contribute to the linear solution of problems, but rather creates whole new constellations of relationship, power, and knowledge out of which arise whole new questions. Postmodernists are suspicious of universal claims or explanations, and point out the fragmentation and discontinuity of human experience. Postmodernism makes difference important. In his recent work on the intellectual history of the twentieth century, Peter Watson also points out that postmodernism is old enough to have generated its own critique, that it has its own kind of universalizing tendencies, in addition to its propensity to endlessly fragment human community into smaller and smaller segments based on more and more specific differences with a consequent return to narrow sectarian politics. Watson suggests that recently a new pragmatic trend has emerged, marked by flexibility, tolerance for ambiguity, and recognition of rapid change, but at the same time a reemphasis on community and groups and a renewal of conversation between science and literature and art. He calls the present time a crossover culture, where people are more free to think with both the tools of analytical science and the discussion of meaning found in religion and literature. In the end he views it as necessary that we begin to think of science as a human enterprise.[13] Watson does not address the place of religion in this conversation, that would be up to us. The United Church of Christ faces this very question in its tension between the ecumenical longing for Christian unity and the inclusion and reconciliation of humanity in all its differences.

Inclusivity and the Possibility of the Beloved Community

The possibility of the beloved community rests squarely on the expansiveness of our inclusivity. The community beloved by us may in fact be very small, but we are called to encompass, as far as we can understand it, the community beloved by God. In the High Tech Era or post modernity, this requires that we engage in the spiritual discipline of hospitality, and that we begin or continue the work of reconciliation among Christian peoples who have historically harmed and have been harmed. Eventually, we are called to work for the reconciliation of all humanity regardless of anyone's participation in the Christian faith. In this way finally the ecumenical calling of the Church will result in its ability to give witness to Christ's work of reconciling the world to God.

Our consideration of inclusiveness of the beloved community, as a foundation for the ecumenical project of the United Church of Christ must rest in Jesus. As the Gospel writers understood Jesus, he was among other things, a person who continually violated the boundaries of conventional hospitality within his Jewish tradition. In both Christianity and Judaism, there are two ways to view hospitality and its role in religious practice. On the one hand, eating together signifies that we are family together, or that our friendships represent trust and love sealed by the breaking of bread. The tradition of God providing food to the Israelites at critical times makes these shared meals a piece of collective memory of this nurture. Therefore, one has to be inside in order to be at the table. In this view, certain suspicious strangers and outsiders are explicitly excluded from breaking bread together with the "children of God." In Christianity, perhaps the majority invite to the Communion Table only those who clearly confess the same faith, at minimum one must be baptized in some Christian church to sit at the table with Christ. Communion signifies Christian unity and is the fruit of ecumenical effort.

On the other hand, the Mediterranean world valued hospitality to the stranger and sojourner. Judaism also preserved a tradition of hospitality to the stranger in their midst. Abraham even created a feast of the best food in the house for three complete strangers. The Gospel's preservation of a tradition of Jesus eating with strangers, particularly socially outcast strangers, provides the rationale for those churches who invite everyone to the Communion Table, with the theological understanding that one may meet Christ for the first time there. The biblical scholar Burton Mack, studying the ancient Q communities of earliest Christianity, argues that the earliest churches consisted of socially inclusive groups of people.

> Meals together would be the perfect occasion of aphoristic discourse, parables, reports, poking fun, and serious discussions about staying alert and living sanely in the midst of cultures in transition. A sense of the unconventional may very well have prevailed, supposing the company were mixed and the conversation somewhat self-reflective. Even if most were

> marginal people, without great investments in social status to lose, the risk may have been both poignant and rewarding. The "spirit" of discourse about the kingdom of God as well as behavior appropriate to it may very well have been generated by social formation at mealtime, an experience some did not want to relinquish just because Jesus was no longer present. A little display of wisdom would still be possible. As things developed, ever greater sagacity would have been required to account for what was taking place.[14]

Following this socially inclusive group as it expanded in the ancient world, Peter Brown describes a group of people who might almost be modern. "The successful businessman, the freedman administrator, the woman whose status and education had slowly improved, found themselves no longer citizens of their accustomed town, but "citizens of the world"; and many, it appears, were finding that the world was a lonely and impersonal place. It is among such people that we find the Christians."[15] Brown thus delineates a movement among alienated and lonely people to find community. He called them "immigrants by heart," separated from their environment by their beliefs, but knowing they shared these beliefs with other small communities all over the empire. It was possible for them to "achieve in a small group 'among the brethren [and sisters]' relationships that were being achieved in society at large at heavy cost of conflict and uncertainty."[16] The Christian invitation to a communal meal, the identity granted to those who sit around the table because there they are known and beloved, gives them both the permission and the confidence to engage in conversation, even conflict, without fear that the community will be destroyed. The presence of the Holy Spirit in drawing together and inspiring the community disrupts the static conventional conversation and grants the grace necessary for peace with diversity.

The community of these "immigrants by heart,"[17] is the essence of *koinonia*. Thinking for a moment about the United Church of Christ as a community of immigrants, from England of the sixteenth and seventeenth centuries, from Germany of the eighteenth and nineteenth centuries, from Africa (and none by choice) from the sixteenth to the eighteenth centuries, from China, Japan, and Mexico, Puerto Rico (some by conquest rather than choice) in the nineteenth century, and from the

Philippines, Micronesia, Samoa, Korea and Senegal in the twentieth century. The only ones who were not immigrants to this part of North America were various American Indians converted by the immigrants, and made, one might say, another kind of immigration from one world to another. All brought parts of languages and cultures with them and have handed down these treasures to their children. *Koinos*, in its Greek connotation, signifies what is communal or common, it can also signify what is ordinary or profane or even ritually unclean. Koine Greek was the common language in which the early Christians wrote to one another. The koinonia they shared was both common meal, common language, and holding things in common. Fundamentally, it was a fellowship of sharing, the sharing of everything that mattered. By the end of the twentieth century, the common language we seek in the UCC, a language that will make possible our koinonia as a community of immigrants by heart, is not a simplistic default language of English, but a more complex language as a style of communication that fosters the ability to listen across barriers of difference.

I do not want to make this sound too simple. The Presbyterian ecumenical theologian Lewis Mudge makes some important points about the problem of sustaining the beloved community in the contemporary situation. He points out that we live in a time when people doubt the capacity of language to convey the reality people desire to see. Rather than expressing any sense of shared reality, our language "speaks us." At the same time we witness worldwide an explosion in the forms of Christian expression and organization. No longer are the old denominational and confessional forms of Christian life the only ecclesiastical categories for thinking about the church. Finally, he argues,

> The subordination of theological language to communal practice and the multiplication of new church forms combine to raise questions about existing ways of expressing the catholicity or universality of Christian faith. If there is one gospel for the whole world, have we words or communal structures for articulating it? Most of us acknowledge that no historic confession or communion alone is adequate to express the wholeness of Christ's people on earth. But attempts so far to build fragile conceptual bridges between these worlds have not produced spans on whose strength many are prepared to stake their lives.[18]

In addition to the postmodern suspicion of language, postcolonial thinkers join the century long analysis of racism in the United States in raising the question of the possibility of any shared common language across the abyss of the terrible and violent histories of slavery and colonization. Memories of anguish passed down from one generation to the next among people of color, renewed by discrimination, ignorance and denial on the part of the heirs of "manifest destiny"[19] and the economic benefits of slavery, combine to make the common language of koinonia difficult if not impossible. Every bit as divisive as the babel of cultural languages are the subcultures of gender and sexual identities. Women and men, straight, lesbian, gay, bisexual, transgendered, and those who are simply not so sure of these things any longer, all find it difficult to communicate their experience, their anxieties, and their sense of self to one another. Fears, ignorance, denials, and privileges like those which separate people of different races, make the common language of koinonia difficult here also. These issues, perhaps because they come so close to home, issues touching the bodies in which we live as profoundly as our skin color, have in their turn proved theologically and sociologically divisive and one need not look very far to find violence and anguish in their histories. Finally, but not last in importance, the means of communication in whatever common language we can share, depend upon the frailty of human bodies, eyes that can see the printed word, ears that can hear what is spoken, hands that can write, legs that can mount the steps to a microphone, a tongue that can shape sound, brains that can remember and reason, all physical systems that can fail us and inevitably will fail each of us. The common language of koinonia will have to overcome the inflexibility of material structures built for efficiency and yet again the ignorance of the circumstances of others, and alas, even again histories of abuse and violence.

Koinonia, the beloved community, will not come easily. In fact, in human terms it may well be impossible. We live in a crowded world, among billions of people who have little chance to form relationships outside of their families and immediate circle of friends, co-workers, and neighbors. Without names or stories, the myriads of "others" we know only as a vast crowd. Koinonia however, rests on the invitation, the calling of God, not on something we do ourselves.[20] For the Christian, the *ekklesia*, the Church, is the body of people called together by God through Jesus Christ in the power of the Holy Spirit. It takes human effort for *ekklesia* to become *koinonia*. Learning the common language requires real listening to others. It requires us to face the truth about broken relationships, disillusionment about history, and the difficulty of forgiveness for things done by ours or other's ancestors. The purpose of Christian *ekklesia* is precisely to bear witness to the reconciliation of the world to God through the resurrection of Christ. The reconciliation of the world to God, something that has already happened, makes possible the reconciliation of human beings with one another—that which seems so impossible. Mudge calls such reconciliation, revelation, as does Karl Barth.[21] In the traditions of the UCC the witness for social justice has always been at the center of our work of reconciliation.

The United Church of Christ has in recent years begun a process of reconciliation and redress in order to witness to God in Christ reconciling the world to God. The apology of the UCC to the native Hawaiian people for the misdeeds of our missionaries and their heirs in the past, and the attempt to redress the wrong is one example of the effort required to create koinonia. Not everyone agrees to recognize missionaries as people with feet of clay. Certainly the UCC has not forgotten the schools they built, the churches they founded, and the effort they made to put the Hawaiian language in written form, making it possible to preserve the language even as they also worked to transform the Hawaiians into English speakers. A common language here requires however, that history be viewed from more than one vantage point, and that the story be presented in more than one language before it can be considered to have become common to us all. Koinonia is based upon the whole story, including the recognition of God's reconciling work. I want to close this section with a word of admonition. I think too often in our thinking about the church we gloss over the deep abyss between the races that still exists. The Consultation on Church Union, now the Churches Uniting in Christ, has recognized antiracism work as one of the marks of the faithful church. That such reconciliation would be indeed a revelation of God gives the project some perspective. But it is also urgent. The African-American philosopher James Baldwin put the urgency in these terms.

> If we—and now I mean the relatively conscious whites and the relatively conscious blacks, who must, like lovers, insist on, or create, the consciousness of others—do not falter in our duty

> now, we may be able, handful that we are, to end the racial nightmare, and achieve our country, and change the history of the world. If we do not now dare everything, the fulfillment of that prophecy, recreated from the Bible in song by a slave, is upon us: *God gave Noah the rainbow sign, no more water, the fire next time.*[22]

Catholicity and the Possibility of Covenant Communion

If our sense of koinonia in the United Church of Christ is the foundation for inclusivity, and lies at the heart of our social justice commitments, what part then does koinonia with other Christian churches, either other congregations than our own within the UCC or other churches in the wider Church, play in our sense of our ecumenical project? Besides a common language, we also participate in covenant communion with other Christians. Besides internal inclusivity, koinonia fosters our relationships with other Christians, and perhaps even other faith traditions.

It is important to delineate the relationship between the beloved community, a local phenomenon, and covenant. I am talking here about the covenant that binds a local congregation's members together, but even more about the covenant that supports the unity of the whole Church. One aspect of that covenant is sometimes understood to be doctrinal orthodoxy. As we saw above, the UCC calls into question, and its traditions have in the past also called into question, creedal teachings that claim universal (or catholic) truth. This questioning does not mean that we completely dispense with these historic testimonies to the Christian faith, but we regard them as exactly that, testimonies. They are not themselves the faith. How then do we participate in ecumenical covenants with churches who regard them as the one agreed upon Testimony and thus as symbolic of the unity of the Church. Particularly we must consider the Apostle's Creed and the Nicene Creed, two statements worked out in hard fought theological controversies in the first six centuries of Christian history.

If in our inclusivity, our understanding that Christ invites to the Table first those we do not expect, those at the margins, what do we make of covenants of belief or practice formulated at the center? The historian Rebecca Lyman, in her study of conversion in Late Antiquity and the early Middle Ages, focused on the conversion of Justin

Martyr,[23] one of the early figures in the emergence of Christian "orthodoxy." She observed that Christian orthodoxy emerged from the margins, not from the dominant culture, a surprising claim.[24] Justin Martyr is commonly recognized as one of the earliest Christian apologists who used Greek philosophical terms to bridge the gap between ancient philosophy and Christian theology, using Greek philosophical terms such as *logos*, the word or reason. Contemporary philosophers regarded such apologists using their language with suspicion. By some Christians, they were accused of corrupting Christian theology with these philosophical categories foreign to the Bible. We find echoes of this accusation in many arguments against creeds found in the traditions of the UCC. However, Lyman characterizes the work of Justin as that of an immigrant from the margins of the Roman Empire (from Syria Palestine) to its center in the city of Rome who was trying to forge a personal identity in a double culture, that of the Hellenistic culture of late antiquity and the emerging Christianity.[25] In Justin's First Apology one can see his use of philosophical terms and style of argument.[26] Lyman argues that immigrant intellectuals such as Justin formulated Christian theology as an expression within the predominant Greek-speaking Hellenistic culture and created an expression of Christianity that the Church came to regard as normative. As a colonial subject of the Roman Empire, moved from the colonies to the center of power, and as a Christian, a member of a persecuted religious minority, Lyman characterizes his "logos Christology" as having possibilities of both assimilation and alienation.[27] The indefinite boundary thus created between Christianity and philosophy provoked within the Church a search for more definition, for instance Irenaeus, also from the margins of the empire and a student of Justin's, began to equate philosophy with heresy.[28] Lyman concludes that rather than identifying a core of universal truth within Christianity, the theological formulations that defined orthodoxy emerged in order to solve perceived problems with these indefinite boundaries between Christianity and culture that were felt particularly by those at the margins rather than by those in the centers of power.

I have come to think that often it is those most in contact with some other way of thinking who want most to clarify the identity, or characterization of their own group. If Lyman is correct, those at the center of a church or a movement have the least need to be precise, and are in least danger of suffering persecution. This may be why martyrs so often come from the margins, they are more exposed to outside view. In the contemporary United Church of Christ, with our celebration of inclusivity, and our reluctance to create a test of faith, we will have to order our beloved community in such a way that the margins are continually drawn into the center. This is one way that covenant functions among us. Ideally it makes every part of the church aware of and attentive to all the other parts. The covenant among us arises as we look around the Table of people Christ has called together. These are not people we thought to invite, but those who have received a call, an invitation, from Christ. Eating together we unavoidably become stamped with our common relationship to Christ and become as my colleague Archie Smith Jr. puts it, "siblings by choice."[29] I might add, by divine choice, not our own. All of our human covenants and constitutions must be measured by this central covenant of communion with the living Christ.

Paul put at the center of the sacrament that which makes this covenant communion real in the Church the Tradition passed down to him, and which he passes down to the next generation. Christ is not calling together just any beloved community, but a beloved community that shares a particular covenant of love with one another, passed down as a Tradition formulated in ancient symbols and expressed in human languages no longer alive today. For some Christians in our day this means that every word and motion must be preserved from one generation to another intact for the covenant to be recognizable. The United Church of Christ, formed out of many complex parts, does not see it this way. But that does not mean that the Tradition does not exist as part of the covenant we hold with one another and with our sisters and brothers in other churches. We maintain that the Tradition helps us to live in the beloved community, but is not itself the goal.

It is told somewhere that the nineteenth-century German Romantic poet Goethe once remarked that "There is no Past that we can bring back to us by the longing for it, there is only an eternally new Now that builds and creates itself out of the elements of the Past as the Past withdraws. The true desire to bring the Past back to us must always be productive and create something new and something better."[30] The more recent philosopher Jacques Derrida puts it slightly differently. When talking of inheritance he wrote, "The radical and necessary heterogeneity of an inheritance . . . is never fully gathered. . . . Its presumed unity, if there is one, can only consist in the *injunction to reaffirm by choosing*. . . . One always inherits a secret which says: 'Read me, will you ever be up to it?'"[31] Those of us who attended Sunday School as children learned sooner or later about the covenant God made with the people of Israel and how over and over they failed to keep it, but God never failed. We will never be up to the covenant we have as brothers and sisters in Christ, but rather than retreat into a small and comfortable family group, the United Church of Christ is called again and again to draw the marginal people into the center and to reappropriate the Tradition translated into fresh language to give form to the beloved community.

Participation in the Mission of God in the High Tech Era and Beyond

Our alternative to the long predicted death of the mainline, modernist Protestant church in America is for the United Church of Christ and other churches like it to create a new way to be a Christian church in the context of (late?) modernity, the High Tech Era. Though postmodern literature, philosophy, and other aspects of culture seem to cut everything loose from its moorings, seem to produce chaos, postmodern conditions may well be a kind of chaos within which God can create something new. I would like to consider whether the ecumenical project of the United Church of Christ can work within a postmodern understanding of our times to further the emergence of the church as a beloved community, one living in covenant communion with God, and participating in the mission of God.

The mission is after all the purpose of all the care we bestow on the beloved community. The ecumenical recognition of our unity in Christ is necessary only because God's mission is diminished by our divisions. The traditional mission of the Church entails proclamation of the Gospel of Jesus Christ, healing the bodies and souls of people, healing the wounded relationships between peoples, and finally bearing witness to the love of God for humanity by creating social structures of justice and integrity. Through the Holy Spirit, who gives the gift of speaking and understanding other languages, we are called to retranslate the Gospel for a new generation, this time a generation in which there are many unfamiliar with traditional Christianity, a generation for whom the social structures of society have failed, a generation brought up with mass media rather than solitary reading as their main form of obtaining information, a generation overwhelmed by the information available and the rapidly changing technologies which contain and transmit it. It is an awesome thing to contemplate what it means to be the Church in this new cultural context. The work of reconciliation is no less daunting, and our need of the Holy Spirit for guidance is no less great. It is not only the alienation of individuals from their sense of self and from their own bodies that stands in need of the healing grace of God, but the chasms between peoples, particularly between the central and privileged and the marginal peoples that are in need of reconciliation. And the work of justice is far less simple than it seemed to our optimistic Social Gospel great grandparents. Too often we simply give up because the questions of fairness are too complex. Nonetheless, this is the mission to which we have been called as a church, and for which we need our faith in Jesus Christ, our unity, our beloved community of trust and renewal, and our discipline of covenant living. As the poet Adrienne Rich suggested, we have no extraordinary power, only the ordinary holy power of love and with that we are called to reconstitute the world.[32] As a church whose focus has been so often on reconstituting the structure of the church, it would pay us not to lose sight of the reasons why we exist, and the mission of God to which we are called.

NOTES

CHAPTER I

1. H. Richard Niebuhr, *The Social Sources of Denominationalism* (Hamden, Connecticut: The Shoestring Press, 1954, reprint of the 1929 edition, Henry Holt and Company, Inc.) chapters on "The Churches of the Middle Class" and "The Churches of the Immigrants."

2. "The Church Union Memoirs of Samuel D. Press," *The United Church Herald* (July 1, 1965) 20-22. He is quoted as saying, "All of the participants [in the St. Louis Collegium] were men of the cloth, and all were Caucasians of American stock. That is to say, there were no representatives of the laity or of the St. Louis Negro Churches included. This was not with intent but by oversight, yet it indicates that our collegium was not 100 percent ecumenical nor a complete work of God."

3. Percel O. Alston, "The Afro-Christian Connection," in Barbara Brown Zikmund ed. *Hidden Histories in the United Church of Christ*. vol. 1 (New York: United Church Press, 1981) 21 36.

4. Bernice A. Buehler, Letter to Robert Moss, November 9, 1972, Robert Moss Papers, UCC Archives 90-3 Box 3 file folder 29. This letter is quoted and discussed more fully below p.110.

5. These include Douglas Horton's *The United Church of Christ* (New York: Thomas Nelson and Sons, 1962); Hanns Peter Keiling's *Der Entstehung der "United Church of Christ"* (USA) (Berlin: Letner-Verlag, 1969); Louis Gunnemann's, *The Shaping of the United Church of Christ* (New York: United Church Press, 1977); *United and Uniting* (New York: United Church Press, 1987); Barbara Brown Zikmund's, *Hidden Histories of the United Church of Christ,* vols. I and II (New York: United Church Press, 1984 and 1987);

Margaret Post's "A History of the United Church of Christ" in the pamphlet *History and Program of the United Church of Christ* (New York: United Church Press, 1986); Dorothy Bass and Kenneth Smith's, *United Church of Christ: Studies in Identity and Polity* (Chicago: Exploration Press, 1987); Daniel Johnson and Charles Hambrick Stowe's, *Theology and Identity* (New York: The Pilgrim Press, 1990) and the Pilgrim Press reprints of Williston Walker's *Creeds and Platforms of Congregationalism* and David Dunn et. al. *History of the Evangelical and Reformed Church.*

6. Margaret Rowland Post, "A History of the United Church of Christ," in Division of Education and Publication, United Church Board for Homeland Ministries, History and Program (New York: United Church Press, 1986 reprinted in 1991) pp. 52. The last sentence is quoted from Norman Goodall in Fred Hoskins, *Congregationalism Betrayed or Fulfilled* (Newton, MA: Andover Newton Theological School, 1962) 7-8. This was Hoskins' Southworth Lecture.

7. Interestingly, the United Church of Christ has not yet seen fit to reprint any of the histories of the Christian tradition such as Milo True Morrill, *History of the Christian Denomination in America* (Dayton Ohio: The Christian Publishing Association, 1912), Durwood Stokes and William Scott's *History of the Christian Church in the South* (Elon College, NC: Elon College, 1973), or J. Taylor Stanley's *History of Black Congregational Christian Churches of the South* (New York: United Church Press,1978).

8. Louis Gunnemann, *The Shaping of the United Church of Christ: An Essay in American Religious History* (Cleveland: The United Church Press, 1999, reprint of the 1977 edition with Foreword and Chapter 9 by Charles Shelby Rooks). The obvious issues of Christian unity as Gunnemann presents them, arising first in the Reformation, certainly form an important and deep foundation of the existence of the United Church of Christ. Following Gunnemann's basic thesis, but expanding the historical view prior to the twentieth century, a full discussion of these Reformation issues as well as the long history of concern and work on ecumenical questions forms the later essay on the United Church of Christ as an ecumenical project.

9. Douglas Horton, *The United Church of Christ: Its Origins, Organization, and Role in the World Today,* (New York: Thomas Nelson and Sons, 1962).

10. Louis Gunnemann, *United and Uniting: The Meaning of an Ecclesial Journey, United Church of Christ 1957–1987* (New York: United Church Press, 1987)

11. Much of the literature in the UCC in the late 1980s and early 1990s displays an uneasiness about a lack of common identity or sense of unity in the UCC, and the perception that each church or even each person goes a separate way. Gunnemann referred to a "persistent thread of self-questioning," "confusion and "the absence of a common language of faith." (Prologue to *United and Uniting*). Thirty-nine seminary professors referred to the mid-

1980s as "a most difficult and urgent time" (Memo to the Executive Council, January 21, 1984, subsequently published in *New Conversations,* Spring 1985). In an article in *Prism* (vol. 5 no. 2, Spring 1990) Browne Barr pessimistically discussed "The Rise and Fall of the United Church of Christ" pp. 80–90.

12. An example of this drift of the national body apart from the local bodies can be found in James M. Gustafson, "The United Church of Christ in America: Actualizing a Church Union" in Nils Ehrenstrom and Walter G. Muelder eds. *Institutionalism and Church Unity* (New York: Association Press (YMCA), 1963) 325-351. Gustafson's discussion of the case of the formation of the United Church Board of Homeland Missions from the two predecessor bodies emphases the primacy of institutional concerns over theological ones, and the way in which the culture of the Congregational Christian Board of Home Missions prevailed over that of the Evangelical and Reformed. The Congregational Christian Board related to the conferences rather than to the local congregations and developed a wide range of social service projects, whereas the Evangelical and Reformed Board related directly to the local church pastors and concerned itself only with programs to strengthen the local church.

13. Dale E. Jones, et. al., *Religious Congregations and Membership in the United States 2000* (Nashville: Glenmary Research Center, 2002) p. 4. Glenmary puts the UCC at 1.37 million full members and 1.69 million adherents in 2000. The current UCC membership figure from the Research Office of the UCC is 1.33 million members. Edwin Gaustad and Philip Barlow, *New Historical Atlas of Religion in America* (New York: Oxford University Press, 2001) p. 388, Figure C.21 gives a similar picture augmented by their excellent maps for the previous decade.

14. Ruth Rouse and Stephen Neill, *History of the Ecumenical Movement, 1517–1948* (Philadelphia: Westminster Press, 1967).

15. "The Bekenntnisparagraph," Elsabeth Slaughter Hilke, *Growing Toward Unity,* Vol. 6, *Living Theological Heritage of the United Church of Christ,* (Cleveland: The Pilgrim Press, 2001) Part IV, Document 55.

16. All three addresses were published in *The Ecumenical Review* (October 1995). Reinhard Groscurth, "Conversion and Identity: The United Churches: Origins, Progress, Relationships," pp. 440-450; Roderick R. Hewitt, "A Present Vocation in Mission and Service: The Challenge to United and Uniting Churches," pp. 451-463; and Rena Karefa-Smart, "The Ecumenical Challenge of United and Uniting Churches," pp. 464-471.

17. Reinhard Groscurth, "Conversion and Identity," *Ecumenical Review* (October 1995) p. 447.

18. Roderick R. Hewitt, "A Present Vocation in Mission and Service," Ecumenical Review (October 1995) p. 461.

19. Hewitt, "A Present Vocation," p. 453.

20. Groscurth, "Conversion and Identity," p. 447.

21. Hewett, "A Present Vocation," p. 455.

22. Burton Mack, *A Myth of Innocence: Mark and Christian Origins* (Philadelphia: Fortress Press, 1988) 115.

23. Ernesto Laclau, "The Uses of Equality," *Diacritics* (Spring 1997) pp 3–17.

24. Nils Karlström, in his chapter "Movements for International Friendship and Life and Work 1910–1925," in Ruth Rouse and Stephen Charles Neill eds. *A History of the Ecumenical Movement 1517–1948* (Philadelphia: The Westminster Press, 1967) confirms this view. "The Conference deliberately made no attempt to reach a doctrinal formulation of Christian unity: unity is not to be sought in the acceptance of one doctrinal system or another. Behind the different interpretations for faith, fides quae creditur, stands faith itself, fides qua creditur, the human heart apprehended by Christ and trusting him. Unity in faith can, therefore, exist even where confessions of faith are different." p. 527.

25. Some of the people in the UCC traditions involved in the Life and Work related ecumenical conferences were John Baltzer, Samuel Press, Reinhold Niebuhr, John C. Bennett and H. Richard Niebuhr.

26. The World Conference On Christian Life and Work, "A Message to All Christians," in Hilke, *Growing Towards Unity,* LTH vol. 6 Part IV Document 59.

27. David B. Barrett, George T. Kurian, and Todd M. Johnson, eds. *World Christian Encyclopedia,* Second Edition, vol. 1. (New York: Oxford University Press, 2001) 772.

28. Dale E. Jones et. al. eds., *Religious Congregations and Membership in the United States 2000* (Nashville: Glenmary Research Center, 2002) 3.

29. Predominantly the UCC churches are found in counties where less than 50% of the population is affiliated with a religious institution. Edwin Gaustad and Philip Barlow, *A New Historical Atlas of Religion in America* (New York: Oxford University Press, 2001) pp. 93–98 and 388–389.

30. The complex issues of becoming a Multiracial, Multicultural Church are discussed in a subsequent chapter.

31. R. Laurence Moore, *Religious Outsiders and the Making of America* (New York: Oxford University Press, 1986) xi.

32. Leonard Sweet, "The Modernization of Protestant Religion in America," in David Lotz ed. *Altered Landscapes: Christianity in America 1935–1985* (Grand Rapids: Eerdmans Publishing Company, 1989).

33. Gary Dorrien, *The Making of American Liberal Theology: Imagining Progressive Religion 1805–1900* (Louisville: Westminster John Knox Press, 2001) xix.

34. Amanda Porterfield, *The Transformation of American Religion: The Story of a Late Twentieth-Century Awakening.* (New York: Oxford University Press, 2001) 2. She echoes a similar conclusion by Wade Clark Roof and William McKinney in American Mainline Religion: Its Changing Shape and Future (New Brunswick: Rutgers University Press, 1987) 6. Commenting on the cen-

tripetal forces in American religious experience they note the "almost total acceptance of the social environment: Americans have traditionally viewed the state, the community, the family, and the marketplace as "God Given."

35. Leonard Sweet, "The Modernization of Protestant Religion in America," in David Lotz, et. al. *Altered Landscapes: Christianity in America 1935–1985* (Grand Rapids: William B. Eerdmans Publishing Company, 1989) 19–41.

36. Sweet, "The Modernization of Protestant Religion," p. 24.

37. Gunnemann, *The Shaping of the United Church of Christ,* p. 13. Gunnemann cites both of these events in his discussion.

38. Gunnemann, *Shaping,* p. 14. Robert Moss's "Address to the Pilgrims" was a key argument for this. Minutes of General Synod IX June 22–26, 1973 pp. 98–101.

39. Amanda Porterfield, *The Transformation of American Protestantism,* p. 123, remarks about a group of students at an American Jesuit University, "Chaos and disorder pervaded their ordinary, everyday life. Their grasp of any mythological structure underlying ordinary life was exceedingly tenuous, if indeed it existed at all." Leonard Sweet, in his essay "The Modernization of Protestant Religion in America," p. 25 notes that "Clergy were fast going from missionizing to merchandising, which helps account in part for the remarkable 1960s phenomenon of clergy picking fights with their congregations as the badge of being prophetic. By the 1960s some modernist clergy treated their parishioners as if they were the enemy rather than racism, sexism, and a host of other injustices . . . . Modernist Protestantism remained hopelessly estranged from the voices of its past, its members having almost entirely forgotten how to live historically in conversation with their classic traditions."

40. I am grateful for work done a few years ago in a conversation with Revs. David Finster and Harold Rucker of the Northern California Nevada Conference of the UCC as part of a larger conversation within the conference committee on Ecumenical Concerns on the question of Biblical Authority in the UCC. In addition, I am persuaded that in the UCC we most often treat the Bible as a source for discerning the Spirit of God, but not as the words of God such that they are completely unambiguous. The Bible's authority rests in its perceived reliability as an inspiration for our Christian lives rather than in its possible role as a law code. Within the UCC, as in most mainline churches, there has been for generations a considerable gap between what the clergy learn about the historical critical study of the Bible and what they are able or willing to teach the laity. Consequently thinking lay people often have to decide either to stop thinking about their questions and accept the Bible in its simple literal surface form, or to stop reading it altogether.

41. I borrow the idea of ecclesial journey from Louis Gunnemann, *United and Uniting: The Meaning of an Ecclesial Journey* (New York: United Church Press, 1987).

42. Lewis Mudge, *Rethinking the Beloved Community: Ecclesiology, Hermeneutics, Social Theory* (Boston: University Press of America, 2001). I think this exact term "beloved community was first suggested to my mind by Mudge, but he got it from Josiah Royce who used it in his *The Problem of Christianity.* However, quite independently, womanist theologians have been using the term. It is from them, I believe that the UCC folks have picked up the term. See particularly Toni Morrison's novel *Beloved* where "Beloved [the main character] becomes a mythic figure for community." Quoted from Karen Baker Fletcher's *A Singing Something: Womanist Reflections on Anna Julia Cooper* (New York: Crossroads Publishing Company, 1994) 208 note 32.

43. Norman Jackson, "Our Christendom Church and God's Mission, Prism (Spring 2000) 21–35.

CHAPTER 2

1. I am well aware that it is not necessarily helpful to single out one of the many issues of human oppression facing the churches. Sexism and heterosexism as well as racism and prejudice about culture need serious and sustained attention. I am convinced that the problem of race is the most difficult for us as a church, and therefore, I have chosen to discuss it first. I humbly admit that I do not understand well enough the connections of all these issues together to treat them as a single question. I do perceive from my experience as a woman in the church and in this society in general that lightness of skin, maleness of body, and a masculine way of presenting oneself in public tend to inspire confidence in one's competence and leadership. Those who differ from these characteristics have to prove themselves and enjoy fewer opportunities for leadership. Masculinity can be cultivated by anyone, but it is understood and expressed differently in different cultures. Nonetheless, women, for instance, can cultivate masculine qualities and be admired for doing so. Lightness of skin and maleness of body are not things one typically can acquire. It appears to me that time after time, the rationale for preferring light skinned men for leadership involves an identification of darker skin color and ambiguous or nonmale body gender with the feminine. The identification always contains associations of weakness, lesser rational ability, and often of provocative, lustful or uncontrolled sexual expression. Unfortunately, the theological traditions of Christianity in which the United Church of Christ participates, along with the cultural conventions practiced among us, make it extremely difficult to proceed with an open conversation about sexuality, and even more difficult to discuss its connections to our constructions of gender and race in our Christian organization and practice. I continue to pray that we receive wisdom from the Holy Spirit as well as wisdom from each other on these matters.

2. "Pronouncement calling the United Church of Christ to be a Multiracial and Multicultural Church" *Minutes of the Nineteenth General*

Synod, 1993, 39–40. The Statement of Christian Conviction of the Proposed Pronouncement can be found in, Fredrick Trost and Barbara Brown Zikmund, eds., *United and Uniting* (Cleveland: Pilgrim Press, 2005), LTH vol. 7, Part VII, Document A. 3.

3. Recent late twentieth century philosophical thinking has helped me shape my thinking about the UCC, though this is not the appropriate venue for putting forward these arguments and ideas in all their technicality. The ideas have to do with recent thinking about the role of postmodern ideas of difference in human experience and thinking, put next to the modernist, unitive ideas underlying the ecumenical vision of the UCC. Levinas and Derrida work with the idea of difference. They point out that Western philosophy has since the Greeks, desired to bring all reality into a unified understanding. Whenever the western mind encounters an Other, it immediately attempts to incorporate that Other into "the Same." The Otherness is too uncomfortable. However, the incorporation goes only one way, the Western mind never conceives of itself being incorporated into the Other's Same, and thus be radically changed. Levinas referred to a kind of otherness which cannot be incorporated into the Same as "alterity." From this some have begun to use the term subaltern to refer to those incorporatable Others who are also under the hegemony or influence of some other cultural power. For this reason, many recent philosophers have embraced the virtue of political conflict as a necessary means of preventing hegemonic incorporation of difference into a seamless Same. Ernesto Laclau is one, who sees such conflict as good and right. In an ideal democracy, representatives of all kinds of difference would be in perpetual dialogue about the ordering and meaning of society. Rather than those with hegemony incorporating difference into a Same, variety would reign. This philosophical work I think describes very well the fundamental dilemmas and ambiguities of life in the United Church of Christ, and also perhaps offers us a few new ways of thinking about ourselves. However, it counters the entire philosophical tradition in which Christianity has expressed its theology and political ideals. Is it possible for us to, and should we, completely rethink the philosophical underpinnings of the faith? If we judged it possible, is it appropriate for us, a marginal Christian community, to call the traditional philosophical expression into question? I raise the questions for the next generations of UCC thinkers to ponder. My apologies to these philosophers for taking their ideas and using them here in boldly simplistic ways. Those readers who would like to explore the complexities of their thought and perhaps also challenge my use of them are welcome to consult the following works: Peter Watson, *The Modern Mind* (New York: HarperCollins Publishers, 2002); Simon Critchley, *The Ethics of Deconstruction: Derrida and Levinas* 2nd Edition (West Lafayette, Indiana: Purdue University Press, 1999); Judith Butler, Ernesto Laclau and Slavoj Zizek, *Contingency, Hegemony, Universality: Contemporary Dialogues on the Left* (London: Verso, 2000); and *Thandeka, The Embodied*

Self: Friedrich Schleiermacher's Solution to Kant's Problem of the Empirical Self (Albany: State University of New York, 1995). Their notes and bibliographies will lead you into the primary sources.

4. Yvonne Delk, excerpts from "The Unfinished Agenda: Racism," *New Conversations,* 1989, 40–44. Frederick Trost and Barbara Brown Zikmund, eds. *United and Uniting,* LTH Vol. VII , Part V Document A.3

5. Fernando F. Segovia, "Minority Studies and Christian Studies," in Eleazar S. Fernandez and Fernando F. Segovia eds. *A Dream Unfinished: Theological Reflections on America from the Margins* (Maryknoll, NY: Orbis Books, 2001) 1–36.

6. Gregory (Pope) to Augustine (601 AD)," Mission Work in England (c.590–604)," in Reinhard Ulrich, ed. *Ancient and Medieval Legacies,* LTH, vol. 1 (Cleveland: The Pilgrim Press, 1995) Part III, Document 49.

7. Gregory (Pope) to Augustine.

8. A good short summary of the concerns of the Reformation is John Payne's introduction to the second volume of the Living Theological Heritage of the United Church of Christ. John Payne, "Reformation Roots," in John Payne ed. *Reformation Roots,* LTH, vol. 2 (Cleveland: The Pilgrim Press, 1997) 1–36.

9. The German Reformed Church had its origins in the reformation of specific areas in Germany where the prince chose the Reformed faith, but also in the migration during times of persecution of Protestant refugees, such as the French Huguenots into territories friendly to Reformed Protestantism.

10. John Eliot, "Dialog. I, Kinsman Piumbukhou Speaks," Margaret Lamberts Bendroth, Lawrence N. Jones, and Robert A. Schneider eds. *Outreach and Diversity,* LTH, vol. 5 (Cleveland: The Pilgrim Press, 2000) Part II, Document 19.

11. Eliot, "Dialog. I, p. 204. Eliot seems unaware that the native people also had their own civil government forming a model of democracy under divine principles as good as that the Puritans offered.

12. The main sources are Mourt's *Relation* which contains two letters mentioning the first Thanksgiving, though not by that name, and Bradford Smith, *Bradford of Plymouth* (Philadelphia: J. B. Lippincott Company, 1951) p. 162–163. This is a somewhat sentimental biography of William Bradford, who relying on the Mourt accounts also embellishes the scene somewhat and notes that there were only about ten surviving women to do most of the work of preparing the feast. Mourt's *Relation of the Beginning and Proceedings of the English Plantation Settled at Plimoth in New England,* (London 1622), on page 90 notes that there were about ninety Indians at the feast.

13. A. Knighton Stanley, *The Children is Crying: Congregationalism Among Black People.* (New York: The Pilgrim Press, 1979) 27.

14. Horace Bushnell, "True Wealth . . ." August 1837 Address to Phi Beta Kappa, New Haven, quoted in Paul Barton, "Inter-Ethnic Relations Between

Mexican American and Anglo American Methodists in the U. S. Southwest 1836–1938" in David Maldonado, Jr. ed. *Protestantes/Protestants: Hispanic Christianity Within Mainline Traditions.* (Nashville: Abingdon Press, 1999) 61 note 6. This essay provides additional insight into the Hispanic Protestant cultural creativity. The original of the Bushnell essay can be found in the *North American Review* (January 1838) 301–302.

15. David Maldonado, Jr. ed. *Protestantes/Protestants* contains significant discussions of this difficulty as it still exists.

16. Stanley, *The Children is Crying,* p. 61–62.

17. "The Vitality of Congregationalism," *Congregationalist and Christian Times,* 1 October 1852, in Elizabeth C. Nordbeck and Lowell H. Zuck eds. *Consolidation and Expansion,* LTH vol. 4 Part III, Document 81.

18. Josiah G. Bishop, "Bases and obligations of Christian Missions" (1914) in Margaret Lamberts Bendroth, Lawrence N. Jones, and Robert A. Schneider eds. *Outreach and Diversity* vol. 5, LTH, Part I, Document 2.

19. Paul A. and E. W. Menzel, "What has Chhattisgarh Done for the Evangelical Synod?" (1934) in Bendroth, Jones and Schneider, *Outreach and Diversity* LTH vol. 5 Part I, Document 3, p. 51.

20. Charles E. Schaefer, "The Larger Meaning of Home Missions," (1914) in Bendroth, Jones, and Schneider, *Outreach and Diversity,* LTH vol. 5, Part I, Document 4.

21. Josiah Strong, *Our Country: Its Possible Future and Its Present Crisis,* rev. ed. (New York: Doubleday, Page, and Co., 1912) 222–223. Quoted in Paul Barton, "Interethnic Relations Between Mexican American and Anglo-American Methodists in the U.S. Southwest, 1836–1938," in David Maldonado, Jr. ed. *Protestantes/Protestants: Hispanic Christianity Within Mainline Traditions* (Nashville: Abingdon Press, 1999) 61 note 6. Strong's *Our Country* contains an entire chapter on the issue, "The Anglo Saxon and the World's Future."

22. A. Knighton Stanley, *The Children is Crying: Congregationalism Among Black People* (New York: The Pilgrim Press, 1979) 100.

23. Segovia, "Minority Studies and Christian Studies," p. 23.

24. Extract from Robert Browne, "Booke which Sheweth the Life and Manners of All True Christians, etc." Middelburg, (1582), in Williston Walker, *Creeds and Platforms of Congregationalism.* Reprint of 1893 edition. (New York: The Pilgrim Press, 1991) 18. I modernized the spelling for clarity.

25. From "The Cambridge Platform" (1648) in Walker, *Creeds and Platforms,* p. 204.

26. From "The Cambridge Platform" Walker, p. 205. The term 'militant' translates better as 'activist' or even 'aggressive' rather than as associated with military might or coercion.

27. *The Heidelberg Catechism,* 400th Anniversary Edition, (New York: United Church Press, 1962) 54. Also in John B. Payne, ed., *Reformation Roots,* (Cleveland: The Pilgrim Press, 1997) LTH vol. 2, Part II, Document 21.

28. *The Evangelical Catechism,* reprint of 1957 edition. (Cleveland: United Church Press, 1991) 54.

29. *Evangelical Catechism* (Revised Edition) 1929, in LTH vol. 4, Part II, Document 55, questions 87 and 90.

30. James O'Kelly, "The Author's Apology," 1798 in Elizabeth C. Nordbeck and Lowell H. Zuck, *Consolidation and Expansion,* LTH Vol. 4, Part I, Document 1.

31. Rice Haggard, "The Sacred Import of the Christian Name," 1804 in Nordbeck and Zuck, *Consolidation and Expansion,* LTH vol. 4, Part I, Document 2.

32. Rosemary McCombs Maxey, "Who can sit at the Lord's Table? The Experience of Indigenous Peoples," in Daniel Johnson and Charles Hambrick-Stowe, *Theology and Identity: Traditions, Movements, and Polity in the United Church of Christ* (New York: The Pilgrim Press, 1990) 51–63.

33. Even as early as Browne's "A Treatise of Reformation without Tarying for Anie," (LTH, vol. 1, Document 28) Puritan leaders castigated a tolerant church for suffering open wickedness. Browne did not specify what kinds of wickedness, except to mention the "solemne feastes, as for their Christmasse and Easter, and Whit-suntides, and of all their traditions received from Baal." Righteousness had a particular cultural form for Browne. Anything that could be associated with paganism was especially dangerous.

34. Maxey, "Who Can Sit at the Lord's Table?" p. 61.

35. James Treat, Introduction to Rosemary McCombs Maxey's "Who Can Sit at the Lord's Table," in James Treat ed. *Native and Christian: Indigenous Voices on Religious Identity in the United States and Canada.* (New York: Routledge, 1996) 38. This emphasis is also characteristic of the Congregational spirit and of the Christian churches' ecclesiology.

36. David Hirano, "Theology Among Asian Americans in the United Church of Christ," *Prism,* (Fall 1986) p. 73.

37. David Hirano, "Theology Among Asian Americans," p. 75.

38. Ismael García, "Hispanic Experience and the Protestant Ethic," in David Maldonado, Jr. ed. *Protestantes/Protestants: Hispanic Christianity Within Mainline Traditions* (Nashville: Abingdon, 1999)158.

39. García, "Hispanic Experience," p. 159.

40. Minutes of the Fourth General Synod of the United Church of Christ.

41. Roger Shinn, "Unsettling Problems," in Douglas Horton et. al. *Reform and Renewal.* (Philadelphia: United Church Press, 1966) 28–29.

42. Shinn, "Unsettling Problems," p. 29.

43. Shinn, "Unsettling Problems," p. 30.

44. Norman W. Jackson, "Our Christendom Church and God's Mission," pp. 21–35.

45. Jackson, "Our Christendom Church," p. 31–32.

46. Jackson, "Our Christendom Church," p. 31.

47. Samuel L. Slie, "The United Church of Christ and the Experience of the Black Church," in Johnson and Hambrick-Stowe eds. *Theology and Identity,* pp. 1 and 47.

48. Benjamin E. Chavis, Jr., "Psalm 141" from *Psalms from Prison* (New York: Pilgrim Press, 1983) 158. Quoted in Slie, "The UCC and the Experience of the Black Church," pp. 48–49.

49. Words from the United Church of Christ Statement of Faith.

50. Lawrence N. Jones, "Black Theology in the United Church of Christ," *Prism* (Spring 1986) p. 65.

51. United Church of Christ Commission on Racial Justice, "Pastoral Letter on Contemporary Racism and the Role of the Church," January 18, 1991.

52. Bennie E. Whiten, Jr. "Race, Ethnicity, and the United Church of Christ: 1985–1995," *Prism,* (Fall 1995) p. 73.

53. Whiten, "Race, Ethnicity, and the UCC" p. 73.

54. Bernice Powell Jackson, "Finding Common Ground: The Roles of Faith, Community and Diversity," *New Conversations,* (Spring 1995) p. 4.

55. Jean Alexander, "Trying to be Honest Across Racial Lines," *New Conversations,* (Spring 1995) p. 9 and p. 11.

56. Eleanor Scott Meyers, "The Ambiguity of Racism: Whiteness and the Relations of Race," *New Conversations,* (Spring 1995) p. 16.

57. Meyers, "The Ambiguity of Racism," p. 19.

58. Hollis K. Wilson, "Reflections of an Affirmative Action Officer (1990–1994)" *New Conversations,* (Spring 1995) p. 44.

59. Wilson, "Reflections," p. 44.

60. Geoffrey Black, "Decision Making and the Multiracial, Multicultural Church: A Case for Discernment," *Prism* (Fall 1999) p. 49.

61. Black, "Decision Making" p. 58.

62. Jones, "Black Theology in the UCC," p. 67. Emphasis mine.

63. Cornel West, *Race Matters.* (New York: Vintage Books, 1994) 159.

CHAPTER 3

1. Very few churches defined by parameters of doctrine manage to enforce uniformity of belief, nor do all of them even try. Just as we know we have congregations and individuals whose theological formulations lie well outside the norms of UCC confessional practice, more doctrinally defined churches also have such congregations and members, and even leaders who with varying degrees of openness dissent from the rest in their theological views. Confessional requirements are not a guarantee of unity in theological thought and witness.

2. For a good introduction to Fundamentalist theology by an insider, written between the two twentieth-century periods of open warfare between Fundamentalists and Modernists in the twentieth century, see J. L. Packer's

Fundamentalism and the Word of God (Grand Rapids: Eerdmans, 1958). Several recent histories of the movement and its influences are available including Martin Marty's multivolume study produced in the 1990s by University of Chicago Press. The term Fundamentals refers to a specific set of theological principles first published in the years following 1910 as a series of pamphlets and later repeated in such documents as the 1910 proclamation of the Presbyterian Church General Assembly (later revoked) and in the formation of the World Christian Fundamentals Association 1919. For those unfamiliar with them, they consist of five principles, "The inspiration and infallibility of Scripture, the deity of Christ, His virgin birth and miracles, His penal death for our sins, and His physical resurrection and personal return." (Packer, p. 28) Two recent comparative analyses of fundamentalism in the three related religions, Judaism, Christianity and Islam put it in the context of Modernity as essentially an antimodern movement. Bruce Lawrence, *Defenders of God: The Fundamentalist Revolt Against the Modern Age* (San Francisco: Harper and Row, 1989) and Karen Armstrong, *The Battle for God* (New York: Alfred P. Knopf, 2000).

3. I will discuss the meaning of orthodoxy later, but for now simply say that here it implies congruence with the creeds of the first ecumenical councils, namely the Apostles' Creed and the Creed of Nicaea.

4. Amanda Porterfield, *The Transformation of American Religion: The Story of a Late Twentieth-Century Awakening* (New York: Oxford University Press, 2001) 203.

5. Martin Marty, "M. E. M. O.," *The Christian Century* (June 28, 2003) 47.

6. This phrase comes from a section title in Brad S. Gregory's *Salvation at Stake: Christian Martyrdom in Early Modern Europe* (Cambridge, MA: Harvard University Press, 2001) 78.

7. As I write this, there are disturbing signs that many in the world of the twenty-first century regard religious plurality as dangerous and are moving again to eliminate rival faiths rather than co-exist with them and return to a principle of civic unity by state religion.

8. The philosophical limitations of this assumption are apparent to anyone familiar with postmodern theory but few practice the discipline of trying to see other points of view, or imagine other truths.

9. Martin Luther, "The Freedom of a Christian" (1520) in John Payne, *Reformation Roots,* LTH, vol. 2 (Cleveland: The Pilgrim Press, 1997) 119. This translation is from Harold J. Grimm ed. *Luther's Works: Career of the Reformer,* vol. 31 (Philadelphia: Fortress Press, 1957).

10. Martin Luther, "Formula of Mass and Communion for the Church at Wittenberg," (1523). in John Payne ed. *Reformation Roots, The Living Theological Heritage,* vol. 2. p.130. The excerpt is from Bard Thomson's *Liturgies of the Western Church* (Cleveland: The World Publishing Co., 1951).

11. When using ancient writings, I find it difficult as a feminist historian always to know when to let exclusive language stand. Here and in the work that follows, if I think it important honestly to let the gendered term remain, I will leave it so, if I change it to clarify its inclusive intent, I will place it in square brackets, [like so]. Luther unfortunately recognized no mothers among the important early theologians.

12. Luther, "Formula of Mass," in Payne, *Reformation Roots* LTH vol. 2, Part 2, Document 6.

13. Martin Luther, "Preface to the Small Catechism,"(1529) in J. Payne, *Reformation Roots,* LTH vol. 2, Part II, Document 8.

14. "The Marburg Colloquy" 1959. LTH, vol. 2, Document 13.

15. Luther, "The Freedom of a Christian," in Payne, *Reformation Roots,* LTH vol. 2, Part II, Document 5. I have put the passage in the plural for reasons of inclusivity.

16. Ulrich Zwingli, "Sixty-Seven Articles," (1523) in J. Payne, *Reformation Roots,* LTH vol. 2, Document 10.

17. Zwingli, "Sixty-Seven Articles."

18. Ulrich Zwingli, "Action or Use of the Lord's Supper," (1525) in J. Payne, *Reformation Roots,* LTH vol. 2, Part II, Document 11.

19. A large portion of the Colloquy of Marburg as recorded by the participants is contained in J. Payne, *Reformation Roots,* LTH vol. 2, Part II, Document 13.

20. The 1997 Lutheran-Reformed Full Communion agreement represents a high point in this effort in North America. Excerpts from the documents related to this agreement may be found in LTH, vol. 7, Part 6. Document B. 1. Excerpts from "A Formula of Agreement Between the Evangelical Lutheran Church in America, The Presbyterian Church (U. S. A.), The Reformed Church in America, and the United Church of Christ on Entering into Full Communion on the Basis of A Common Calling." Published in a pamphlet by The Lutheran-Reformed Joint Coordinating Committee, 1996.

21. Jane Dempsey Douglass, *Women, Freedom, and Calvin* (Philadelphia: The Westminster Press, 1985) 117.

22. John Calvin, *Institutes of the Christian Religion* III, xix, 11. John T. McNeill ed. Ford Lewis Battles tr. (Philadelphia: The Westminster Press, MCMLX) 844. The last sentence is changed according to Jane Douglass's usage in *Women, Freedom, and Calvin,* p. 118 for inclusivity. Douglass elaborates on her principles for using inclusive language in historical texts in the same volume pp. 8–9.

23. Jacobus Arminius was a Calvinist theologian who diverged from Calvin particularly on the matter of predestination. Calvin taught the doctrine of predestination, that God, knowing and governing everything, has predestined some souls to eternal life and others to eternal death. He derived this view, as Luther did, from Paul and Augustine. It was a particularly useful theological

doctrine in the face of the problem they identified as works righteousness, the idea that people could earn God's favor by doing good. The result of the doctrine was the necessity of viewing God as terribly arbitrary. It even seems to make God responsible for human evil. Arminius chose to use other possibilities in the theological and biblical record to argue that we can do something toward our own salvation by choosing to respond "yes" to God's grace and God's call. We are Christians by positive response to the call of God, he argued. Calvin was particularly concerned to preserve the absolute freedom of God. He also wanted, as all Reformers did, to emphasize that salvation comes by faith in the grace of God, not from doing good deeds, that we are only able to do good because of God's grace at work in us.

24. Robert Browne, "Treatise of Reformation without Tarying for Anie." Payne, Reformation Roots, LTH, vol. 2, #28.

25. Humanism in the period of the Renaissance needs to be distinguished from the philosophical stance labeled humanism or secular humanism in more recent times. Renaissance Humanism was a movement characterized above all by an interest in literature, in human reflection on the world and on religious and ethical truth. One of the most influential projects of the Renaissance Humanists was the recovery of the original languages of the Biblical text. They sought out the Greek and Hebrew manuscripts instead of using the customary Latin text. They also looked for the earliest manuscripts in their desire to find the first edition or the earliest possible text of the Bible, the one closest to the original inspiration. In addition, they were interested in translating that text into the vernacular languages. It was the Humanists who also recovered an interest in history, in questioning the claims of tradition using documents as evidence. They thus uncovered the forgery of the Donation of Constantine, a document that had been thought to give the Pope secular jurisdiction over large territories in the Italian peninsula. In their interest in ethics, the Humanists were alarmed by the corruption of the church in many of its higher levels, and the ignorance of the clergy in its lower levels and were among the strongest advocates of reform. They were not however nonreligious people. They were people of deep faith who nevertheless understood human reason to be an important tool for discerning the truth.

26. The experimental method entails a systematic investigation of a question about the physical world or the world of human behavior. The key element of the method is the design of experiments and observations that will answer a particular, well defined question. The experiment needs to be reproducible, providing the same results each time when performed under the same conditions by any person. This goal of this systematic investigation is to understand the laws which govern the physical world and make it reliable and predictable. The experimental method rests on the assumption that like conditions and processes always produce like results, that the processes at work in the physical world do not change from day to day. The experimental method is applied to

human life based on the same assumptions but with less satisfactory results, because experiments with human subjects about aspects of human behavior were and are complicated by the inability of the experimenter to completely control the conditions sufficiently to reproduce the experiment. Nonetheless, the Enlightenment produced a body of knowledge that made possible enormous technological development in the subsequent two centuries.

27. Jonathan Edwards, *A Treatise Concerning Religious Affections,* John E. Smith ed. (New Haven: Yale University Press, 1959) Part III.

28. The words "myth" and "legend" have also shifted meaning over time. In the Enlightenment thought they have the connotation of untruth. They are either fanciful inventions, or misunderstandings, but either way they are not true and therefore harmful. In contemporary times, after much academic investigation of myth and legend and their use in many societies, as well as in the literature of many cultures, we have recovered a sense of the kind of truth conveyed in myth and legend, not usually factual truth, but symbolic truth, understandings of the human psyche or the collective unconscious for instance, or poetic attempts to articulate experiences of the divine, or records of historical events preserved in larger than life form but not completely separated from other evidence.

29. After the Reformation, as the Protestants became severely divided and associated with the rising nation states, Protestant theology focused on illuminating and elaborating ever smaller points of difference in an effort to maintain clearly separate theological identities. Many put these theological differences openly in the service of national identity.

30. Philip Jacob Spener, *Pia Desideria.* Trans. Theodore Tappert. (Philadelphia: Fortress Press, 1964) 87–122. Also in LTH vol. 4, Part II, Document 39.

31. An account of this union, prepared during the union negotiations between the Evangelical Synod of North America and the Reformed Church in the United States, can be found in the article by C. Schieler, "Wie die Union der lutherischen und reformierten Kirchenkörper entstanden ist," *The Theological Magazine* (of the Evangelical Synod) (January 1, 1934) 38–44. A good English language account is Theophil W. Menzel, "European Background–Evangelical," in David Dunn et. al. *A History of the Evangelical and Reformed Church* (New York: The Pilgrim Press, 1990) rev. ed. pp. 147–157.

32. Here "affections" refers not simply to feelings of liking something or someone, but rather all feelings including both emotions and feelings derived from the senses.

33. Jonathan Edwards, *Religious Affections.* John E. Smith ed. (New Haven: Yale University Press, 1959) Part III.

34. Jonathan Edwards, "The State of Religion," (1744) in Charles Hambrick-Stowe ed. *Colonial and National Beginnings,* LTH vol. 3, Part I, Document 9.

35. Edwards, "The State of Religion."
36. Edwards, "The State of Religion."
37. Edwards, *Religious Affections,* p. 291.
38. Edwards, *Religious Affections,* p. 411.
39. Edwards, *Religious Affections,* p. 298.
40. The best short discussion I know of the complexities of Edwards' thought is William A. Clebsch, *American Religious Thought: A History* (Chicago: Chicago University Press, 1973). He makes this point particularly in the second chapter, "The Sensible Spirituality of Jonathan Edwards," p. 17–18. A more recent and longer work on Edwards is George Marsden, *Jonathan Edwards: A Life.* (New Haven: Yale University Press, 2003).
41. Clebsch, *American Religious Thought,* p. 18.
42. Clebsch, p. 18.
43. Clebsch, p. 21. Clebsch here points out that Harriet Beecher Stowe recognized this as Edwards' contribution in her book *Old Town Folks* (Boston: 1897) p. 229.
44. Clebsch, p. 191 note 18.
45. W. H. Walsh, "Immanuel Kant," in Paul Edwards ed. *The Encyclopedia of Philosophy* (New York: Macmillan Publishing Company, Inc., 1967) vol.4, p. 322.
46. Immanuel Kant, "Foundation of the Metaphysics of Morals," in *The Foundation of the Metaphysics of Morals and What is Enlightenment?,* trans. Lewis White Beck. (Indianapolis: The Bobbs-Merrill Company, Inc., 1959) 9.
47. Kant, "Foundation of the Metaphysics of Morals," 17.
48. W. H. Walsh, "Immanuel Kant," p. 306.
49. Immanuel Kant, "What is Enlightenment?" in *The Foundation of the Metaphysics of Morals and What is Enlightenment?,* trans. Lewis White Beck., 86–87.
50. Thandeka, *The Embodied Self: Friedrich Schleiermacher's Solution to Kant's Problem of the Empirical Self.* (Albany, NY: State University of New York Press, 1995) is an excellent discussion of this particular problem. Especially important is the relationship between human reason and religious experience that underlies the attempts by theologians such as Edwards and Schleiermacher to understand the Christian faith using both modes of knowing.
51. Thandeka, *The Embodied Self,* pp.100–104. This reliance on immediate awareness compares to such thinking in Edwards, and has a mystical quality.
52. Friedrich Schleiermacher, *On Religion: Speeches to Its Cultured Despisers,* trans. John Oman, (New York: Frederick Ungar Publishing Co., 1955) 139.
53. Schleiermacher, *On Religion,* pp. 148–149.
54. "F. D. E. Schleiermacher on the "Natural Heresies" of Christianity," in Alister McGrath ed. *The Christian Theology Reader* 2nd ed. (Malden, MA: Blackwell Publishers, Ltd., 2001) 286–287.
55. These documents may be found in volumes 2 and 3 of The Living Theological Heritage of the United Church of Christ.

56. Reinhard Groscurth, “Conversion and Identity, The United Churches: Origins, Progress, Relationships,” *The Ecumenical Review* (October 1995) 440–450.

57. George W. Dunn, “Correspondence,” Raleigh, N. C., Dec. 11, 1879, *Herald of Gospel Liberty,* (21 February 1880) p. 3, reprinted in Nordbeck and Zuck eds. *Consolidation and Expansion,* LTH vol. 4, Part I, Document 23.

58. In the Living Theological Heritage volume *Consolidation and Expansion* several other documents contain such summaries, for example, David Millard’s “Six Principles and the Evolution of a Denomination 1834;” and “Manifesto at the General Convention” and “Basis of Union” 1874.“Plan of Union of the General Convention 1890.”

59. Joseph Badger, “Address” *Christian Palladium* (1 May 1834), 1–2 reprinted in Nordbeck and Zuck eds. Consolidation and Expansion LTH vol. 4, Part I, Document 16.

60. Simon Clough, “Creeds Rejected,” *Christian Palladium* (15 March 1838) reprinted in LTH vol. 4, Part I, Document 27.

61. James Hastings Nichols ed, *The Mercersburg Theology.* (New York: Oxford University Press, 1966) 3–10. James I. Good, *History of the Reformed Church in the U. S. in the Nineteenth Century* (New York: The Board of Publication of the Reformed Church in America MCMXI) viii, dates the movement more precisely as the “Liturgical Controversy” 1844–1878. He was a member of the party in the church opposed to the Mercersburg liturgy. Don Herbert Yoder, “Christian Unity in Nineteenth-Century America,” in Ruth Rouse and Stephen Charles Neill eds. *A History of the Ecumenical Movement, 1517–1948,* second edition (Philadelphia: Westminster Press, 1967) pp. 246–247. Yoder gives slightly different dates, 1836 to 1871. 1836 (actually 1837) was the year the Reformed seminary moved to Mercersburg and 1871 perhaps because the results of the First Vatican Council made Protestant and Catholic unity even more difficult to imagine.

62. For the influences of the Mercersburg theology on the United Church of Christ Book of Worship, see A. Hale Schroer, “The Spirit of Mercersburg in the Book of Worship,” *Prism* vol. 4 no. 2 (Fall 1989) 23–33.

63. J. H. Nevin, letter to Henry Harbaugh, ca. 1860, reprinted in LTH vol. 4, Part IV, Document 88.

64. John Williamson Nevin, “Antichrist and the Sect,” in Nichols, ed. *The Mercersburg Theology,* p. 101–102.

65. Philip Schaff, *The Principle of Protestantism,* John W. Nevin trans. (1845), Bard Thompson and George H. Bricker, Eds. (Philadelphia: United Church Press, 1964) 73–74. Emphasis in the original. It is difficult not to be taken aback by the anti-Jewish rhetoric common in the theology of the day.

66. Schaff, *The Principle of Protestantism,* 228.

67. Gary Dorrien argues for this middle way in *The Making of American Liberal Theology: Imagining Progressive Religion 1805–1900* (Louisville:

Westminster John Knox, 2001) xxi-xxii. Dorrien writes: "My account accents the mediationist character of liberal theology. The "third way" rhetoric of early American liberal Christianity was not merely a rhetorical posture. The early American liberal theologians abhorred the tradition smashing terror and "infidelism" of the French Revolution. . . . Channing, Parker, and Bushnell believed that orthodoxy and infidelism were closely related, often as cause and effect . . . They reasoned that the problem was not the Enlightenment, but rather the ecclesiastical power of a discredited orthodoxy that refused to reform. . . . [Liberalism] steered a faithful, but critical path between the literalistic dogmatism of Christian orthodoxy and the antireligious dogmatism of modern rationalism."

68. The Oxford English Dictionary in its long article on the word "man" indicates that it is never unambiguously generic. It derives from a very old Indo-European, Teutonic word that in its earliest appearance seems to have meant human being, and at that time there was separate vocabulary for man and woman as having separate gender. However, modern English fails to distinguish between man as human being and man as adult male human being. The inclusive language question has its origin in the effect of this ambiguity on women's sense of identity, agency, and value in society.

69. Rev. Bernice A Buehler to Robert Moss November 9, 1972. United Church of Christ Archives, Robert Moss Papers, Box 3 File Folder 29. Quoted by permission from the United Church of Christ Archives.

70. Robert Moss to Rev. Robert K. Nace, December 5, 1975. United Church of Christ Archives, Robert Moss Papers, Box 3 File Folder 29. Quoted by permission from the United Church of Christ Archives.

71. The texts of all three forms of the Statement of Faith may be found in the *Book of Worship* (Cleveland: The United Church Office for Church Life and Leadership, 1986) pp. 512–514 and in many other places in United Church of Christ literature.

72. More about this in Chapter 5. See Gary Dorrien, *The Making of Protestant Liberal Theology in America* for a general discussion.

73. Craig R. Prentiss ed., *Religion and the Creation of Race and Ethnicity* (New York: New York University Press, 2003).

74. The problems of poetry in hymns and the desire to let authors speak for themselves have not yet been resolved.

75. This quick move to a Unitarian position on the Trinity, or to language for God that kept the trinitarian form without the classical creedal language seemed easy at the time, but ignored centuries of Christian struggle, including fighting wars, over the meaning of the words. It is no surprise that feminist solutions to problems of exclusive language in Christian theology and liturgy have reopened old controversies.

76. This is not out of the question. For instance Andrew Walls in his recent work *The Cross-Cultural Process in Christian History* (Maryknoll, NY: Orbis

Books, 2002) p. 29 argues that Christianity survives by translation and retranslation into new cultural forms. "It is as though there is some inherent fragility, some built-in vulnerability, in Christianity, considered as popular profession . . . this vulnerability is also linked with the essentially vernacular nature of Christian faith, which rests on a massive act of translation, the Word made flesh, God translated into a specific segment of social reality as Christ is received there."

77. Jacquelyn Grant, *White Women's Christ and Black Women's Jesus: Feminist Christology and Womanist Response* (Atlanta, Ga.: Scholars Press, 1989).

78. A basic understanding of this theological position can be found quickly in "Nominalism" in Jerald C. Brauer, ed. *The Westminster Dictionary of the Christian Church* (Philadelphia: The Westminster Press, MCMLXXI) 606–607.

CHAPTER 4

1. Wade Clark Roof and William McKinney, *American Mainline Religion: Its Changing Shape and Future* (New Brunswick: Rutgers University Press, 1987). McKinney is himself a member of the United Church of Christ.

2. Throughout this chapter I wish to distinguish the adjective "liberal" from the noun "liberalism." Liberalism indicates a conscious, deliberate choice to define one's theology, politics, economics, or ethical positions in liberal terms and to act accordingly in the world. However, a person or church may exhibit characteristics one could describe as liberal without adopting a comprehensive liberalism. From the Reformation to the present, the definitions of "liberal" and "liberalism" have shifted and multiplied and we can use neither term satisfactorily without being aware of their complexity.

3. Roof and McKinney, *American Mainline Religion,* p.86–87.

4. Roof and McKinney, *American Mainline Religion,* p. 85.

5. Roof and McKinney, *American Mainline Religion,* p.86.

6. Charles Sanders Peirce (1839–1914) was an important American philosopher. He published a series of six essays in *Popular Science Monthly* (1877–1878) on the subject of doubt and belief. *Popular Science Monthly* is still in print, but those who have read it recently will rarely have found in it anything this theologically useful. The entertainment of doubt is still present in the work of UCC theologians. The recent book by James M. Gustafson is a particularly interesting case in point. James M. Gustafson, *An Examined Life: The Grace of Self-Doubt* (Minneapolis: Fortress Press, 2004).

7. One of the results of the Medieval Christian Crusades against the Muslims in the Holy Land was a growing knowledge of the Arabic culture and the high development of their intellectual traditions in medicine, astronomy, chemistry (alchemy), and their use of Aristotle's philosophy. This inadvertent fertilization of European culture with new ideas set the stage for the Renaissance and the Reformation. In addition to the Crusades, merchants

traveling in eastern Asia brought back from China inventions such as gunpowder, paper money, and the printing press. These new technologies served both the spread of new ideas and the development of centralized national power. The Church struggled to cope with these new ideas and the new context they created, and though the Church survived, it ended up splintered and weakened and finally, in Europe and much of North America, returned to its original status as a religion outside the centers of power even if it still has respect and influence.

8. James Turner, *Without God, Without Creed: The Origin of Unbelief in America* (Baltimore: Johns Hopkins University Press, 1985) p. 267. Turner put it this way: "Unbelief emerged because church leaders too often forgot the transcendence essential to any worthwhile God. They committed religion *functionally* to making the world better in human terms and *intellectually* to modes of knowing God fitted only for understanding this world. They did this because, trying to meet the challenge of modernity, they virtually surrendered to it."

9. An older but good summary of this arrangement can be found in R. W. Southern, *Western Society and the Church in the Middle Ages* (Baltimore: Penguin Books, 1970).

10. Since this office of the church is currently a center of critical conversation in ecumenical circles, I will elaborate on its etymology here. The earliest Judeo-Christian uses of the term *episcopé* are found in the Septuagint, the Greek translation of the Hebrew Scriptures used in both the Greek-speaking synagogues and in the early churches.

The Septuagint uses the term episcopé to translate another word from Hebrew. *Phakad* or *Pekuthah* has two meanings. The first is a visitation of divine power such as in Genesis 50:24. (Then Joseph said to his brothers, "I am about to die; but God will surely come to you . . .(*episcopé*)) , or Job 10:12 (You have granted me life and steadfast love, and your care (*episcopé*) has preserved my spirit).

A second use of the word *phakad* in the Septuagint suggests a more familiar meaning. The Septuagint uses the term in Numbers 4:16 (Eleazar son of Aaron the priest shall have charge (episcopé) of the oil for the light . . .). Other meanings include to attend to, visit graciously, (Is. 23.17, Gen. 50.24, Je. 15.15) - to seek with interest (Is 26..16), - to observe with special interest, to see how someone fares (Job 10.12), - to lay a charge upon , muster, appoint, (1 Sam 17.18), - to visit to search or test (Job 7.18), - to visit to punish (Jeremiah 6.6).

The possible reasons for the Greek–speaking Jewish scholars use of the term *episcopé* for the Hebrew *pekuthah* can be found in its use in the wider society of the ancient Hellenistic world. Its pre-Christian use can be found in Plato's Republic. Plato uses *episcopé* to refer to the guardians of the people, the philosopher kings. Officials of many religions in the Roman Empire were called *episcopos*, carrying a general meaning of leader, guardian, or overseer.

In the Gospels, the word also refers to a visitation of divine power as in Luke 19:44 (. . . you did not recognize the time of your visitation (*episcopes*) from God), and in the Epistles, in 1 Peter 2:12 (. . . glorify God when he comes/visits (episcopes) to judge). We find the more specific meaning of *episcopé* with which we are used to dealing, namely *episcopé* as oversight of the church, in the Pastoral Epistles, though it also appears in Acts and even the Old Testament.

11. All of these documents in English translation may be found in John B. Payne ed., *Reformation Roots,* LTH, vol. 2. For the purposes of this work, I have not sought out the texts in the original languages, though that exercise greatly improves one's understanding of the issues involved in these theological developments.

12. Ulrich Zwingli, "Sixty-Seven Articles," (1523) in J. Payne, *Reformation Roots,* LTH vol. 2, Part II, Document 10.

13. "The Marburg Colloquy," (1529) in Payne, *Reformation Roots,* LTH vol. 2, Part II, Document 13.

14. William Farel and John Calvin, "The Geneva Confession" (1536) in Payne, *Reformation Roots,* LTH vol. 2, Part II, Document 16.

15. Calvin, Letter to Pierre Viret, April 7, 1549. Translated with variations by William Bouwsma, *John Calvin a Sixteenth Century Portrait* (New York: Oxford University Press, 1988) 23.

16. Bouwsma, *Calvin,* 185.

17. The magisterial reforms were those carried out with the blessing or at the behest of the civil government. Luther relied on the protection of his prince, the Swiss city councils acted to reform their churches, the English monarchs removed the Church of England from the jurisdiction of the Pope. Most of the Roman Catholic reforms were also magisterial because of the close alliance between the Catholic church and the rulers of the time. The nonmagisterial Protestant reformers, primarily the Anabaptist groups and the Socinian Unitarians, deliberately separated themselves from secular society and participation in civil life and faced considerable persecution. The nonmagisterial Catholic reformers had little immediate effect on the whole Church though they were able to reform certain dioceses and religious orders.

18. John Calvin, *Institutes of the Christian Religion,* John T. McNeill ed., Ford Lewis Battles, tr. (Philadelphia: The Westminster Press, MCMLX) vol. 1. Book Two, chapter XI, section 13.

19. "The Examination of Mrs. Anne Hutchinson" (1637) Charles Hambrick-Stowe, *Colonial and National Beginnings,* (Cleveland: The Pilgrim Press, 1998) LTH, vol.3, Part I, Document 3. p. 57.

20. Martin Luther, "An Appeal to the Ruling Class of German Nationality as to the Amelioration of the State of Christendom," (1520) in John Dillenberger ed. *Martin Luther: Selections from his Writings* (Garden City, NY: Anchor Books, 1961) 407–408.

21. Martin Luther, "The Pagan Servitude of the Church (or more commonly, The Babylonian Captivity of the Church," (1520) in Dillenberger, ed. *Martin Luther,* p. 349. I retained the masculine pronoun in this translation of Luther's work because it is clear to me that he had no intention of according to women the same privileges of preaching and administering the sacraments that he explicitly gives to male laity under certain circumstances, nor does he explicitly include women in the body of members qualified to choose a person from among them to do these things representing the church.

22. "The Examination of Mrs. Anne Hutchinson" (1637) Hambrick-Stowe, *Colonial and National Beginnings,* LTH, vol.3, Part I, Document 3.

23. "The Examination of Mrs. Anne Hutchinson," in Hambrick-Stowe, *Colonial and National Beginnings,* LTH, vol. 3, Part I, Document 3.

24. The people of Massachusetts eventually recognized their error with regard to Hutchinson and to the Quaker Mary Dyer. Their statues now stand at the entrances to the Massachusetts State House in tribute to their stand for freedom of conscience.

25. "The Cambridge Platform," (1648) in Hambrick-Stowe, *Colonial and National Beginnings,* LTH, vol. 3 Part I., Document 6, p. 103–104.

26. Jonathan Edwards, "The State of Religion," in Hambrick-Stowe ed., *Colonial and National Beginning,* vol.3 (Cleveland: The Pilgrim Press, 1998) 147.

27. Edwards, *Religious Affections,* pp. 266 and 357.

28. William A. Clebsch, *American Religious Thought: A History* (Chicago: University of Chicago Press, 1978) 15–16.

29. Here Clebsch is following H. Richard Niebuhr, *The Kingdom of God in America.* 187–195. Quoted in *American Religious Thought* 191 note 22. Most United Church of Christ members know only Edwards' dramatic sermon "Sinners in the Hands of an Angry God," probably because we find it in the American literature anthologies we study in school, and we are startled to find that the theology in that sermon does not reflect the main stream of his theological thought.

30. Clebsch, *American Religious Thought,* 16.

31. Jonathan Edwards, "The Nature of True Virtue," in Clarence H. Faust and Thomas H. Johnson, *Jonathan Edwards: Representative Selections, with Introduction, Bibliography, and Notes* Revised Edition (New York: Hill and Wang, Inc., 1962) 349. A selection from "The Nature of True Virtue" can be found in nearly every collection of Edwards writings.

32. James Turner, *Without God, Without Creed: The Origin of Unbelief in America,* provides a searching look at this phenomenon.

33. I suspect that in this regard I should confess to being somewhat Tillichian in my theological method.

34. Friedrich Schleiermacher, *On Religion: Speeches to its Cultured Despisers,* tr. John Oman, (New York: Frederick Unger Publishing Company). The argument is woven throughout the speeches, but stated particularly well in the sec-

ond speech "The Nature of Religion." "Through the gradual operation of the fellowship between knowledge and feeling, they have arrived at the immediate feeling that there is nothing even in their own nature that is not a work of this Spirit, an exhibition and application of these laws. In virtue of this feeling, all that touches their life becomes truly a world, a unity permeated by the Divinity that fashions it." pp. 57–58.

35. Friedrich Schleiermacher, *The Christian Faith.* Trans. by H. R. Mackintosh and J. S. Stewart from *Der christliche Glaube nach den Grundsätzen der evangelischen Kirch im Zusammemhang dargestellt,* 2nd ed, Berlin, 1830. (Edinburgh: T & T Clark, 1928) 12.

36. Schleiermacher, *The Christian Faith,* 320.

37. Schleiermacher, *The Christian Faith,* 289.

38. Schleiermacher, *The Christian Faith,* 427.

39. Friedrich Schleiermacher, "A Letter . . ." in Elizabeth Nordbeck and Lowell Zuck eds. *Consolidation and Expansion.* LTH, vol. 4, Part II, Document 37.

40. The EKU united in July 2003 with fourteen other Landeskirchen (state churches) to form Die Union Evangelischer Kirchen (UEK).

41. "The Christians," in Nordbeck and Zuck, *Consolidation and Expansion,* LTH, vol. 4, Introduction to Part I, p. 6.

42. Rebecca Miller, "Duty of Females," (1841) Nordbeck and Zuck, *Consolidation and Expansion,* LTH, vol. 4, Part I, Document 11.

43. George W. Dunn, "Correspondence," Nordbeck and Zuck, *Consolidation and Expansion,* LTH, vol. 4, Part I, Document 23. One could also mention the American Missionary Association schools of the Congregational churches though Dunn does not. They also encouraged those who attended their schools to join their churches.

44. This issue of Schleiermacher's pantheism persists, and forms one piece of twentieth century rejection of liberalism. To clarify, Schleiermacher never claimed to be a pantheist. In the Christian Faith he wrote, "let us accordingly hold Pantheism fast to the usual formula of One and All: then God and the world will remain distinct at least as regards function, and thus such [human beings], since [they] reckon [themselves] as belonging to the world, can feel [themselves], along with this All, to be dependent on that which is the corresponding One. Such states of mind can scarcely be distinguished from the religious emotions of many a Monotheist. At any rate, the distinction . . . between a God who is outside of and above the world, and a God who is in the world, does not particularly meet the point, for nothing can strictly be said about God in terms of the antithesis between internal and external without imperiling in some way the divine omnipotence and omnipresence." (p. 38) Schaff argued that Schleiermacher derived his position from Spinoza (1632–1677), the Jewish philosopher, who, basing his thought in Medieval arguments particularly those of Maimonides and the Scholastics, argued that the Creator of the world was imminent in it, continuing to create, rather than transcendent

and simply the first cause. Spinoza thought that the mind and the body were the same thing, unified by one substance. That unity was an expression of the divine. (For more guidance to Spinoza's thought see Alisdair MacIntyre, "Spinoza," *Encyclopedia of Philosophy* (New York: Macmillan Company, 1967) vol. 7, pp. 530–541). Schleiermacher followed him in this line of thought. This is not the same as claiming that everything is divine. A more recent student of Schleiermacher, Thandeka, argues that panentheist would be a better term for Schleiermacher's thought. She quotes Charles Hartshorne's definition (in *The Divine Reality: A Social Conception of God* (New Haven: Yale University Press, 1948) p. 89: "'panentheism' is an appropriate term for the view that deity is in some real aspect distinguishable from and independent of any and all relative items and yet, taken as an actual whole, includes all relative items." (Thandeka, *The Embodied Self*, p. 123 note 26.)

45. Philip Schaff, "German Theories of Development," from *What is Church History?* (Philadelphia: 1846) in James Hastings Nichols ed. *The Mercersburg Theology.* (New York: Oxford University Press, 1966) 155–156.

46. These of course were following the Arminian strain in Calvinism, the ideas which influenced the Wesleys, but against which the orthodox Calvinists maintained their view of Predestination.

47. Gary Dorrien's characterization of nineteenth-century liberal theologians as trying to hold a " 'third way' between the authority-based orthodoxies of traditional Christianity and the spiritless materialism of modern atheism or deism" (*Imagining Progressive Religion* p. xiii) seems to me to fit a figure like Finney. Charles Hambrick-Stowe in his biography of Finney wrote, "Charles Finney certainly did not embrace every element of typical evangelical religion (e.g., he was not a premillennialist), but in many ways he was a mediating figure. He held conflicting tendencies together by his zeal for souls, his passion for justice, and his prayerful love of God." (Charles Hambrick-Stowe, *Charles G. Finney and the Spirit of American Evangelicalism* (Grand Rapids: William B. Eerdmans Publishing Company, 1996) xiv.

48. Finney detailed the methods in his *Lectures on Revivals.*

49. Horace Bushnell, *Christian Nurture*. Reprint from the 1861 edition. (Cleveland: The Pilgrim Press, 1994) 65–68.

50. Bushnell, *Christian Nurture*, 82–83.

51. Bushnell, *Christian Nurture*, 10.

52. Bushnell, "Christian Nurture," in Margaret Lamberts Bendroth, Lawrence N. Jones, and Robert A. Schneider eds. *Outreach and Diversity.* LTH vol. 5, Part I, Document 11.

53. Bushnell, "Preliminary Dissertation on the Nature of Language as Related to Thought and Spirit," from *God in Christ* (Hartford: 1849) in Sidney E. Ahlstrom ed. *Theology in America: The Major Protestant Voices from Puritanism to Neo-Orthodoxy* (Indianapolis: The Bobbs-Merrill Company, Inc., 1967) 332–333.

54. Bushnell, "On the Nature of Language," 348.

55. Turner, *Without God, Without Creed,* 182–183.

56. Charles Darwin, *The Autobiography of Charles Darwin 1809–1882,* Nora Barlow ed. (New York: W. W. Norton and Company, 1958) pp. 92–93.

57. Darwin, *The Autobiography* p. 94.

58. Gary Dorrien, *Imagining Progressive Religion* discusses this trend in several places, most particularly in his treatment of Henry Ward Beecher.

59. It is important to note that Marx and others made extensive use of Judeo-Christian traditions of justice in developing their thought. They were most against the connections of the church as institution with the economic privilege of the upper classes.

60. Washington Gladden, "The Church and the Social Crisis," Bendroth, Jones, and Schneider, eds., *Outreach and Diversity,* LTH, vol. 5, Part II, Document 50.

61. Elmer Arndt, "Towards the Development of a Social Consciousness," Bendroth, Jones, and Schneider, eds., *Outreach and Diversity,* LTH, vol. 5, Part II, Document 54.

62. H. Richard Niebuhr, *The Church Against the World* (Chicago: Willett, Clark and Company, 1935). I used the introduction reprinted in Sidney E. Ahlstrom ed. *Theology in America: The Major Protestant Voices From Puritanism to Neo-Orthodoxy* (Indianapolis: The Bobbs-Merrill Company, Inc., 1967) 590–618.

63. H. Richard Niebuhr, *The Church Against the World,* 615. The concept of loyalty is strongly suggestive of Josiah Royce's philosophy of community.

64. This theology is outlined most clearly in Reinhold Niebuhr, *Moral Man and Immoral Society: A Study in Ethics and Politics* (New York: Charles Scribner's Sons, 1932).

65. Henry P. van Dusen, *The Vindication of Liberal Theology: A Tract for the Times* (New York: Charles Scribner's Sons, 1963) p. 18. "Here we confront a divided voice among "liberal" Christians themselves. Many who gladly confess themselves "liberals in theology" have been at pains to deny that "Liberalism" is a Theology. Rather, they maintain, it is an "outlook," an "approach," a "point of view," a "spirit"—the "liberal spirit" in Theology. Thus, my revered teacher and predecessor, Dr. Henry Sloane Coffin: "By "liberalism" is meant that spirit which revers truth supremely, and therefore craves freedom to ascertain, to discuss, to publish, and to pursue that which is believed to be true, and seeks fellowship in its discovery." ["Can Liberalism Survive," in *Religion in Life* (Spring, 1935) 194.] Assuredly that is the outlook which animates theological liberals, which sets them on their quest and guides them throughout their course."

66. In 1973 the United Church of Christ dismissed its Theology Commission, lodging that work with the newly created Office of Church Life and Leadership. However, the OCLL staff never enjoyed sufficient time and resources for disciplined theological work. Perusing the theological justifica-

tions for action taken in UCC settings reveals increasingly shallow discussions, sometimes only passing references to Jesus' command to love our neighbors or the prophet's call for "justice to roll down like waters."

67. "The Dubuque Declaration," *New Conversations* (Spring 1985) 17. The document was adopted by the Board of Directors of the United Church People for Biblical Witness, in Dubuque, Iowa, November 17, 1983. Gerald R. Sanders, in his commentary in the same volume explains, "The Dubuque Declaration is neither so presumptuous to be called a "creed" nor pretentious enough to be called a "confession." It is a declaration. A declaration attempts to set before the church certain teachings that appear to be endangered in the life of the church. . . . The Dubuque Declaration has six major concerns, which it sets before the United Church of Christ. In these statements are affirmed: the Lordship of Christ; the Trinitarian faith as confessed by the Church catholic; the sacrificial atonement of Christ Jesus; the Holy Scripture as the infallible rule for the faith and practice of the church; one is redeemed through the free grace of Christ Jesus; and being called to works of mercy, piety, and justice for all tongues and races." p. 18.

68. "A Most Difficult and Urgent Time," *New Conversations* (Spring 1985) 2–3.

69. "The Craigville Colloquy Letter," *New Conversations* (Spring 1985) 7–10.

70. James R. Smucker, "Response: Christians for Justice Action," *New Conversations* (Spring 1985) 44.

71. Susan B. Thistlethwaite, "Theological Ferment in the United Church of Christ," in Dorothy C. Bass and Kenneth B. Smith eds. *The United Church of Christ: Studies in Identity and Polity* (Chicago: Exploration Press, 1987) 51.

72. Barbara Brown Zikmund quoted in Thistlethwaite, "Theological Ferment," 52.

73. Don Armstrong, Mal Bertram, Bob Lee, Clyde Miller, Valerie Russell, Donna Schaper, and Bill Webber, "The Prophet Speaks to Our Times," in New Conversations (Spring 1985) 25.

74. Here I would like to acknowledge with gratitude several conversations I have had with Sharon Thornton, Professor of Pastoral Theology at Andover Newton Theological Seminary. Sharon first pointed out to me the difference between the doubt of the believer and the doubt of the cynic.

75. Andrew F. Walls, *The Cross-Cultural Process in Christian History* (Maryknoll, NY: Orbis Books, 2002) 47.

CHAPTER 5

1. Executive Council for the United Church of Christ, *The Constitution and Bylaws of the United Church of Christ* (Cleveland: United Church Resources, 2001). This document is also easily accessible on the United Church of Christ Web site.

2. *The Constitution and Bylaws of the United Church of Christ,* 2001.

3. "The United Church of Christ Statement of Faith" can be found in several places, perhaps most readily in the *Book of Worship* (New York: United Church Resources, 1986) 512, on the United Church of Christ Web site, or in *United and Uniting,* LTH, vol. 7, Part 1, Document B.1.

4. "In 1983–84, amendments to the Constitution and Bylaws of the United Church of Christ introduced new language of "covenantal relationship" to describe the manner in which the partners are to work with one another." Office of Church Life and Leadership, *United Church of Christ Manual on Ministry: Perspectives and Procedures for Ecclesiastical Authorization of Ministry* (Cleveland: United Church of Christ Office for Church Life and Leadership, 1991, reprint of 1986 edition) 6.

5. United Church of Christ, *The Constitution and Bylaws of the United Church of Christ* (Cleveland: Executive Council of the United Church of Christ, 2000) 3.

6. Philippians 2:7.

7. I am aware that in Biblical scholarship the identity of this scroll is debatable.

8. *The Oxford English Dictionary* article for "church" contains a lengthy discussion of the roots of the word in Teutonic and Anglo-Saxon descriptions of Christian meeting places, derived from the Greek *kyrios* (lord) or the Lord's house, and thus originally referred to the building rather than the people.

9. John Calvin, *Institutes of the Christian Religion* tr. Ford Lewis Battles (Philadelphia: The Westminster Press, 1960) II.10.4.

10. Calvin, *Institutes of the Christian Religion* IV.8.6.

11. In a long argument, Calvin puts forward the view that "infant baptism best accords with Christ's institution and the nature of the sign." *Institutes* IV.11.

12. Jeremiah 31:33.

13. Original sin is a concept subject to many debates within the UCC. Some regard it as an outmoded, even dangerous idea. Others find it helpful in understanding the human condition. In these chapters I use it descriptively when the theologian I am discussing used the term. Those who find it a useful theological term, particularly with regard to social structures of racism, corporate greed, war and dysfunctional families from which individuals cannot extract themselves do not necessarily hold all of the corollary positions Calvin and others have held. I do not think Augustine and others in the early centuries were right to connect original sin to sexuality and primarily to the sexual lives of human beings. That Augustinian concept I think has done much harm, and therefore, I urge anyone who finds the term useful to be careful to think through its connotations and definitions because it comes to us with such a weight of former meanings.

14. Calvin laid out his theology of God the Redeemer in the second book of the Institutes. He subscribed to Anselm's theology though he relied mainly on Augustine. He followed the basic outline of Anselm, based in the feudal society's concern for honor, that the incarnation was necessary to satisfy the insult done to God's infinite honor in Adam's disobedience because a finite human being could not do it. But Calvin also made use of older ransom or rescue atonement theology, that God in Christ paid a ransom to save us from our condition, and then defeated the powers of sin and death in the resurrection. See an excerpt from Anselm's *Cur Deus Homo* in LTH, vol. 1, Part III, Document 56.

15. William Ames, Introduction to "The Marrow of Theology, in Payne, *Reformation and Roots,* LTH vol. 2, Part III, Document 31. The whole book is well worth reading, William Ames, *The Marrow of Theology* trans. and ed. John D. Eusden (Boston: The Pilgrim Press, 1968).

16. I am aware that there are at least two understandings of the development of covenant theology in the Puritan communities of the colonial era, one put forward by Congregational historians such as Williston Walker in his *Creeds and Platforms of Congregationalism* and Gaius Atkins and Frederick Fagley's *History of American Congregationalism.* They place the formation of the covenant idea in the separatist movement and the Pilgrims. The other interpretation is that of Perry Miller, an intellectual historian of Puritanism, but not a Church Historian. He tended to locate the origin of covenant theology in Massachusetts Bay among the non-separatist Puritans using ideas and practices emerging from both communities of Puritanism. The Pilgrim, or separatist colonies had such a short history before the arrival of the much larger number of nonseparatist Puritans that I think it would be difficult to trace a truly distinctive tradition of covenant among the separatists. However, the separatist ideal served and continues to serve those in the UCC who want to maintain a strictly congregational polity. See Theodore Louis Trost, *Douglas Horton and the Ecumenical Impulse in American Religion.* (Cambridge, MA: Harvard University Press, 2002).

17. The reference to the monarchy of Christ dates back to antiquity when early Christians referred to Christ as the emperor in order to counter the claim of the emperors to divinity.

18. Robert Browne, "A Treatise of Reformation without Tarying for Anie," (1582) in Payne, *Reformation Roots,* LTH vol. 2, Document 28, p. 472.

19. For our purposes, we do not need to go into the history of the English Parliamentary conflict with the King and the evolution of the modern English state. The Puritans played an important role in those developments because they controlled Parliament at a crucial time.

20. "The Westminster Confession of Faith" in Philip Schaff, *The Creeds of Christendom with a History and Critical Notes* vol. 3 (New York: Harper and Brothers Publishers, 1877) 616–617. The Confession is presented in both English and Latin.

21. "The Cambridge Platform," (1648) in Charles Hambrick-Stowe, *Colonial and National Beginnings,* LTH vol. 3, Part I, Document 6.

22. "The Cambridge Platform," LTH vol. 3.

23. "The Cambridge Platform," LTH vol. 3.

24. "The Saybrook Platform," (1708) LTH vol. 3, Part I, Document 8.

25. The Heidelberg Catechism Question 74 (Are Infants also to be baptized?) Payne, *Reformation Roots,* LTH, vol. 2, Document 21, p. 343.

26. They had called out from among them Philip Boehm as "Reader" who could maintain Sunday worship with services of the Word and could provide a small amount of pastoral care. However, he was not ordained.

27. John Philip Boehm, "The Consistories of the German Reformed Churches . . . to the Classis of Amsterdam," (1728) in Hambricke-Stowe, *Colonial and National Beginnings,* LTH, vol. 3, Part II, Document 18.

28. Boehm, "Consistories to the Classis."

29. The organization of this Synod is laid out in the "Synodal-Ordnung" in LTH vol. 3, Part II, Document 22.

30. "Synodal-Ordnung" Preamble, LTH vol. 3.

31. "The Half-Way Covenant: Result of the Synod," in LTH vol. 3, Document 7. The Half-Way Covenant was put forward during the Synod of 1662 that met to discuss whether the churches could baptize the children of baptized, but unregenerate parents (those who could give no evidence of an experience of grace as adults), and to define the nature of "consociation" among the churches. The synod decided that the children of unregenerate but baptized parents still fell under the original covenant relationship of their parents even though the parents were not admitted to communion.

32. "Pastoral Letter to the . . . German Reformed Church," (1846) in LTH vol. 3, Part II, Document 27. This is a long letter and contains important details about this theological position and addresses other parts of the controversy about baptism. For the purposes of this chapter, I simply want to point out the way in which covenant is understood.

33. Theophil W. Menzel, "Frontier Beginnings (– 1866)," in David Dunn et. al. *A History of the Evangelical and Reformed Church* (New York: The Pilgrim Press, 1990) p. 170.

34. John Locke, "Selections from Two Treatises of Government" in T. V. Smith and Marjorie Greene eds. *From Decartes to Locke* (Chicago: The University of Chicago Press, 1940) 471. I am not sure that Locke included women in his thinking so I have not suggested our inclusion in this quote.

35. The word "autonomy" comes into English directly from the Greek *autonomia,* meaning self (*auto*) governing (*noma*). The word implies both that the "self" regulates itself, but also that it develops its own principles of action or laws.

36. Robert Browne, "A Treatise of Reformation without Tarying for Anie" 1582, in Payne, *Reformation Roots,* LTH vol. 2, Part III, Document 28. p. 475.

37. Browne, "A Treatise of Reformation without Tarying for Anie." p. 472.

38. Henry Jacobs, "Principles and Foundations of the Christian Religion," (1604 or 1605) in LTH vol. 2, Part III, Document 29.

39. Jacobs, "Principles and Foundations."

40. Jacobs, "Principles and Foundations."

41. John Robinson, "A Just and Necessary Apology,"(1625) in LTH, vol. 2, Part III, Document 30.

42. Robinson, "A Just and Necessary Apology." Here it is obvious that Robinson is an Aristotelian rather than Platonic thinker. His argument here derives from Medieval Nominalism where reality belongs only to particular things not to ideas. See LTH vol. 2, note 5, p. 519. Many of the Reformers were influenced by Nominalism, as was the developing scientific method. The theology developed in the thirteenth century and beyond. It aroused suspicion in theological circles because one argument nominalists could make was that the Trinity as an idea had no reality, only the individual members of it could be thought to have reality. Nominalism also fostered a tendency either to place faith in the Scriptures, a kind of literalism that gave reality only to the particular revelation contained there, or to place faith in the mystical experience of a particular individual. "Nominalism" in Jerald C. Brauer, ed. *The Westminster Dictionary of the Christian Church* (Philadelphia: The Westminster Press, MCMLXXI) 606–607. See also Chapter 3 above.

43. Robinson, "A Just and Necessary Apology."

44. Among the meanings of this word are reckoning, concern, explanation, relation, principle, manner, style, reason, order, theory, or conviction.

45. William Ames, *The Marrow of Theology,* trans. by John D. Eusden (Boston: Pilgrim Press, 1968) Book I, chapter XXXII, "The Church Instituted," pp. 178–179. Also found in LTH, vol. 2, Document 31, pp. 530–531.

46. William Ames, *The Marrow of Theology.* p180.

47. Ibid. Note here the idea echoed in John Locke, of government as a covenant among the people for the common good. This idea grew from a long tradition in English government of agreements between ruler and people for the common good, for instance in the Magna Carta (1215).

48. William Ames, The Marrow of Theology, p. 159.

49. "The Westminster Confession of Faith," in Schaff, *The Creeds of Christendom,* vol. 3 p. 657.

50. Ibid.

51. "The Westminster Confession of Faith," in Schaff, *The Creeds of Christendom,* vol. 3, p. 669–670.

52. The Puritans regarded the catholic church or the church universal as both visible or invisible. That is invisible because the elect are known only to God, and visible in that by their outward behavior others recognize the presence of Christ. The church is also regarded as either militant or triumphant.

The church triumphant consists of those who are in heaven, the church militant consists of those still battling evil in this world.

53. "The Cambridge Platform,"in Hambrick-Stowe, *Colonial and National Beginnings,* LTH, vol. 3, Part I, Document 6.

54. "The Cambridge Platform." The church is necessary for the expression of the Christian faith. "Saints by calling must have a visible political union amongst themselves or else they are not yet a particular church, as those similitudes hold forth which Scripture makes use of to show the nature of particular churches." p. 98.

55. "The Cambridge Platform."

56. Rice Haggard, "The Sacred Import of the Christian Name," in Nordbeck and Zuck, *Consolidation and Expansion,* LTH, vol. 4, Part I, Document 2. He typically did not capitalize the "c" in Christian.

57. Rice Haggard, "The Sacred Import of the Christian Name."

58. "The Last Will and Testament of the Springfield Presbytery," (1803) in Nordbeck and Zuck, *Consolidation and Expansion,* LTH, vol. 4, Part I, Document 5.

59. "Manifesto at the General Convention," (1874) in LTH, vol. 4, Part I, Document 21.

60. Ibid.

61. Simon Clough, "Creeds Rejected," (1838) in LTH, vol. 4, Part I, Document 27.

62. Ira Allen, "Principles of Union," in LTH, vol. 4, Part I, Document 30.

63. Nicholas Summerbell, "The Christian Pulpit" (1869) in LTH, vol. 4, Part I, Document 35.

64. A. A. Bright, "Revised Ritual of the Christian Church," Hilke, *Growing Toward Unitis,* LTH, vol. 6, Document 27.

65. "The Evangelical Catechism," (1867) in LTH, vol. 4, Document 53, Question 102.

66. Friedrich Schleiermacher, "A Letter [to Klaus Harms]" (1818) in LTH, vol. 4, Part II, Document 37.

67. Elizabeth Nordbeck and Lowell Zuck, "The German Evangelicals" in LTH, vol. 4, p. 206. For more about Spener and pietism, see Chapter 4 above.

68. "The question which immediately confronts us is: whether and to what extent the *Kirchenverein,* as the self styled daughter of the Union Church of Prussia, espoused the theological position of the mother Church. The usual premise in discussions of this nature is that historical affinity must be tested by theological criteria. We may agree that the sociological demands of the frontier may sufficiently account for modifications in the field of liturgy and organization which occur in an immigrant Church; for a vital compromise does not seem immediately to be involved in adjustments of this kind. It is different however in the field of doctrine. A theological age required, and some theological minds still seem to insist, that the validity of a Church depends upon the purity of its theo-

logical succession and upon the rigor with which the traditions of the fathers are revered. . . . Interconfessional spirit pervaded the outstanding German missionary societies and caused them to avoid abstract theological controversies. . . . Nor did the American environment into which *Kirchenverein* pastors were thrust stimulate theological interests. . . . Free from theological predilections, *Kirchenverein* pastors were not inclined to have recourse to dogmatic formulas, but rather found their inspiration and security in the Scriptures." Carl E. Schneider, *The German Church on the American Frontier,* pp. 404–406.

69. Schneider noted, "It was generally contended, usually on the basis of some Scriptural reference such as 1 Cor. 14:33, that the primary purpose of a constitution was to insure law and order; which, however, even the most perfect instruments were not always able to secure." pp. 234–235.

70. "The Evangelical Catechism (Revised Edition)," (1939) in LTH vol. 4, Part II, Document 55. The original version of the Catechism includes one or more illustrations from Scripture.

71. "The Heidelberg Catechism," (1563) in Payne, *Reformation Roots,* LTH, vol. 2, Part II, Document 21.

72. The American Reformed churches could be compared to the Hungarian Reformed Church, some of whose members fled to the United States during the early twentieth century, and became part of the Reformed Church in the United States. As a state church, for a long time in the Hungarian Reformed tradition, only the clergy governed the church (Kirk), and the word "church" referred to the whole and not to the individual congregation. Imre Revesz, *History of the Hungarian Reformed Church* trans. George A. F. Knight, (Washington, D. C.: The Hungarian Reformed Federation of America, 1956) 35 ff.

73. "On the Frontier of a New Land," in David Dunn et. al., *A History of the Evangelical and Reformed Church* (New York: The Pilgrim Press, 1990 reprint of the 1961 edition, Philadelphia: Christian Education Press, 1961) pp 40–41.

74. John Williamson Nevin, "The Church Movement: Seventh Article," (1868) in Nordbeck and Zuck, *Consolidation and Expansion,* LTH, vol. 4, Part IV, Document 90.

75. Douglas Horton, *The United Church of Christ: Its Origins, Organization, and Role in the World Today* (New York: Thomas Nelson & Sons, 1962) 190.

76. Jon Fogle, "Integrated Pastoral Leadership: Taking Expectations and Ecclesiology Seriously," *Prism,* vol. 12, no. 2, (Fall 1997) 83–96.

77. Viewing ecclesiology as a branch of Christology is also a common starting point in ecumenical discussions of the subject. One Orthodox theologian puts it this way, "The essence of Christianity and the Church should be sought in the very person of the Lord on which the Church was founded. But if this principle is accepted, then the revelation in Christ ceases to be a system of ideas . . . and becomes a truth *ontological in character.*" John D. Zizoulas, *Eucharist Bishop Church: The Unity of the Church in the Divine Eucharist and*

the Bishop During the First Three Centuries. Trans. Elizabeth Theokritoff from the 1976 original (Brookline, Massachusetts: Holy Cross Orthodox Press, 2001) 15. Zizoulas goes on to argue for the essential role of the episcopacy in the unity of the church, an argument with which the UCC might not agree fully. Nevertheless, his grounding ecclesiology in Christology echoes the Mercersburg ecclesiology and other thought within the UCC.

78. Robert Paul, *Freedom with Order: The Doctrine of the Church in the United Church of Christ.* (New York: United Church Press, 1987) 6–7.

79. See for instance Ruben A. Sheares II, "A Covenant Polity," in Johnson and Hambrick-Stowe, *Theology and Identity.* pp. 67–78.

80. Clyde Steckel in consultation with the Ecclesiology Subcommittee of the General Synod Committee on Structure, "Background Paper: United Church of Christ Ecclesiology," (1997) Trost and Zikmund, *United and Uniting,* LTH, vol. 7, Document 8. A. 1

81. The first complete articulation of this consensus may be found in Faith and Order Paper 111, *Baptism Eucharist and Ministry* (Geneva: World Council of Churches, 1982), and subsequent related positions are contained in *The COCU Consensus and Churches in Covenant Communion* (Princeton, NJ: Consultation on Church Union, 1989 revised in 1995), and in Keith F. Nickle and Timothy Lull, *A Common Calling: The Witness of Our Reformation Churches in North America Today* (Minneapolis: Augsburg Fortress Press, 1993).

82. The word in Greek (*epi* - over; *scopé* - see, sight) literally means over-see, over-look, over-view, or super-vision. It refers to the "big picture" or the ability to see the whole. It also has connotations of evaluation and judgement and power.

83. One notable exception is the Hungarian Reformed Church, present in the United Church of Christ as the Calvin Synod.

84. I have written more extensively on this in a position paper for the Parish Life and Leadership Ministry Team, "The Role of the Laity in Priestly and Episcopal Ministry" in *United Church of Christ Ministry and the Law: Three Position Papers for Study and Discussion Throughout the United Church of Christ,* (Cleveland: Parish Life and Leadership Team, 2003).

85. Friedrich Schleiermacher, *The Christian Faith,* English translation of the second German edition, H. R. Mackintosh and J. S. Stewart eds. (Edinburgh: T & T Clark, 1928) §145, p. 667.

86. In theory a local church may ordain its own clergy without consulting the Association, though those clergy will have no standing within the larger church. See the discussion of the ordination of Antoinette Brown below.

87. For the most part those churches who complain about this do not recognize the extent to which their own congregations do not abide by the agreements either, even when their bishops theoretically have the power to enforce them. This illustrates first the semicongregational format of nearly every North American church by virtue of the voluntary nature of religion in

America and the lack of state support for the churches. The laity exercise considerable enforcing power by their ability to support financially what they approve and to fail to support what they disapprove. Second, it suggests that no church polity is purely one kind or another, but that congregational, presbyterian, and episcopal kinds of church order are always found in some mixture. This may actually be the ground for any consensus that has developed.

88. Randi J. Walker, "Episcopé or Oversight," (1998) in Trost and Zikmund, *United and Uniting*, LTH, vol. 7, Part 3, Document C.6.

89. I discussed two such instances in *Emma Newman, A Frontier Woman Minister* (Syracuse, NY: Syracuse University Press, 2000) Chapters 4 and 5.

90. Rollin Russell, "UCC Conferences and the Council of Conference Ministers," *Prism* (Fall 1994) 59–64.

91. Russell, "UCC Conferences," p. 63.

92. John W. Lynes, "Nurturing the Flock: The Role of Conferences in the Restructured UCC," Prism (Fall 2000) 40–49.

93. It is important to note here that I am talking theologically about the role of the Conference and Association ministers. It is also undeniable that they have a more informal kind of power that has nothing to do with theology and everything to do with how many financial resources the Association or Conference controls and how those financial resources are used to strengthen the churches and their mission. The decision about who receives funds has a kind of coercion about it that is real, but not well articulated theologically. The UCC has both richer and poorer conferences and also has its share of leaders who use this wealth to influence the mission of the whole church.

94. At the beginning it is only fair to acknowledge that I (a straight woman) am in full theological and practical support of the inclusion of both women and lesbian, gay, bisexual and transgendered (LGBT) people in the life and ministry of the Church. I recognize that there are a few biblical passages that seem to condemn both of these positions. My reading of the biblical record is that the overwhelming message of the Bible in both its testaments is one of love, particularly love expressed toward the stranger (those unlike us), recognizing that they are capable of love and that our responsibility as human beings is to act with justice and mercy toward each other. I also acknowledge in my passion for the ecumenical work of our church that our positions of affirmation and inclusion of both women and LGBT persons in the ordained ministry and in our theological formulations are a stumbling block to our ecumenical relationships. Some would argue either that we rescind our affirmation of such (particularly LGBT) ordinations and our development of inclusive theological language in order to preserve our ecumenical relationships. Others would argue that we should let go of ecumenical relationships with churches that deny these positions. I believe we must hold both our understanding of God's inclusive community and our ecumenical commitments. I am willing to live in the tension between them though I recognize that others in the UCC are not.

95. Catherine Brekus, *Strangers and Pilgrims: Female Preaching in America 1740–1845.* (Chapel Hill: University of North Carolina Press, 1998) discusses the many women who were preaching by the middle of the nineteenth century. The Christian Connection along with the Universalist churches were the most open to women. Since the Christians did not always ordain their preachers and had a high view of the role of the laity in the life of the church, women were more prominent than in denominations where the worship leadership and preaching were prerogatives of the ordained.

96. This congregation is no longer listed as such in the UCC Yearbook.

97. Moorland's ordination was noted in several sources, but the most complete record of her career I have been able to find is in Ruth Ewers Haberkorn, "The First Ordained Congregational Woman in the United States," *Journal of the Illinois State Historical Society* (September 1942) 288–294.

98. Marilyn Hedges-Hiller, "A Trickle of Ordained Women," *Bulletin of the Congregational Library,* (Winter and Spring/Summer 2000) 4–16.

99. I have looked into the deliberations of two Associations on this matter and the discussion of their debate may be found in *Emma Newman, A Frontier Woman Minister* (Syracuse, NY: Syracuse University Press, 2000).

100. For one illustration see, Walker, *Emma Newman, A Frontier Woman Minister,* 162–167.

101. The classic expression of this position is Donald G. Bloesch, "A Faithful Church: Concerns of the Biblical Witness Fellowship," in Johnson and Hambrick-Stowe, *Theology and Identity* pp. 132–138, and in the Dubuque Declaration.

102. A more complete discussion of this literature can be found in Kevin Carr, "Gay Theology and the UCC: A Journey of Change and Growth," Unpublished paper in the Pacific School of Religion collection of UCC History Papers vol. VIII 1997, in the author's possession.

103. An important discussion of this issue in Biblical Studies in general can be found in Mary Ann Tolbert, "When Resistance Becomes Repression: Mark 13:9–27 and the Poetics of Location," in Fernando Segovia and Mary Ann Tolbert eds. *Reading from this Place* vol. 2 (Minneapolis: Fortress Press, 1995) 331–346. Tolbert writes, "The Bible's 'truth' for today must be evaluated on the basis of its ethical impact, its blessing or its curse on God's creation as a whole." p. 347.

CHAPTER 6

1. I am grateful for a short phone conversation with Lydia Veliko on August 18, 2003 on these questions.

2. "'With a Demonstration of the Spirit and of Power'(1 Cor. 2:4): The Life and Mission of the United and Uniting Churches," Background and Overview materials for the 7th International Consultation of United and Uniting Churches, September 2002. One of these united and uniting churches has

learned particularly painful lessons in this regard. The Dutch Reformed Church in South Africa, a united church, also for many years supported apartheid. The contradiction between the claim of Christian unity and the denial of the unity of the human race became evident eventually to the whole world.

3. Ibid. These questions face every United and Uniting Church.

4. I am not going to attempt a complete discussion of ethics here, but the Church cannot dispense with serious ethical as well as theological reflection on these matters.

5. Jesus' well-known prayer for the unity of his followers in the Gospel of John Chapter 17, "that they all may be one, as You and I are One," has been a central Christian concern but not always understood in the same way by all. Even the record of the Council of Jerusalem in the Biblical texts illustrates the difference of opinion about its outcome. Paul, writing to the Galatians (1:11–2:2), tells how he first proclaimed a Gospel he had received directly from Jesus Christ and did not consult many others about what he was preaching, fourteen years later, went to Jerusalem with Titus to lay before the other apostles the gospel he was proclaiming among the Gentiles to make sure he "did not run in vain." Paul reported the result of the council to be that Titus was not compelled to be circumcised, and they asked only that in their preaching that they remember the poor. On the other hand, the writer of Acts, writing about the same council (Chapter 15), told of a long debate among the apostles about the inclusion of the Gentile Christians and in the end decided that circumcision was not necessary and laid down two principles of Christian practice based in the Torah, abstention from what has been sacrificed to idols, from blood and from what has been strangled, and abstention from fornication. Neither account mentions doctrine, but their accounts of the agreements about practice differ significantly.

6. There is not space in this work to delineate the evidence completely, but recent studies of late antiquity point to the explosion of interest in many religions in the first three centuries of early Christianity and the common practice of people either experimenting with several faiths during a lifetime (St. Augustine is a prime example) or holding more than one faith at the same time, including Christianity, Judaism and Pagan traditions together. In addition, Christian doctrine was fluid during this period. W. H. C. Frend, *The Rise of Christianity* (Philadelphia: Fortress, 1984) discusses this phenomena and provides good bibliography for the primary sources.

7. To this end, a new ecumenical organization has arisen in the United States, Christian Churches Together in the U.S.A This group resulted from an initial meeting of ecumenical leaders from the Evangelical, Orthodox, Pentecostal, Mainline Protestant, and Roman Catholic churches, including the United Church of Christ, in Baltimore, September 7–8 2001. Lamenting the divisions of the body of Christ, the diffuse and diminished voice of the churches in society, the churches' lack of faithfulness to each other, and that no ecumenical body currently includes the full spectrum of Christians in the

U.S., they envision a new ecumenical organization with a common witness and they issued an invitation to all U. S. churches to join with them. The draft basis statement reads, "Christian Churches Together in the U.S.A. gathers together those church and Christian communities which acknowledging God's revelation in Christ, confesses the Lord Jesus Christ as God and Savior according to the Scripture, and in obedience to God's will and in the power of the Holy Spirit commit themselves to seek a deepening of their communion with Christ and with one another; to fulfill their mission to proclaim the Gospel by common witness and service in the world for the glory of the one God, Father, Son, and Holy Spirit." From "Christian Churches Together in the U.S.A.: An Invitation to a Journey," April 6, 2002, Chicago, Illinois.

8. Bruce Lawrence, *Defenders of God: The Fundamentalist Revolt Against the Modern Age* (Columbia, South Carolina: University of South Carolina Press, 1995, reprint of San Francisco: Harper and Row, 1989 edition) 17.

9. Leonard I. Sweet, "The Modernization of Protestant Religion in America," in David Lotz, ed. *Altered Landscapes: Christianity in America, 1935–1985.* (Grand Rapids, Michigan: Eerdmans Publishing Co. 1989) 19–41.

10. Sweet, "The Modernization of Protestant Religion in America," p. 26.

11. Lawrence pointed out the tendency for moderns to categorize experience, creating taxonomies organized by exclusive descriptions, it's either this or that. Counting, comparing and systematizing Lawrence identified as particularly modern phenomenon. Comparison is characteristically made in terms of dyads that are either completely opposite to each other, or at least opposing in some way such as "thought/action, tradition/modernity, continuity/change, nature/culture, primitive/civilized." *Defenders of God*, pp. 28–29.

12. A good study of this phenomenon is Dean R. Hoge, Benton Johnson, and Donald A. Luiden, *Vanishing Boundaries: The Religion of Mainline Protestant Baby Boomers* (Louisville: Westminster/John Knox Press, 1994).

13. Peter Watson, *The Modern Mind: An Intellectual History of the 20th Century* (New York: Harper Collins, 2001) pp. 667–681 and 770–772.

14. Burton Mack, *A Myth of Innocence: Mark and Christian Origins* (Philadelphia: Fortress Press, 1988) 82.

15. Peter Brown, *The World of Late Antiquity* (W. W. Norton and Company, 1971) 62.

16. Brown, *The World of Late Antiquity*, p. 66.

17. Not only is the term "Immigrants by heart" from Brown, but also might find an echo in Rita Nakashima Brock's work on Christology, *Journeys by Heart.*

18. Lewis S. Mudge, *Rethinking the Beloved Community: Ecclesiology, Hermeneutics, Social Theory* (New York: University Press of America, 2001) 3.

19. Those familiar with the way in which U. S. history is ordinarily presented will remember that manifest destiny ideology expressed American belief that God had destined the White Anglo-Saxon race to inhabit and rule over the whole North American continent from sea to shining sea with its superior

religion (Protestantism) and its superior political system (representative democracy). This destiny also eventually encompassed numerous Native American peoples, the northern provinces of Mexico, Puerto Rico, Hawaii and the Philippines and continues to play a part in U. S. foreign policy today.

20. I suppose here I am unabashedly Calvinist, but an Arminian Calvinist. The call always comes from God, and I think we can really choose to hear it or not. I try to remember two things in addition, one is that not everyone will hear the call the way I hear it, God calls to each in his or her own language, and the other is that not everyone will respond in the same way, and I may not be able to tell what lies between another's heart and God.

21. Mudge, *Rethinking the Beloved Community,* p. 11.

22. James Baldwin, *The Fire Next Time* (New York: Vintage Books, 1993 reprint of 1963 Dial Press edition) 105–106.

23. Justin Martyr's "First Apology" (c. 155) can be found in Reinhard Ulrich, *Ancient and Medieval Legacies,* LTH, vol. 1, Part I, Document 11.

24. Rebecca Lyman, "The Politics of Passing: Justin Martyr's Conversion as a Problem of 'Hellenization,'" forthcoming in *Seeing and Believing: Conversion in Late Antiquity and the Early Middle Ages,* ed. Anthony Grafton and Kenneth Mills (Rochester: University of Rochester Press).

25. Lyman, "The Politics of Passing," manuscript, pp. 4–5.

26. The footnotes in the LTH version of the Apology also remind us that this is not a new project with the apologists, but that the New Testament authors were already engaged in this conversation with philosophy.

27. Lyman, "The Politics of Passing," manuscript, p. 18.

28. Ibid. p. 18. If you compare the language and argument of Justin's "First Apology" with Irenaeus' "The Faith in Scripture and Tradition" from *Against Heresies* (c. 189) found in LTH vol. 1, Part I, Document 3, you can see that Justin is much more comfortable with philosophical language whereas Irenaeus uses biblical language.

29. Archie Smith, Jr and Ursula Ridel Pfaeflin, "Siblings: Race Gender and Violence" (St. Louis: Challice Press, 2004).

30. This quote from Goethe I found in Charles P. Curits, Jr. and Ferris Greenslet eds. *The Practical Cogitator: The Thinkers Anthology* (Boston: Houghton Mifflin Company, 1962) 147. They cite it as a quote reported by Goethe's friend Chancellor von Mueller from a conversation on November 4, 1823 when someone toasted Memory, p. 651.

31. Quoted in Keith Jenkins, *Refiguring History: New Thoughts on an Old Discipline.* (New York: Routledge, 2003) 29–30. Jenkins points out that our inheritance from our traditions is never ours until we find a way to be what we inherited, rather than try to preserve that inheritance.

32. Adrienne Rich, *The Dream of a Common Language: Poems 1974–1977* (New York: W. W. Norton and Company, 1978) The end of the poem "Natural Resources," p. 77.

INDEX